BATTERED WOMEN'S JUSTICE

The Movement for Clemency and the Politics of Self-Defense

SOCIAL MOVEMENTS PAST AND PRESENT

Robert D. Benford, Editor

"America for the Americans":
The Nativist Movement in the United States
by Dale T. Knobel

The American Peace Movement: Ideals and Activism
by Charles Chatfield

The Animal Rights Movement in America:
From Compassion to Respect
by Lawrence Finsen and Susan Finsen

The Anti-Abortion Movement and the Rise of the Religious Right:
From Polite to Fiery Protest
by Dallas A. Blanchard

Civil Rights: The 1960s Freedom Struggle
by Rhoda Lois Blumberg

Controversy and Coalition: The New Feminist Movement
by Myra Marx Ferree and Beth B. Hess

Family Planning and Population Control:
The Challenges of a Successful Movement
by Kurt W. Back

Farmers' and Farm Workers' Movements:
Social Protest in American Agriculture
by Patrick H. Mooney and Theo J. Majka

The Gun Control Movement
by Gregg Lee Carter

The Hospice Movement: Easing Death's Pains
by Cathy Siebold

Let the People Decide: Neighborhood Organizing in America
by Robert Fisher

Profiles in Power:
The Antinuclear Movement and the Dawn of the Solar Age
by Jerry Brown and Rinaldo Brutoco

The Rise of a Gay and Lesbian Movement
by Barry D. Adam

BATTERED WOMEN'S JUSTICE

The Movement for Clemency and the Politics of Self-Defense

Patricia Gagné

Twayne Publishers
An Imprint of Simon & Schuster Macmillan
New York

Prentice Hall International
London Mexico City New Delhi Singapore Sydney Toronto

Battered Women's Justice:
The Movement for Clemency and the Politics of Self-Defense
Patricia Gagné

Copyright © 1998 by Twayne Publishers

Twayne Publishers
An Imprint of Simon & Schuster Macmillan
1633 Broadway
New York, NY 10019

Library of Congress Cataloging-in-Publication Data
Gagné, Patricia.
    Battered women's justice : the movement for clemency and the
politics of self-defense / Patricia Gagné.
        p. cm. — (Social movements past and present)
    Includes bibliographical references and index.
    ISBN 0-8057-9150-7 (alk. paper)
    1. Abused women—United States. 2. Abused women—Legal status,
laws, etc.—United States. 3. Women murderers—United States.
4. Battered woman syndrome—United States. 5. Self-defense (Law)—
United States. 6. Clemency—United States. I. Title.
II. Series.
HV6626.2.G34   1998
362.82'92'0973—dc21   98-17893
                                                          CIP

This paper meets the requirements of ANSI/NISO Z3948–1992 (Permanence of Paper).

10 9 8 7 6 5 4 3 2 1

Printed in the United States of America

1/00

Contents

Acknowledgments

No act of research and publication is a solo endeavor, and this book is no exception. I am deeply indebted to a number of people who have helped and supported me over the past several years while I have worked on this project. First, I want to thank all the women and men who comprise the clemency movement for making time for lengthy interviews, for helping me contact other activists, for giving me personal files of newsletters, newspaper articles, and correspondence, and for reading and commenting on earlier drafts of this work. Without their openness and desire to help, this work would not have been possible. Several people in the movement went beyond the pale in assisting me with this research: Lety Sierra and Sue Osthoff of the National Clearinghouse for the Defense of Battered Women, Margaret Byrne of the Illinois Clemency Project, and Samy Dyer, who helped me contact Ohio clemency recipients.

Thanks also to former Ohio first lady Dagmar Celeste for suggesting that the Ohio clemencies needed to be researched and for providing entrée to the community of feminists that comprise the battered women's clemency movement. Thanks to former Ohio governor Richard Celeste for making time to talk with me and granting me unlimited access to his files, housed at the Ohio Historical Society. Thanks also to my dissertation committee, Verta Taylor, J. Craig Jenkins, and Joe Scott, for their guidance and encouragement in earlier stages of this work.

Several undergraduate and graduate students and faculty members at the University of Louisville assisted me. Susan Rector Austin conducted all of the legal research on the case law that I analyze in chapter 3. The development of legal theories and defense strategies has been an integral part of this movement, and my research would have been incomplete without Susan's commitment, skill, and attention to detail. My thanks also to Professor Lisa Ivancic and Jeff Blum, who helped me to understand legal terminology and theory. Carla Rich provided hundreds of hours creating graphics and putting the text, notes, and references into proper format. C. Anthony Just also assisted with graphics. Deanna McGaughey helped me analyze interview data from the clemency recipients, and Mamee Evans and Teresa Smith assisted with coding interview data. Their work made the volumes of data I collected far more manageable. Thanks also to Jon Rieger for his encouragement through this process.

I am also grateful to Tom Keil, chair of the Sociology Department, for his support while I researched and wrote this book. Reductions in teaching and service gave me the time I needed to complete this project. Thanks also to my colleague and friend Richard Tewksbury for his support at every stage of this project, and to the many friends and colleagues who provided fun and relaxation at appropriate intervals. Thanks to Jim Beggan, Mark Austin, Allen Furr, and Cindy Negrey. Working with such good friends is priceless.

This project was supported by a number of grants and fellowships. From The Ohio State University Center for Women's Studies I received support from the Elizabeth Gee Fund for Research on Women, and from the Sociology Department at OSU I received a Research Intense Summer Fellowship. These two sources of financial and academic support made my initial research on the Ohio movement possible. In addition, the University of Louisville provided support through two Project Completion Grants from the Office of the Vice President for Research and Development of the College of Arts and Sciences and a grant from the Research on Women Grant Program. The support of these respected institutions made me believe in myself and the project's potential. I am deeply grateful to all of these sources for their assistance.

I want to thank Robert D. Benford and Anne Davidson at Twayne Publishers for giving me the opportunity to complete and publish this work. From our very first interactions, Rob assured me that this book would be a collaborative effort that would result in a fine finished product. Rob, a uniquely gifted editor, gave me the freedom I needed to work inductively with the data while providing insightful guidance with analysis and invaluable suggestions for clarification. His gentle suggestions for improvement inspired me with the confidence I needed to complete this work.

Special thanks to my friend Mark Richard, who read this manuscript several times, providing an insightful critique of my analysis, valuable commentary about the political context of each state, and meticulous copy editing. His deep understanding of history and contemporary politics, together with his support of my work, gave me the confidence I needed to undertake an examination and analysis of the political climate in each state.

Each one of these people, and others too numerous to mention by name, have contributed greatly to the research, writing, and publication of this book. This endeavor has been one of immense intellectual, emotional, and spiritual discovery. I cannot adequately express in words my deep gratitude to all who have helped me along the way.

Chapter One

Introduction

In December 1990 Ohio governor Richard F. Celeste granted clemency to 25 women who were incarcerated for killing or assaulting abusive partners or stepfathers.[1] Calling the cases "genuine tragedies," Celeste cited "battered woman syndrome" (Walker 1984) as grounds for his decision.[2] The clemencies angered prosecuting attorneys and other detractors but were greeted with astonished applause by supporters.[3] Whether angered or pleased, few who were aware of the feminist activism surrounding this issue should have been surprised.

On the surface, Celeste's actions appeared to be an act of mercy by an outgoing public official; however, the clemencies were made possible by a background of feminist activism. Celeste's decision set a precedent that has been followed by governors in five states, who have reviewed multiple applications or granted clemency to groups of women. Activists in at least 34 other states have worked to organize battered women inmates to raise public awareness, apply for clemency, and pressure authorities to review their cases. The result has been a nationwide movement for clemency for battered women who have killed or assaulted the men who abused them.

Despite the feminist activism behind these clemency decisions, little academic attention has been devoted to the study of the battered women's clemency movement. I hope to address this void in the literature by drawing upon data from case law from throughout the United States and discussing movement strategies to achieve fair trials for women accused of killing those who abused them. After an analysis of legal strategies, I summarize case study data from seven states where clemency movements have been fully mobilized and discuss the national organizations that have worked to disseminate information among activists and loosely coordinate the movement. I analyze the sociological factors that aided or impeded mobilization to gain the release of groups of incarcerated battered women, and finally, I discuss the theoretical implications of this movement.

Overview of the Movement

The battered women's movement began with an emergent awareness of wife abuse as a social problem. The early goals of the movement included creating shelters where battered women could be empowered to regain control of their lives. Activists encouraged police to arrest and prosecutors to bring charges against abusive men, educated the public about wife abuse, and worked to reform the law pertaining to family violence. Since the mid-1970s, feminists have challenged gender biases in self-defense law and devised effective defense strategies for battered women charged with killing or assaulting abusive men. During the 1980s, many movement founders established careers within which they sought to advance feminist goals through positions of authority. The operation of shelters was left to a new cohort of women, some of whom were less interested in challenging the patriarchy than in implementing programs oriented toward individual solutions to the problem. During that transitional period, the social-change focus of many shelters in the United States was threatened, leading many analysts to conclude that the movement had been, or was in danger of being, co-opted (Ferraro 1983; Johnson 1981; Schechter 1982; Tierney 1982).

Although these authors did not clearly define co-optation, it referred to a shift away from a collectivist organizational model, which emphasized challenging the patriarchy through individual empowerment and social change, and toward a hierarchical "mental health/social welfare" model that focused on treating individual clients (Davis 1988). This shift in strategy was informed by different theories about the definition and cause of the problem. Those from a mental health background believed the problem was one of "family violence," in which women and men were equally capable of abusive behavior. The cause of violence was generally thought to be a disruption in the family system. If equilibrium could be restored to the family, it was believed, then the violence would stop. Feminists, on the other hand, believed that "wife abuse" was one of many forms of male violence against women in society and that although women sometimes used violence against men, it was usually in self-defense. Feminists assumed that violence against women was rooted in a patriarchal system that condoned violence against women. To end wife abuse, the patriarchy itself needed to be challenged and dismantled. In the interim, individual women could be empowered and drawn into the movement (Walker 1990).

Assumptions that the movement had been co-opted came largely from analysts' narrow focus on shelters rather than on activists, social movement communities, informal networks, and national organizations. By widening the focus and drawing upon more than one theoretical framework, the activism of feminists throughout the United States becomes visible.

Theoretical Framework

Studies concluding that the battered women's movement had been co-opted in the late 1970s and early 1980s were based on the dominant theoretical framework in that period's social movement literature, resource mobilization theory (see McCarthy and Zald 1973; Zald and Garner 1987). Resource mobilization theory provides the conceptual tools necessary to examine social movement organizations, the most efficient means of organizing to achieve a specific goal, and interactions between activists and authorities (Gamson 1975; Gerlach and Hine 1970; McCarthy and Zald 1977; Piven and Cloward 1977; Zald and Garner 1987). In addition, it provides a theoretical method of examining the political process in which social movements are involved and the opportunity structures that enhance or impede their chances of success (McAdam 1982; Tilly 1978). But although resource mobilization informs some aspects of social movements, it has a tendency to direct attention away from other factors and to neglect certain types of activism. Resource mobilization theory presumes that social movements are separate from institutionalized politics and personal life. Because of its focus on movements as outside challengers (Gamson 1975) and its suppositions of a separation among personal life, the civic arena, institutionalized politics, and social movements, resource mobilization falls within the tradition of liberal democratic political theory, dating from the Enlightenment period of Western political thought (Acklesberg 1988; Ferree 1992; Phelan 1989).

Since initial examinations of the battered women's movement were published, new social movement theory has been introduced, shifting the focus of social movements toward issues of movement culture and communities, collective identity, and collective action frames (see Laraña, Johnston, and Gusfield 1994; Morris and Mueller 1992). Additionally, feminist theorists have challenged the tenets of liberal democratic theory, arguing that women's lives differ from men's in sociologically salient ways and that theories assuming a separation between public and private spheres and behaviors overlook much of women's activism (Acklesberg 1988; Alonso 1988; Benhabib and Cornell 1987; Collins 1990; Epstein 1989; Ferree 1992; Smith 1990). Because of the feminist dictum that the personal is political, new social movement and feminist theories are more conducive to the analysis of the battered women's movement, because they allow an examination of activism in all aspects of life rather than focusing exclusively on activism associated with social movement organizations.

Most analyses of the battered women's movement have concentrated on shelters and other social movement organizations rather than on the small group settings where "processes of collective attribution are combined with rudimentary forms of organization to produce mobilization for collective action," otherwise known as the "micro-mobilization context" (McAdam, McCarthy, and Zald 1988, 709). I do not contest that co-optation has been an issue for the battered women's movement, nor that some shelters were transformed into social service agencies with little interest in challenging the patriarchy. This is an important facet of the movement's history, but it is only one aspect. Whereas researchers focused on shelters, activists developed new strategies based on an emergent understanding of the issues. These activists developed networks and resources and created new political opportunities to bring about social change.

It is not fruitful to discard resource mobilization theory because of its assumptions about separations among the arenas of personal, civic, and political life. Resource mobilization theory provides a perspective through which to examine networks, organization, and the political process, but it assumes that the oppression of excluded groups can be addressed entirely by pressuring authorities. Among groups for whom oppression is based on identity and experiences in the home, areas in which the state is reluctant to intervene, grievances can be only partially redressed through political participation (Phelan 1989). Other aspects of oppression, including those that occur in arenas the state considers private, must be addressed by empowering individuals to resist violence and abuse. But individual resistance is not enough.

The movement must also challenge ingrained beliefs that are the cultural foundations of the institutions that perpetuate oppression. Although these goals are central in the mobilization of identity-based movements, a new social movement theoretical framework precludes an examination of the social policy and structural goals of movements such as that of battered women's clemency.

In my examination of this movement, I draw upon concepts from resource mobilization, new social movement, and feminist theories. I discard the postulate of separate spheres that is a central premise of resource mobilization theory but retain its conceptual elements pertaining to networks, organization, and political process. I draw upon feminist and new social movement perspectives to understand identity, community, personal politics, career activism, the creation of new democratic spaces (Cohen 1985), and the hypothesis that divisions between personal, civic, and political domains are artificially constructed. My aim in this book is to present a new model of social movement organization that takes into account the following factors: (1) identity transformation and empowerment of incarcerated battered women; (2) the emergence of prison social movement communities; (3) feminists' movement into careers in which they have been able to carry out a feminist agenda (see also Whittier 1995); (4) the role of collective action frames in uniting disparate groups of activists; (5) the implications of personal politics on the roles of public office holders and their spouses; (6) the role of social movement organizations and social movement communities in coordinating the work of disparate groups; and (7) the importance of considering the political opportunity structure while mobilizing.

By drawing upon the concepts offered by these three theoretical perspectives, a more accurate and dynamic picture of the battered women's and clemency movements emerges. I hope that this model will enhance the examination of other social movements assumed to be co-opted or dead, for which activists have continued to work to achieve goals in arenas less visible than public protests and social movement organizations.

The Focus of This Book

The chapters that follow document the history of the battered women's movement and the role it played in creating legal defense strategies for women who killed or assaulted abusive partners and in securing large-scale clemency reviews for women incarcerated for such crimes. I draw upon the Ohio movement as a precedent-setting case study, then discuss and analyze events in six other states where large-scale clemencies were achieved or attempted. Ohio was the first state to achieve a large-scale clemency review, because of a feminist network that existed within state government and because of the activism and leadership of the first lady, Dagmar Celeste. Because of the opportunities they created for themselves, feminists in that state were able to accomplish what other movements only hoped to do. Once the first "mass" clemency was achieved, activists in other states were able to draw upon the experiences of those who had succeeded and seek their advice. They could argue to governors in their states that clemency was less risky because of the precedent.

Before clemency became a movement goal, feminist legal activists worked for two decades to challenge laws that they argued prevented women from fully defending themselves when on trial for killing abusive men. One focus of their efforts was to challenge self-defense law so that women who had killed could describe the danger with which they had lived and explain the basis of their honest and reasonable belief that force was needed to defend their lives. Initially the movement focused on differences in gender socialization and physical stature and used strategies geared toward examining the androcentric social context of the homicide. Within only a few years, however, some activist attorneys and psychologists began to frame their legal-defense strategies within the language of battered woman syndrome. Such courtroom strategies were used despite the urgings of other activists to exercise extreme caution in deciding when to present such evidence. As is perhaps obvious, using battered woman syndrome to support legal defense strategies has been a source of controversy in the battered women's movement.

Throughout the 1980s, the presentation of self-defense strategies centered on the admission of evidence of death threats or serious bodily harm outside the immediate scope of the homicide and on battered women's assessments of danger at the time they killed their abusers, even if the homicide occurred when an attack was not taking place. The movement's goal was fair trials for women who had killed abusive men. The way to attain it was to make all evidence in a case available to the court. Many defense attorneys used the language of battered woman syndrome, not because they believed women were mentally ill but because it had the potential to meet legal rules of evidence. While more effective defense strategies were being devised, clemency emerged as a movement goal. Feminists believed that women who were in prison for defending their own or another's life did not belong there and that clemency would provide partial justice in an otherwise gender-biased system.

In this book, I provide a descriptive summary of a movement that has drawn upon psychological, sociological, and feminist analyses of gender inequality in its efforts to challenge the law and gain equity for battered women charged with or incarcerated for crimes against their abusers. Although my aim has been to document and analyze the history of the battered women's clemency movement, I have attempted to do so in a way that will enable social movements scholars to navigate the intricacies of the movement with relative ease; those whose primary interest is in wife abuse and clemency, on the other hand, will be able to read past the theoretical elements. In chapter 2, I explain the prevalence of intimate violence against women in the contemporary United States and place those statistics within the historical context of a legal system designed to encourage men to "discipline" their wives. I provide a history of the battered women's movement in the United States and explain how activists turned their attention toward women who had killed violent and abusive mates. To understand this turn of events, I provide the clinical definition of battered woman syndrome as well as show how some feminists have worked for its use in court, and I give an overview of self-defense law.

In chapter 3, I provide an overview of a series of precedent-setting political trials that took place in the 1970s and 1980s and analyze the strategies and barriers to gender equity in the courtroom. In that chapter, I provide an analysis of the pragmatic use of battered woman syndrome as well as the potential pitfalls of its use in the development of any self-defense strategy. Included in this chapter is a summary of legal reforms that the movement has achieved and an analysis of self-defense strategies that movement activists have advocated, implemented, and criticized.

In chapter 4, I provide a case study of the Ohio battered women's movement, placing events and strategies in that state within the context of the nationwide movement. I include an analysis of transformations in the shelter branch of the movement; the events that led activists in that state to become involved in issues regarding women who kill; the decision by movement founders to pursue their activism through careers in government, law, and psychology; and finally, how clemency was advocated, organized, and achieved in that state. In chapter 5, I describe the strategies and achievements in six states where activists have attempted or attained large-scale clemency reviews, or where clemency procedures have been reformed to provide greater access to battered women. I identify factors that played a role in the success or failure of the movements examined in this book.

In chapter 6, I analyze the strategies and tactics of the seven previously described statewide clemency movements, drawing upon a synthesis of resource mobilization, new social movement, and feminist theories. Finally, in chapter 7 I discuss the lives of 11 of the 26 Ohio women who received clemency. It is for these women and others like them that the battered women's movement and the clemency movement have fought for justice. Their courage and activism helped to convince governors and parole board members that large-scale review of the cases of incarcerated battered women was right and just. It is through the lives and actions of these and other battered women activists that the movement has been disseminated into arenas in which it is most likely to have an impact.

Chapter Two

The Historical, Social, and Legal Context of the Clemency Movement

Legalized violence against wives existed at least as far back as the late Roman period (Dobash and Dobash 1979). Throughout history, laws have recognized the right and duty of husbands to control and discipline family members, even if it meant killing them (Dobash and Dobash 1979; Martin 1976; Pleck 1987). The first American reform against family violence was the Puritans' *Body of Liberties* in Massachusetts in the seventeenth century. The legality of disciplinary measures and accepted levels of violence was not clarified in the United States, however, until the mid-nineteenth century, when a husband's right to beat his wife was gradually eroded by local police courts and state supreme courts (Pleck 1987; 1989).

The Puritans established the *Body of Liberties* to reinforce hierarchy within the family and society and to limit "illegitimate" violence (Pleck 1987; 1989). The Puritans sought to protect less powerful members of the family and society only if they were seen as blameless for violence against them, and they sought to punish those who were sinful, stubborn, or disobedient. These laws were an expression of concern for social order but were rarely enforced. When they were, offenders received light sentences. The physical punishment of wives was permitted under Puritan law, but wives were never granted the legal right to discipline their husbands. In other colonies, there was little interest in controlling family violence. In the postcolonial period, citizens were more concerned with protecting the family from state intervention than with protecting family members from each other.

In the eighteenth century, legal scholars, reflecting the philosophy upon which liberal political theory is based, distinguished between public and private behavior. In 1769 Jurist William Blackstone wrote that "crime was an act that produced mischief in civil society, while private vices were not the legitimate subject of law" (Pleck 1989, 28). Until the mid-nineteenth century, there were few laws regarding wife abuse or other forms of family violence. It is frequently argued that common law in the United States followed the English "rule of thumb," which permitted a man to beat his wife with an instrument no thicker than his thumb. Although the legal decision upon which that rule was based was never recognized in England (Pleck 1989), it appears that Puritan and United States laws were heavily influenced by the notion of "acceptable" levels of violence against wives.

In the United States, concern about wife abuse and other forms of family violence and efforts to criminalize such behaviors have occurred when domestic abuse was perceived as threatening the social order, when the defense of the traditional family and beliefs favoring family privacy were weakest, or when social movements brought attention to the issue (Pleck 1987; 1989). Wife assault was rendered illegal in legislation passed in Tennessee in 1850 and in Georgia in 1857. Those laws permitted the punishment of wife beaters at the misdemeanor level. In a series of appellate court decisions that began in Mississippi in 1824, followed by North Carolina in 1864 and 1868 and by other states later in the century, "moderate" forms of wife assault were declared legal and more serious forms illegal. Nonetheless, the courts were concerned with preserving family privacy and did little to punish assailants or protect victims.

Appellate court decisions were one product of the temperance and feminist movements' efforts to draw attention to wife abuse, but feminists believed divorce was the solution to the problem of wife beating. In the antebellum period of the nineteenth century, these movements drew public attention to wife abuse, but both regarded family violence as a consequence of alcohol abuse and believed that women were responsible for their husbands' moral rehabilitation. Concern with family violence and the neglect of children was the result of middle- and upper-middle-class fears of social disorder in the wake of the wave of immigration of the late nineteenth century (Pleck 1987; 1989). Those who spoke out against wife abuse framed their arguments in terms that defended the family from "brutish men" (Pleck 1987).

Throughout most of the twentieth century, wife abuse has been perceived as a private problem. Violent families are believed to deviate from "normal" families. As with temperance activists and feminists in the nineteenth century, the issue of the patriarchal control of women has been sidestepped, the problem individualized, and the myth of the supportive, loving household sustained. Despite abundant evidence that violent behavior toward wives had existed for centuries, the social problem of wife abuse as a form of patriarchal domination was not recognized until the early 1970s (Schechter 1982; Tierney 1982).

The battered women's movement began in 1972. Feminists in Chiswick, England, renovated an abandoned house and opened a women's center (Dobash and Dobash 1988; Pizzey 1977). In their activism, these feminists began to encounter women in need of a place to escape violent relationships. As a result, the center was transformed into what is believed to be the first shelter in the world specifically for women seeking refuge from violent relationships (Dobash and Dobash 1988; Pizzey 1977). Like feminists elsewhere, Chiswick activists had little understanding of the issues confronting battered women or the scope of the problem.

The first shelters in the United States were sponsored by Al-Anon groups to assist families of alcoholics and, similar to nineteenth-century efforts, focused on alcoholism as the cause of violent behavior within the family (Ferraro and Johnson 1985; Johnson 1981; Schechter 1982; Tierney 1979). They did little to publicize the problem. The reframing of wife abuse as a social problem rather than a personal one was the result of feminist activism (Bograd 1988; Schechter 1982; Tierney 1982). As awareness of the problem spread during the late 1970s, services for battered women proliferated. As shelters emerged, the need for stable funding sources became apparent. Shelter providers were overwhelmed with demands for refuge, and in an effort to provide continuous services they turned to foundations, mental health boards, charitable organizations, and government agencies to pay for rent, utilities, supplies, and staff (Schechter 1982).

In the United States, what is believed to be the first shelter specifically for battered women (as opposed to wives of alcoholics) was established in 1974 in St. Paul by the feminist group Women's Advocates (Johnson 1981; Martin 1976). The shelter was an outgrowth of a consciousness-raising group established in 1971 (Schechter 1982). In 1976, two formerly battered women living in Boston opened their apartment to women seeking refuge from violent relationships. They were soon joined by members of Cell 16, one of Boston's earliest radical feminist groups (Schechter 1982). In 1975, a group of feminists in Cleveland from an array of women's groups, including the Free Clinic, the Rape Crisis Center, and WomenSpace (an umbrella organization of women's groups in the area), began meeting to decide how to provide emergency shelter for battered women. In 1976 they established a hot line to provide support and information to battered women. In December 1976, the new group—Women Together—received its first foundation grant and opened the first shelter in Ohio in the home of then lieutenant governor Richard F. Celeste and his wife, Dagmar Celeste.

Fewer than half of the existing shelters in the United States during the 1980s were founded by or directly related to feminist groups or ideology (Ferraro 1981). Of the remainder, approximately 25 percent were founded by church groups and 25 to 30 percent by YWCA or other civic organizations (Johnson 1981). Feminists were responsible for establishing more shelters than any other single group, but as others brought in new ideological orientations the provision of services became more diverse. The presence of shelters that employed scientifically recognized methods of therapy and hierarchical forms of organization put pressure on feminists to alter their service model (Schechter 1982). The presence of nonfeminist shelters led to assertions that the movement had been co-opted.

Ideological Orientations
in the Battered Women's Movement

Kathleen Tierney (1979) identified three overlapping but distinct philosophical orientations in the battered women's movement as it existed in the 1970s. They were social service/community mental health, feminism/civil rights, and legal advocacy. These orientations are loosely correlated with the three dominant social scientific perspectives on wife abuse and family violence.[1]

The first perspective focuses on intra-individual explanations for family violence, including mental illness and substance abuse (Burgess and Draper 1989). The second perspective is comprised of social-psychological theories, which suggest that family violence is rooted in individual characteristics, including low self-esteem (Gelles and

Straus 1988; Walker 1979), learned helplessness (Walker 1977–1978), battered woman syndrome (Walker 1984) substance abuse (Gelles 1974; Gelles and Straus 1988; Sonkin, Martin, and Walker 1985), childhood experiences with family violence (Straus, Gelles, and Steinmetz 1980), frustration-related aggression (Gelles and Straus 1979), and the desire to maintain tension in a relationship (Gelles and Straus 1979). These individual traits are examined within the family system, based upon a theory that asserts that family violence results from stressors external to the family (Kalmuss and Seltzer 1986) and from the interactive dynamics of the family, which establish power, resources, and the behavior that is acceptable to family members (Giles-Sims 1983; Neidig and Friedman 1984).

The mental health branch of the movement has relied more heavily on these perspectives, to the exclusion of macro-level explanations or feminist theories. Intra-individual and social-psychological perspectives treat family violence as an anomaly, caused by individual pathology or family dysfunction. The social-psychological perspective focuses on the family as the context for violent behavior. Adherents believe that counseling individual family members and families can eliminate violent behavior. Services based upon this model tend to be hierarchical, employ licensed professionals to provide treatment, and assume that individual family members must find solutions to their problems. With the exception of those who take advantage of legislation designed to protect victims while they work through their problems, service providers that draw upon this perspective have little interest in changing the larger society.

The third perspective focuses on the macro level of analysis and contends that wife abuse and other forms of interpersonal violence are functions of social structures and arrangements (Burgess and Draper 1989). The feminist perspective focuses primarily on the macro level of analysis, contending that wife abuse is a form of social control made possible by the cultural acceptance of violence against women and the unequal distribution of resources between women and men, and men use it to protect and advance their interests as men. Feminist examinations of the psychological or social-psychological factors of wife abuse are embedded within the social context. Initially, the feminist branch of the battered women's movement focused on making changes at the macro level, with intervention at the individual level geared toward pragmatic assistance and the empowerment of women as a means of achieving social change.

According to the feminist perspective, the emancipation of women in general, and battered women in particular, requires the expansion of consciousness at three levels (Mies 1983). The first level entails raising the individual woman's consciousness of her suffering *as a woman*. Among battered women, this might include an understanding that abuse did not occur because of reasons given by her partner; it happened because she was female, and if she had been born male she would not have experienced such violence. The second level involves the creation of collective consciousness. This is achieved first through understanding one's personal history and then through an emerging consciousness of shared experiences. Many battered women are ashamed that they have been beaten. They keep the abuse a secret. When they learn that there are other women who have been beaten and that their experiences are similar, isolation is diminished and a sense of group membership and collective consciousness emerges. At the third level, individual and collective consciousness are combined with the study of women's social history and an understanding of women's place in society. When women reach this level of consciousness, they are empowered. The result is the politicization of identity and activism to create social change. This third level is similar to McAdam's concept of "cognitive liberation" (1982), which similarly results in greater insurgency.

Feminists' initial goal in the battered women's movement was to eliminate violence against women by challenging androcentrism in society. Until society could be changed, they relied upon the provision of refuge for women seeking escape from abusive relationships. In battered women's shelters, they provided the pragmatic assistance needed to establish independent living arrangements. Because they believed empowerment would occur through interaction with women who had similar experiences, they hired survivors of wife abuse to staff the shelters. They offered regular rap sessions for shelter residents instead of individual therapy. Collectivist principles of organization ensured that women could have a maximum amount of self-determination.

By the end of the 1970s, as feminists successfully raised public awareness of wife abuse as a social problem, government entities and foundations began to seek out shelters and services for battered women (Tierney 1982). Feminist shelter providers were faced with an overwhelming demand for services, and mental health workers began to view "family violence" as part of their professional domain. Funding sources solicited applications from battered women's programs as a way of enhancing their own status by providing services to a less stigmatized population. The requirements of such programs demanded that applicants provide evidence of organizational accountability (Tierney 1982). Mental health professionals learned that offering services to victims of family violence could be lucrative. Feminists were forced to compete with the social service model by hiring professional staff members and establishing hierarchical forms of organization or to forego funds required to remain in operation. Most compromised (Tierney 1982).

Because of the need to present an air of accountability, many feminist shelters gave way to a mental health model during the late 1970s, and by the early 1980s the majority of shelters in the United States had shifted away from a feminist model or were created based on a mental health model (Ferraro 1983; Johnson 1981; Schechter 1982; Tierney 1982). Nonetheless, feminism has been maintained in or found its way back to battered women's shelters, particularly in areas where feminist networks are strongest (Schechter 1982; Tierney 1982). Activists have developed feminist therapies for victims (Rosewater and Walker 1985) and perpetrators (Adams 1988; 1991). They have produced analyses of wife abuse that examine intra-individual factors and the dynamics of the violent relationship within the larger patriarchal context and developed feminist interventions for problems of mental illness and substance abuse, along with ways to help individual family members. Their focus on power inequities within the relationship, the need for social change at the macro level, and personal transformation and empowerment for victims of violence has remained.

The third branch of the movement has focused on legal reform. Activism in this branch of the movement has drawn upon a feminist perspective, examining individual traits and the interpersonal dynamics of violent relationships within the social context and challenging androcentric biases within the law. This branch has been the one perhaps most overlooked in the social movement literature. In the 1970s it successfully criminalized wife abuse in jurisdictions that had previously condoned it and established spouse abuse as a separate crime under the law. In the late 1970s and 1980s activist lawyers filed class-action lawsuits to improve police response to women's calls for help (see Jones 1991a; 1991b). Activists worked to institute mandatory or preferred arrest laws and legalized warrantless misdemeanor arrest laws in domestic violence cases. Their efforts brought changes in police policy and training procedures, both of which now encourage offi-cers to arrest the perpetrator and assist the victim, and made protec-tion orders more readily available for victims.

As these efforts suggest, the battered women's movement has shifted its emphasis from one in which solutions to the problem of wife abuse were sought outside established institutions, via an under-ground railroad of safe homes and shelters (Ferraro and Johnson 1985), to one in which solutions are sought within established institu-tions, with social and legal change as the primary goals. Over 25 years these three orientations have managed to find common ground.

Understanding these philosophies is important for at least two rea-sons: first, the argument that the movement has been co-opted has been based on the shift in some shelters to hierarchical models of or-ganization and a focus on the mental health of battered women. Among some feminists, this was perceived at worst as "blaming the victim" and at best as shifting the focus back onto the individual (Bush 1992; Davis 1988; Ferraro 1983). Clearly, many feminist shelters have undergone a dramatic transformation from the early days of hot lines and safe homes. In the eyes of many analysts and activists, the shift from structural change to individualized treatment is evidence of co-optation (Ferraro 1983; Johnson 1981). Nonetheless, a focus on shel-ters assumes that organizations, not activists, are what compromise the movement.

Second, the focus on mental health issues, particularly as it has in-tersected with self-defense law, has been a complex problem for femi-nists, mental health professionals, and legal experts (see Browne 1993; Schneider 1986). These issues are central to clemency because in states where the earliest large-scale commutations were granted, advocacy on behalf of incarcerated battered women was framed in terms of battered woman syndrome. Since the clemencies in Ohio and Maryland, however, most clemency activists have distanced them-selves from the syndrome. Instead, they have framed their arguments for clemency in terms of social justice, using the syndrome on a case-by-case basis.

Within the movement, debate surrounding battered woman syn-drome tends to center on one issue. Some feminist clinicians argue that the syndrome is a psychological subcategory of post-traumatic stress disorder (PTSD), the existence of which can be revealed by psychological tests and clinical interviews (Walker 1984). Accord-ingly, behaviors that accompany battered woman syndrome are normal responses to ongoing abuse, similar to reactions of terrorist hostages (Graham, Rawlings, and Rigsby 1994; Graham, Rawlings, and Rimini 1988). Many argue that experts must explain to jurors what the syndrome is and, if possible, testify that a particular defendant had the psychological profile of one experiencing it. Those who oppose the unlimited use of battered woman syndrome to support a claim of self-defense argue that its implied psychological pathology suggests that battered women who kill are less rational than men who kill and that it has the potential to work against defendants who are less than perfect (Browne 1987; Schneider 1986). Women who are addicted to drugs or alcohol, or who have prostituted themselves, abused their children, dropped charges against the abuser, left and returned, or previously been charged with assaulting the abuser are more likely to be perceived by juries as deserving punishment because they do not appear to be helpless and "innocent." Further, opponents caution that the unbridled use of battered woman syndrome creates the potential for backlash, which will harm women who have reacted to violence with some degree of agency rather than with helplessness (Dutton 1993). Finally, they contend that use of the syndrome, except in specific cases in which it is warranted, keeps the focus on the woman who "failed" to leave the relationship rather than on the abuser and the social context of their relationship.

Battered woman syndrome was initially introduced at trials in support of self-defense strategies because it had the potential to meet legal rules of evidence. Expert witnesses and attorneys have tended to take a clinical approach to its use. Advocates of its legal recognition argue that the syndrome can be used to educate judges and jurors about violent relationships and, perhaps more importantly, the social context in which it existed. As the syndrome has gained recognition by courts, some feminists have worked to expand its use, moving away from a psychological focus to a more contextual analysis of the dangers with which battered women live. At the same time, activists have worked to develop other innovative defense strategies and to shift the focus from the victim and toward the factors that effectively trapped her in the relationship.

Battered woman syndrome was used as the rationale for the earliest clemencies because it was recognized by the courts. In some states, governors and legislators understood and were sympathetic to it. In no state where large-scale clemencies have occurred has the syndrome been advocated or employed as a clinical screening instrument for women applying for review. By framing their advocacy for clemency in terms the public could understand and might accept, feminists in Ohio, working from within the administrative branch of government, were able to set a precedent for less-well-positioned feminists. The benefit of battered woman syndrome is that, now that its scientific legitimacy has been established, it is something that judges, parole boards, and some governors accept. Before we can fully appreciate the way the syndrome has been used, as well as objections to it, we must examine what it entails.

Battered Woman Syndrome and the Dynamics of Violent Relationships   Research conducted over the last three decades has provided a clear idea of what battered women encounter in abusive relationships. Much of this research has been conducted by psychologists, with a view to understanding the mental state of the abused and the dynamics of the battering relationship. Other research has examined the context of the relationship, emphasizing gender biases in all major social institutions, dominant ideologies, and socialization patterns of children. The result is a body of literature with components that have usually been complementary.[2]

Studies examining battered women and abusive relationships have identified patterns and behaviors particular to abusive relationships, including the cycle of violence and battered woman syndrome (Walker 1977–1978; 1979; 1984; 1987). Battered woman syndrome has become important in the mental health and criminal justice systems' converged response to wife abuse. This convergence has been possible to the extent that examinations of battered woman syndrome expand beyond its clinical definition to the social-psychological dynamics of abusive relationships and the social context in which abuse occurs. It explains the psychological and behavioral responses of the victim and demands an understanding of the inequality between women and men in intimate relationships and in society.[3] To fully comprehend battered woman syndrome, we need to understand why battered women stay with abusive partners. To do so, we must examine gender inequality in society.

A Social-Psychological View of Wife Abuse   Research has identified several factors common to abusive relationships, including an escalation in the frequency and severity of abuse over time, the cyclical nature of the relationship, the jealousy of the batterer, and the extent to which he will go to control his partner (Browne 1987; Martin 1976; Walker 1979; 1983; 1984; 1987). Abusive relationships frequently begin with minor forms of violence. Such incidents usually are followed by excuse making, apologies, and promises that it will never happen again. Over time, the violence tends to increase in severity and frequency, with incidents again followed by apologies, excuses, and promises. This cyclical pattern, referred to as the cycle of violence (Walker 1979; 1983; 1987), is comprised of a tension-building phase, resulting in a violent incident, followed by a "honeymoon" phase, during which the abuser becomes apologetic or during which there is simply an absence of violence. During the honeymoon phase, the abuser seems to become the person the victim wants him to be, giving her hope of genuine change. Over time, the tension-building phase becomes more common and the abuse more frequent and severe, and the honeymoon phase declines. By the time battered women realize that the promises are empty, it is too late.

Abusers often attempt to control and isolate victims in an effort to guard the secret of abuse and because of their jealousy of any attention their partners may give or receive from family, friends, or coworkers. Victims often isolate themselves in an effort to conceal the abuse, placate the abuser, and control any unexpected circumstances that might provoke his anger (Browne 1987). This isolation results in victims being cut off from sources of support or any potential avenues of escape that may have existed.

When battered women attempt to placate their abusers or control violent outbursts, they learn that nothing will stop the abuse, and that fighting back or attempting escape may make the violence worse (Browne 1987; Walker 1978–1979, 1983). Although it has been argued that many women abandon efforts to stop or escape violence (Walker 1978–1979), more recent research has focused on the survival strategies of battered women (Ewing 1987; Graham et al. 1994; Graham et al. 1988; Walker 1987).

Battered women commonly experience the same psychological reactions to long-term abuse exhibited by hostages, prisoners of war, and victims of terrorism (Graham et al. 1988, 1994). Abusive mates often exhibit the same pattern of cruelty, followed by acts of kindness, that terrorists or other captors do. Because victims' physical and psychological survival is dependent upon the captor's whims, hostages often experience "traumatic bonding" with those holding them. They become acutely aware of the captor's body language and other cues and begin to view the world from the captor's perspective. Their defin-

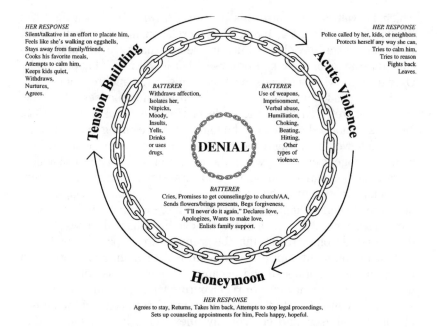

HER RESPONSE
Silent/talkative in an effort to placate him,
Feels like she's walking on eggshells,
Stays away from family/friends,
Cooks his favorite meals,
Attempts to calm him,
Keeps kids quiet,
Withdraws,
Nurtures,
Agrees.

Tension Building

BATTERER
Withdraws affection,
Isolates her,
Nitpicks,
Moody,
Insults,
Yells,
Drinks
or uses
drugs.

DENIAL

HER RESPONSE
Police called by her, kids, or neighbors.
Protects herself any way she can,
Tries to calm him,
Tries to reason
Fights back
Leaves.

Acute Violence

BATTERER
Use of weapons,
Imprisonment,
Verbal abuse,
Humiliation,
Choking,
Beating,
Hitting,
Other
types of
violence.

BATTERER
Cries, Promises to get counseling/go to church/AA,
Sends flowers/brings presents, Begs forgiveness,
"I'll never do it again," Declares love,
Apologizes, Wants to make love,
Enlists family support.

Honeymoon

HER RESPONSE
Agrees to stay, Returns, Takes him back, Attempts to stop legal proceedings,
Sets up counseling appointments for him, Feels happy, hopeful.

Cycle of Violence
Lenore Walker, 1979. *The Battered Woman.* N.Y.: Harper & Row. "Florida Domestic Violence Law," 1996. Tallahassee, Fla.: The Florida Bar, 16–26.

ition of reality becomes dependent upon the captor. Similarly, battered women may view the world from the batterer's perspective. Police, family members, social service workers, or friends attempting to help the woman escape may be looked upon as threatening to the relationship or incapable of understanding that the batterer is himself a victim whom only the abused woman is able to understand.

When battered women try to escape such relationships, their partners frequently hunt for and threaten them with worse harm or death if they try to escape again (Browne 1987). These dynamics commonly make severely battered women perceive their partners as omnipotent, capable of finding them wherever they hide (Browne 1987; Graham et al. 1994; Walker 1987). Battered women are more likely to be killed after they have left a violent relationship than while they are living in it (Browne 1987; Jones 1994; Walker 1987). This indicates that the terror with which these women live is not irrational. In violent relationships, women learn that they are unable to predict the outcome of their behavior, because abusers' responses are random and directed toward total control, and that self-defense or escape will only make matters worse.

Researchers have found that after being repeatedly and unpredictably exposed to abuse, individuals tend to develop psychological characteristics that affect their behavior, even after the original trauma has ended (see, for example, Graham et al. 1988, 1994). Believing they have no control over the situation and that they are unable to escape or predict the outcome of their behavior, persons experiencing PTSD engage in behaviors that help to ensure their survival (Walker 1987).

Before a clinical diagnosis of PTSD may be made, the *Diagnostic and Statistical Manual of Mental Disorders, 4th Edition* mandates that six criteria must be met:[4] (1) there must be a recognizable traumatic stressor that would be expected to evoke major symptoms of mental illness to those exposed to it, and the response must involve intense fear, helplessness, or horror; (2) the individual must reexperience the past traumatic events without willfully thinking of them. Such experiences might include daydreams, flashbacks, recurring nightmares, or intrusive thoughts, involving a sense of powerlessness or loss of control; (3) the individual must experience a numbing of emotions and avoidance of reminders of the abuse, resulting in a disturbance in interpersonal relationships; (4) the individual must manifest a combination of symptoms, resulting in a heightened arousal response. This may involve difficulty falling or staying asleep, irritability, difficulty concentrating, hypervigilance, or an exaggerated startle response; (5) the duration of the disturbance must be more than one month;[5] and (6) the disturbance must cause significant distress or impairment in social, occupational, or other areas of functioning. The psychological and behavioral characteristics of battered woman syndrome include denial of the severity of the abuse; a sense of imminent danger, resulting in constant anticipatory terror; an acute awareness of the body language and cues of the abuser; a preoccupation with the abuser and efforts to placate him; and efforts to conceal the abuse, resulting in a disruption of interpersonal relationships.

Many victims become preoccupied with avoiding danger. Because they have learned that violence is random and unpredictable, battered women tend to engage in behaviors that have the greatest probability of ensuring their safety. Because their safety depends on the perceived kindness of the abuser, victims of domestic violence may thwart others' efforts to intervene and may view neighbors, family members, or the police as enemies who have angered the batterer and endangered their safety. When victims believe that abusers are going to kill them, they react with behaviors that ensure their survival. Some of the actions individuals experiencing PTSD engage in, such as killing or attempting to kill the abuser, might strike disinterested individuals as extreme, irrational, or premeditated, particularly if the victim has escaped and returned or resisted others' efforts to intervene. If a victim has been punished—for trying to placate the abuser, escape, or defend herself—when threatened with death, she may believe homicide is the only action that will ensure her survival.

A Feminist Critique of Battered Woman Syndrome   Opposition to the wholesale clinical application of battered woman syndrome to all women who kill abusive mates is not based on the belief that no clinical reactions occur; rather, it is founded on the belief that the danger to which battered women react is real and deadly. Critics of the syndrome argue that women's reactions are reasonable and that these women should not have to be labeled mentally ill to have their actions judged as such. Instead of focusing on the woman's perceptions, they advocate an examination of the social context that entraps women in violent relationships.

Battered woman syndrome is gender specific. It is one result of women's difficulties in defending themselves against spouses who are larger, stronger, and better trained to fight. It is related to women's economic dependence on their spouses, their difficulties in supporting themselves and their children, and their socialization to be passive and dependent and to put the needs of others before their own (Gillespie 1989; Gilligan 1982). Although not all abused women experience battered woman syndrome, its presence is related to women's experiences in a misogynist society. Feminist expert witnesses argue that evidence of the syndrome introduced in court can educate judges and juries about the woman's perceptions at the time she committed the homicide. Other feminists argue that the focus should be on women's experiences and the society that permits such violence to occur. Battered woman syndrome has the potential to be used both ways.

Prevalence of Wife Abuse

Every year approximately 2.5 million of the women in the United States, age 12 or older, are raped, robbed, or assaulted or are victims of attempts or threats of such crimes. Approximately two-thirds of such attacks are committed by acquaintances (Snell 1994). Among married couples, more than three million spouses severely assault their partners one or more times each year (Straus and Gelles 1988). The incidence among cohabitating couples is even higher (Stets and Straus 1989). Women are approximately six times more likely than men to experience violence committed by an intimate partner (U.S. Department of Justice 1995). Although some men are abused by their female partners (Gelles and Straus 1988), the violence men inflict against women is more frequent and severe (Berk et al. 1983; Browne 1987; Straus 1980). Between 22 and 35 percent of the women in hospital emergency rooms are there because of symptoms related to abuse (Warshaw 1990). Twenty-five percent of women seen by psychiatric emergency services are victims of domestic violence, and 25 percent of obstetrical patients are in abusive relationships (Dickstein and Nadelson 1989).

When women leave violent relationships, they may be in worse danger than if they had stayed. Among female victims, those separated from their partners for six months or less are three times more likely to be physically assaulted than are women who are divorced from their partners, and about 25 times more likely than are married women (U.S. Department of Justice 1995). Women commit less than 15 percent of all homicides in the United States, but when they do kill, it is often to defend themselves from men who have repeatedly beaten them (Browne 1989). When women are victims of homicide, they are significantly more likely to be killed by an intimate partner than are male victims. In 1992, approximately 28 percent of female victims in the United States were known to have been killed by a current or former intimate partner, whereas only 3.5 percent of males fit this category (U.S. Department of Justice 1995). Approximately half of all women inmates have been physically abused at some time in their lives (Bureau of Justice Statistics 1994; Correctional Association of New York 1991). Whether or not such women are in prison for killing or assaulting the men who abused them, most need services to help them cope with their experiences so that when they are released from prison, as most eventually are, they will be able to live free of violence.

Policing of domestic violence has improved over the last two decades. Policies have shifted from arrest as last resort to mandatory arrest in some areas and preferred arrest in others. Many districts have implemented mandatory domestic violence training sessions for police officers. Victim assistance units help women negotiate the criminal justice system and secure protective orders. Nonetheless, arrest has mixed results. Sometimes it deters further violence; sometimes it increases the likelihood of recurrence (Sherman, Schmidt, and Rogan 1992). Protective orders are more readily available to battered women but cannot stop someone from harming or killing another person. They may even increase the risk or seriousness of future violence. Whether they have a negative or only a null effect, weak enforcement is the reason such orders are ineffective (Sherman et al. 1992).

There are numerous reasons jurisdictions place batterers in court-ordered counseling, including jail overcrowding and a desire to preserve the family. Victims often prefer therapy to a jail sentence. After being ordered into counseling, if a batterer misses a specified number of sessions he may be ordered to serve a jail sentence. Although this policy provides apparent assistance to victims, research has shown low success rates, as measured by documented repeat offenses (Sherman et al. 1992). Despite efforts to improve policing and the prosecution and treatment of batterers, women continue to live in a system that is unable to protect them, expects them to leave an abusive spouse, does not provide adequate resources to those trying to escape, and fails to understand the psychological responses of those who refuse to leave, even when leaving seems possible to outsiders. When battered women do leave abusive relationships, the legal system and shelters are often unable to keep them safe from men intent on stalking, harming, and killing them. Although many women escape violent relationships each year, others are trapped.

Self-Defense Law

Many battered women live with violence and abuse for years. It is when they feel their lives, or the lives of their children, are endangered that they defend themselves by killing or attempting to kill the abusive partner (Browne 1987; Walker 1987). Frequently, however, the homicide does not meet the legal criteria of self-defense, which include the following: (1) the honest and reasonable belief that (2) one is in imminent or immediate danger of death or serious bodily harm, (3) that the use of force is necessary to avoid danger, and (4) that a reasonable amount of force was used to repel the attack (Gillespie 1989; Thyfault 1984; Van Cleave 1994). A reasonable amount of force is legally defined as the least amount necessary to repel the assailant, considering the level of danger posed and the available means of deterrence. In a minority of jurisdictions, the defendant must demonstrate the absence of an escape route unless the crime occurred in her or his home (Browne 1987; Fiora-Gormally 1978; Gillespie 1989; Maguigan 1991). In most jurisdictions an individual is not legally required to escape from her or his own home, but many people expect a woman to leave an abusive relationship and are uneasy when she takes action to defend herself, even if she is in serious danger (Browne 1987).

Women who kill their abusers, like all others who claim to have killed in self-defense, must convince juries that they reacted in a "reasonable" manner. In most jurisdictions, reasonableness is measured in terms of the circumstances surrounding the homicide. The defendant's actions are judged in the context of experiences with the abuser and her perceptions at the time of the crime (Maguigan 1991). This type of test is subjective. In a minority of jurisdictions, a less context-specific, "reasonable man" standard is used (see Gillespie 1989). This standard is objective. The standard of reasonableness is based upon legal theory that assumes that one person will not ambush another, that combatants will be equally armed, and that both are of equivalent size, strength, and fighting ability (Gillespie 1989).

Battered women who kill their abusers tend to do so in one of two situations. The first is a "traditional confrontational case," which refers to a situation in which the battered woman kills (or tries to kill) her partner while she is under physical attack. The second is a "nontraditional confrontational case" (hereafter "nonconfrontational"), in which the woman kills her partner after a fight or when no altercation is taking place (Bates 1991).[6]

When a woman who kills her abuser claims she acted in self-defense, two defense strategies may be employed. In the first type, "perfect self-defense," the woman must show that she honestly *and* reasonably believed she was in imminent danger of serious bodily harm and that the use of force was necessary to avoid injury or death (Gillespie 1989; Van Cleave 1994). If her belief is found to be honest and reasonable and the danger she faced was imminent, then her actions are to be judged "justifiable" and she is legally entitled to be acquitted of all charges.

If the woman repelled her partner's attack in a confrontational situation, using reasonable force, the introduction of evidence of past abuse and expert testimony about battered woman syndrome might not be necessary to support a claim of self-defense; however, it could assist the judge and jury in understanding why she used what might seem to be excessive force. Because women in heterosexual relationships are normatively smaller and weaker than their partners, it is unlikely that the use of nondeadly force—for example, hitting back—will have a deterrent effect. Therefore, women sometimes use weapons to compensate for the physical differences between them and their partners. Because they are terrified of the consequences of defending themselves, women sometimes use more force than necessary to repel the attack. For example, if a man has repeatedly and severely beaten his partner over a long period of time, when he threatens to kill her and begins coming toward her she may pick up a gun. Rather than shooting once to repel the danger, she may shoot repeatedly, following him when he attempts to retreat.

This is what happened to one of the women interviewed for this book. Her partner had bought her a gun so she could protect herself from men he believed were bothering her. He had threatened to kill two of her male coworkers, had taken her car away from her, and had beaten her when she did anything he did not like. When she shot her partner the first time, he was coming toward her, threatening to kill her. She shot him a second time when he began throwing furniture. She shot again and again, missing most of the time, following him out of her apartment. She attempted to reload the gun while he was in the ambulance. Her actions sound excessive unless one understands the context of their relationship and her perceptions when she was shooting at him. When I interviewed her a year after her release from prison, she said, "When I shot him the first time and I realized he wasn't dead, he was still alive, he was . . . going to kill me. He said it . . . and that's why I followed him out. . . . And when he went in the [ambulance] . . . I was cut off. Here he is, alive! He's not dead! He's going to kill me."[7] When a bystander convinced her to give up her gun, she begged him not to let the abuser come out of the ambulance and kill her.

In the second defense strategy, imperfect self-defense, the woman must show that she honestly, but not reasonably, believed she was in imminent danger of serious bodily harm and that the use of force was necessary (Gillespie 1989; Van Cleave 1994). Imperfect self-defense is most likely to be argued in cases of homicides that occurred in nonconfrontational situations. Although the woman's belief that she was in danger may have been authentic, it may be judged by a jury to have been unreasonable. For example, in some situations a man may beat his wife and children over many years. Although the wife may have called the police on many occasions, sought help from clergy, and left home, over time she may have learned that help was not available and that permanently escaping from the relationship with several children was impossible for her. When the severity of abuse escalated, she may have honestly believed that her life or her children's lives were in danger.

This was the case for another woman interviewed for this book. She was married for 23 years, through the early 1980s. Throughout her marriage, when this woman called the police to protect her and her children from her husband's rampages, the police told her there was nothing they could do. Her priest told her to pray for her husband. Most of the community knew what was happening, but no one intervened. During her marriage, the woman fled frequently with her children, hiding in motels until she thought it safe to go home. When her husband beat her youngest child with a chain, threatened another child with a knife, and beat him with a blackjack, she hired someone to kill him. The jury was not permitted to hear about the history of her relationship with her late husband, nor were they allowed to know that the police had failed to help. They never heard about her efforts to protect her children. They were not given the opportunity to learn about the dynamics of violent relationships or this woman's state of mind when she hired the killer. The jury had to judge her actions according to the standards of self-defense law that focus on the imminence of danger and the reasonableness of response. They did not know she was trying to protect her children from a man who had beaten his family for more than 20 years, so they convicted this woman of murder and sentenced her to serve 25 years to life.

It is for nonconfrontational situations, such as the one just described, that it is most important for the jury to learn about the history of abuse and that expert testimony is most needed, and it is for these situations that such evidence is least likely to be permitted, unless specifically set forth by law (Bates 1991). Unless jurors know about the history of abuse and the problems a woman experienced in trying to end the violence or escape the relationship, they might find that the homicide was premeditated. If they are given an opportunity to learn about the relationship, the social context in which it occurred, and the woman's psychological reaction to abuse, however, they may be more likely to find that the homicide was either justifiable, if they are convinced the woman honestly and reasonably believed the danger was imminent, or excusable, if they think her perceptions were honest but not reasonable. In cases in which juries believe the homicide was excusable, women tend to be found guilty of lesser degrees of murder or of manslaughter and sentenced to shorter prison terms.

The greatest obstacle facing women in nonconfrontational situations is meeting the criteria of "imminence." Although the introduction of expert testimony and evidence of past abuse can help reduce the level of conviction for women tried in such cases, jurors wishing to acquit these women must go outside the law (Miller 1994). Because of these limitations, Miller has argued that to address the circumstances of all battered women who kill and to remedy the gender biases in self-defense law, statutes should be revised to provide for circumstances of "imminent or unavoidable" danger. Because battered women are often threatened with death or serious harm if they attempt to leave, and because the homicide rates of women who leave their abusers are higher than for those who stay, danger may not always be imminent, but it is certainly unavoidable.

Despite the criteria established in self-defense law, battered women who kill abusive partners tend to resort to such violence as a final attempt to protect themselves from further physical or mental harm or when they believe their life or their children's lives are in danger (Walker 1984). Because battered women become expert at reading the verbal and nonverbal cues their partners provide, they are frequently able to predict if and when a beating is about to occur (Walker 1979, 1984). Believing a beating is imminent or unavoidable and that it will result in death or serious injury, many battered women strike first. They believe they are acting in self-defense, even though according to the criteria established in law the homicide frequently meets the criteria for murder.

Feminists throughout the United States have argued that for battered women to receive fair trials, the law must be reformed to permit jurors to consider all aspects of the legal defense that is offered. To accomplish this, two reforms are necessary. First, defendants must be permitted to introduce all evidence that will educate jurors about the history and social context of the relationship and the state of mind of the woman when she committed the homicide. Jurors should not be limited in their decision about self-defense, nor in the type of self-defense; rather, the facts should be put before them, and they should be permitted to decide on a defendant's guilt or innocence. Second, feminists argue that society itself must be transformed so that jurors no longer bring to their deliberations stereotypes of battered women and women who kill.

Feminists have debated how battered woman syndrome should be used in legal defense strategies for women who have killed abusive partners. Although positions are not dichotomous, there has been an ongoing "frame dispute" (Bedford 1993) surrounding battered woman syndrome almost since the beginning of the battered women's movement. The dispute has been less prominent in the clemency movement, but it is present. Despite this controversy, legal recognition of battered woman syndrome and the right to introduce expert testimony became a goal of many feminist trial court activists in the battered women's movement, beginning in the late 1970s and continuing through the 1990s. Several states have passed legislation ensuring a defendant's right to introduce evidence of abuse and/or expert testimony about the syndrome when on trial for killing or assaulting a person who has abused her.

Why Clemency?

Many women in prison are serving sentences for crimes committed in an era when police were reluctant to arrest batterers, shelters were rare, and society widely assumed that a battered woman must have done something to deserve abuse. At trial these women were prevented from introducing evidence and testimony that might have helped a judge and jury understand the danger they were in, how they were trapped in the relationship, and why they honestly and reasonably believed they had to kill to prevent serious bodily harm or death. Some of the clemency recipients I talked with spoke of being triply victimized: first by their partners, second by a system that failed to protect them, and third by courts that refused to permit them to fully defend themselves at trial. All expressed deep remorse for their crimes, and most said they still loved and missed the men they killed; all believed that clemency was the only form of justice they had experienced.

Clemency is a generic legal term that includes any executive act that reduces or alleviates a penalty for a crime. Such acts include reprieves, which delay the penalty; commutations, which decrease sentences; pardons, which reduce penalties and expunge the crime from the record; or conditional pardons, which forgive the crime once certain conditions have been met. Clemency has become a goal of individual states' battered women's movements for three reasons. First, in most circumstances, homicide is a crime against the state, not the federal government. Second, there is no federal binding legislation or case law that pertains to battered women's rights when they are on trial for killing or assaulting their abusers. Most criminal law pertaining to homicide is written and administered at the state and local levels. Laws that govern such cases and rules applying to executive clemency vary from state to state. Third, feminists recognize that clemency is one way of achieving partial justice for women who were prevented from fully defending themselves at trial. Helping battered women escape abusive relationships is one tactic the movement can use in its efforts to achieve justice for abused women. Clemency is another.

Chapter Three

Political Trials and Legal Reform

The Celeste clemencies and the feminist activism that brought them about were part of a nationwide movement to challenge the gender biases in self-defense law and achieve justice for women convicted under androcentric laws. This activism was not only an effort to address the concerns of individual women; it sought to demonstrate how self-defense laws prevented women from receiving fair trials. In the course of devising effective legal defense strategies, activists worked to raise public awareness of the issues surrounding the trials of women who had defended themselves from men who had abused them.

The legal defense branch of the battered women's movement has been steeped first in radical feminism and later in cultural feminism. Although it used the courts to bring about change, its goal was not liberal reform but rather transformation of the assumptions underlying criminal law. The legal defense branch of the battered women's movement emerged from feminist activism surrounding the trials of women who had defended themselves or their children from strangers. As strategies were formulated, information about the feminist analysis of self-defense law began to be informally distributed to attorneys defending women who had "fought back" and to activists and social service providers working with such women.

As the demand for information grew, feminist attorneys founded a national organization—the Women's Self-Defense Law Project—with the goal of disseminating information and educating attorneys about gender biases in self-defense law and legal strategies for challenging and overcoming them. In the late 1970s, the Women's Self-Defense Law Project was the only national organization exclusively focusing on challenging gender biases in self-defense law. It effectively went out of existence in 1980, leaving an organizationally based leadership void in the legal defense branch of the movement. Nonetheless, the Women's Self-Defense Law Project had a major impact on the future goals and direction trial activists would take.

The Project advocated incorporating evidence of the social and physical differences between women and men into self-defense strategies and interpretations of imminence and reasonable force. Grassroots trial court activists drew upon and deviated from the example set by Project attorneys. Many grassroots activists advocated that expert testimony about battered woman syndrome be admitted into evidence to educate judges and juries about the defendant's perceptions and actions in light of the physical and social differences between the sexes. They reasoned that the syndrome would provide a means by which evidence of past abuse and the social context of the relationship could be introduced.

The unrestricted use of battered woman syndrome has never been advocated as a defense strategy by a national organization. Though national leaders have argued for its use in specific circumstances, for example, as a strategy for introducing evidence to a jury, they have worked to avoid psychological explanations for women's behavior. Nonetheless, some psychologists and legal scholars have advocated the syndrome's use and argued for an expanded version of the definition of battered woman syndrome (Callahan 1994; Dutton 1993). Others have advocated for testimony that shows similarities among the psychological reactions of battered women, prisoners of war, hostages, and other victims of terror (Browne 1993; Graham et al. 1994).

While feminist legal scholars and those associated with the Women's Self-Defense Law Project were cautioning against the wholesale use of expert testimony on battered woman syndrome, grassroots defense attorneys, shelter activists, and expert witnesses were advocating expert testimony for women. These efforts were an unintended outgrowth of the influence of defense theories and strategies the Women's Self-Defense Law Project developed. With a void in national leadership, the syndrome became a way to bridge the discursive gap between activists and the judicial system.

In the first part of this chapter, I examine the nationwide efforts of feminist attorneys, legal scholars, and activists to challenge and transform self-defense law over the last two decades. I describe the major national organizations that worked to coordinate the work of activist attorneys, examine resulting case law, and analyze transformations in movement goals and strategies. Throughout this chapter I argue that in addition to seeking pragmatic solutions to the legal problems facing individual women, the goal of the legal defense branch of the battered women's movement has been to demonstrate the extent to which the legal system has condoned male violence toward women, prevented women defendants from receiving fair trials, and served as a tool of political oppression against women. Trends in legal strategies show that the institutional barriers presented by the courts, together with concerns about keeping battered women out of prison, led to a greater grassroots focus on pragmatic solutions at the expense of exposing gender biases in the law and society.

Conceptual Framework

One of the central tasks facing a social movement is to formulate a collectively held belief system about the issues to be addressed. In many cases, the movement must transform the issue from a private malady to a social problem. Leaders must theorize about social causes underlying the problem, social agents responsible for perpetuating it, and social conditions that must be altered for the problem to be solved (see Tierney 1982). This process has been referred to by Snow and Benford (1992) as "framing." Collective action frames are dynamic efforts by movements to "package" an issue by creating a sense of injustice and attributing blame for it to a particular social group or agent (Snow and Benford 1992). In an informal sense, a movement creates a theory about the source of and solutions to the problem and presents it to the public or authorities or both. Master frames are more abstract theories that guide the discourse of movements within the social movement sector (Snow and Benford 1992). Like theories to a paradigm, the collective action frames of individual movements are likely to adhere to the discourse of the larger master frame.

The master frame of the movements of the 1960s and early 1970s focused on structural and cultural inequality, with goals such as equal rights, justice, and freedom from oppression. When the battered women's movement began in the mid-1970s, the cycle of protest that had begun in the 1950s was reaching the end of its heyday (Jenkins 1987). When the battered women's movement became well established in the late 1970s, the cycle of protest was in decline (Jenkins

1987) and the antifeminist backlash was gaining momentum (Craw-ford 1980; Faludi 1991). Mental health professionals began to reframe battered women's issues in nonoppositional terms and to encroach on the movement (Johnson 1981; Schechter 1982). The master frame of that cycle of protest began to shift toward personal development, and many radical feminists began to turn toward cultural feminism (Echols 1989).

Whereas radical feminists were social constructionists in orienta-tion and sought to eliminate the sex-class system, cultural feminists based their discourse on essentialist premises, with an emphasis on elevating women's inherent virtues and stressing women's spiritual growth (Echols 1989). Radical feminists focused on the similarities be-tween the sexes and the social forces that resulted in differences. Cul-tural feminists focused on the differences, attributing much of the dis-similarity in behavior to differing reproductive capacities (e.g., Smith 1990). When women exhibit behaviors similar to those men tradition-ally engage in, cultural feminists focus on the patriarchal forces that result in such conduct.

Within the legal defense branch of the battered women's move-ment, there has been a great deal of overlap between those who argue in favor of introducing evidence that shows a defendant's actions to have been reasonable and those who advocate introducing expert tes-timony on battered woman syndrome to demonstrate the reasonable-ness of the defendant's perceptions. These groups represent different strategies within a feminist dialogue about the direction the move-ment should take. They are united by the feminist collective action frame and by pragmatic legal goals.

To effect social change, a movement must create an alternative vi-sion of the world and convince others to believe in and follow that view (Dobash and Dobash 1992). To enhance their chances of mobi-lizing potential participants, persuading bystanders, and achieving their goals, activists must develop a collective action frame that agrees with something the public already believes, a process referred to as "frame alignment" (Klandermans 1992; Snow et al. 1986). Alterna-tively, the movement must convert the public to its collective action frame, a strategy that is likely to require greater resources (Klander-mans 1992). In movements in which there are no pragmatic repercus-sions for holding out, ideological purity has fewer consequences, but when individuals' lives are endangered or when people are on trial or in prison, the issues take on greater immediacy.

In the late 1970s, feminist attorneys and legal scholars focused on sociological trends that resulted in gender differences and the injustice of requiring women to meet legal standards established by and for men. These activists argued that because of physical and socialized differences, laws that require women to use equal force in the face of imminent danger are biased. Early feminist legal successes on behalf of women who defended themselves had a significant impact upon the efforts of the battered women's movement to devise new self-defense strategies for women who killed abusers.

While self-defense activists were drawing upon sociological and feminist research, three trends that transformed the political-opportunity context of the movement were occurring. First, a greater emphasis on battered women's mental health had found its way into the movement, particularly within shelters and safe homes. Second, the women's movement was shifting away from radical feminism's emphasis on personal empowerment and structural change and toward the cultural feminist analysis of inherent gender differences. Third, the governmental leadership surrounding feminist issues that characterized the Carter administration fell victim to Ronald Reagan. Battered women needed to find ways to translate their experiences into terminology the courts would admit into evidence.

Within communications, critical theory explains the way that oppressed groups are silenced in society. "Muted group" theory (Ardener 1975; 1978) argues that language has a bias that reflects the experience of males and "mutes" the lives, experiences, and voices of women. The assumptions of muted group theory are that men and women have different experiences in life, based on the gender division of labor. Men are politically dominant in society, and their systems of perception are hegemonic, preventing women's perceptions from becoming institutionally adopted. Therefore women must translate their experiences into terms that coincide with the male worldview to participate in public life (Kramarae 1981; Littlejohn 1996). This translation process is similar to that of frame alignment, which presents new visions in old terminology that dominant groups are more likely to understand and accept. A problem is that by translating rather than challenging, a social movement may lose its oppositional character.

Because rules of evidence regarding the admission of expert testimony were established within a framework that recognizes scientific knowledge above other types, activists needed to translate their expertise about women's reactions to abuse into scientific terms to get their evidence admitted. To do this, many grassroots activists shifted from using arguments about the socialization of girls and boys, differences in physical stature, and arguments about battered women toward using the more scientific psychological "syndrome," ultimately recognized by the American Psychological Association.[1] At the same time, national leaders and legal scholars warned against dependence on clinical definitions of the syndrome and continued to advocate legal defense strategies that focused on the context of the relationship.

Among grassroots lawyers and expert witnesses, the shift from radical to cultural feminist analyses occurred because they were more easily aligned with rules of evidence. By shifting from a discourse of oppression to that of a psychological syndrome, attorneys and expert witnesses thought they could align their arguments with beliefs that women are more gentle and must be driven to a psychologically abnormal state in order to kill. As with most efforts to bridge the differences between worldviews, something got lost in the translation.

The benefit of recognition of the syndrome is that once it was established as a scientific profile, it fit within barriers established by the courts. Unlike other governmental entities, courts are limited to recognizing only certain types of expert testimony evidence, under specific circumstances. According to the *Federal Rules of Evidence* and case law (*Dyas v. United States* 376 A2d 827, D.C. 1977), expert testimony may be admitted under the following conditions: (1) scientific, technical, or other specialized knowledge must assist the jury in understanding the evidence; (2) a witness must be qualified by the court as an expert by demonstrating that she or he has a specific type of knowledge, skill, experience, training, or education that the average person lacks; (3) the expert's knowledge must be outside the jury's understanding; (4) there must be general acceptance of the expert's methodology within the scientific community; (5) the expert's testimony must do more to reveal the facts of the case than to prejudice the jury. In legal terms, it must be more probative than prejudicial; (6) unless given specific permission by the court, expert witnesses may not testify that the defendant did or did not have battered woman syndrome.[2] In some jurisdictions, defendants must present evidence at a preliminary hearing,[3] to establish that they are battered women,[4] that the proposed expert is qualified to offer an expert opinion,[5] and that the testimony is relevant and otherwise admissible (Andersen and Read-Andersen 1992, 376; endnotes in original).

Expert testimony about battering has been accepted by courts throughout the nation and has been successfully presented on behalf of numerous defendants. An expanded, nonclinical definition of the syndrome may provide a venue through which radical and cultural feminists' collective action frames may be presented in court. It allows radical feminism's emphasis on social conditions as the root of wife abuse to be introduced. Cultural feminists' belief that women's homicidal acts are one result of misogynist social conditions may be allowed as evidence. Battered woman syndrome may, when it is used in an expansive, nonclinical way, encompass the collective action frames held by national leaders and grassroots activists of the legal defense branch of the battered women's movement.

Nonetheless, the syndrome tends to be misinterpreted to mean that a battered woman who stays with an abusive mate is mentally ill. The problem with battered woman syndrome is its failure to incorporate a complete analysis of women's response to violence, the similarity of battered women's psychological profiles to other victims of terrorism, and the social context that entraps women in abusive relationships. It has shifted legal understandings of the problem from the androcentric biases in self-defense law and onto the battered woman, whose actions are judged within the confines of self-defense law.

The National Battered Women's Movement

In the late 1970s, one national organization devised policy and loosely coordinated the strategy of the battered women's movement. The National Coalition against Domestic Violence (NCADV) was founded in 1978 in Washington, D.C., as a "membership organization for local programs and state coalitions."[6] It grew out of earlier opportunities for feminists to meet and discuss wife abuse, including the 1977 White House meeting on families and the 1977 International Women's Year conference. NCADV was founded in January 1978 during a workshop entitled "Consultation on Battered Women: Issues of Public Policy," sponsored by the United States Commission on Civil Rights. The workshop was organized because feminist aides to President Carter had decided that "We needed women on the inside and activists from the outside exerting pressure and supporting one another " (Schechter 1982, 136). NCADV's role was to coordinate the collective action frames and activities of groups outside government. Its goal was to provide a national voice for local programs, define the philosophy behind the movement, and advocate on behalf of constituents of under-represented groups.

By the mid-1980s, NCADV experienced internal division over the acceptance of a Department of Justice grant and subsequent governmental efforts to control the content of educational materials published by the organization. Despite these problems, NCADV was active in establishing movement policy and coordinating testimony before the federal government. Nonetheless, its effectiveness decreased and it played only a minor role in the emergent development of defense strategies for battered women.

The Women's Self-Defense Law Project   From the mid- to late 1970s, feminist attorneys took on a number of precedent-setting cases for women who had fought back against men who assaulted or threatened them or their children. These cases brought feminist attorneys into contact with a community of legal defense activists that became the core of the legal defense branch of the battered women's movement. In 1978 the Women's Self-Defense Law Project was founded by feminist attorneys Elizabeth Schneider and Susan Jordan, with assistance from the Center for Constitutional Rights and the National Jury Project.

The Project's goal was to help lawyers in the United States more effectively represent female victims of violence who had defended themselves (Bochnak 1981; Schneider 1986; Schneider et al. 1978). Project activists consulted on more than one hundred cases, working on case analysis, development of defense theory and expert testimony, and preparation of witnesses. It developed legal and educational materials, led training seminars for lawyers and others, and served as a public education resource on women's self-defense issues (Schneider 1986, 195). In the late 1970s it was the most important resource center for attorneys representing women who had defended themselves. Its work was supported by the American Civil Liberties Union (ACLU), which provided amicus curiae (friend of the court) briefs in several cases.

In the mid-1970s, attorneys who would later organize the Women's Self-Defense Law Project successfully argued cases within the feminist theories discussed earlier. At the same time, these activists challenged the "reasonable man" standard of self-defense law in states with more objective criteria, arguing that women might reasonably perceive danger in situations in which a man might not (Schneider et al. 1978). Between

1978 and 1980, the Project provided assistance to trial lawyers and loosely coordinated the goals and strategy of the legal defense branch of the movement. It never formally went out of existence, but it discontinued services sometime during 1980 (interview, 27 December 1996).

The legal defense branch of the battered women's movement was initially a loose national network of attorneys, feminist activists, and an emergent community of feminist psychologists. These activists were affiliated through local shelters and hot lines, victim advocacy centers, statewide networks, and feminist communities within the American Psychological Association and bar associations. This social movement community exchanged information through the Women's Self-Defense Law Project and the National Center on Women and Family Law (a project of the Legal Services Corporation). They also communicated through traditional methods of legal research and friendship networks among attorneys and psychologists. In 1978 in Washington, D.C., a clinical psychologist attempted to introduce expert testimony about "battered women" at the trial of a woman who had killed her abusive husband.[7] That testimony drew upon research regarding the social-psychological dynamics of violent relationships and the resulting psychological profile of women victims. With this case, the focus began to shift from feminist sociological theories toward the relationship itself. By 1980 one successful effort had been made to introduce evidence of "battered woman syndrome," ironically to oppose the insanity defense of a man who tried to kill his wife.[8] In 1981 the admission of expert testimony was upheld by two appellate courts.[9] Previously, the most common reasons trial courts had given for excluding expert testimony were that the information such witnesses could provide was not beyond the understanding of the average juror and that the scientific methodology for establishing battered woman syndrome was not established.[10]

Whereas attorneys associated with the Women's Self-Defense Law Project presented evidence to demonstrate the gender biases in self-defense law, many attorneys in the 1980s turned to expert testimony on battered woman syndrome as a way to educate the jury about women's perceptions of the reasonableness of their actions. The syndrome had the potential to be used to discuss such sociological factors as lack of police protection, women's lack of physical and self-defense training, and economic disparities between the genders, but it tended to be interpreted more narrowly in court.

The benefit of focusing on a "syndrome" was that once professional activists could show that the methodology surrounding it had been scientifically established, attorneys could more readily overcome structural barriers in the legal process and introduce evidence in support of a claim of self-defense. The problem is that it moved the focus away from the gender inequities in the law and society and toward the relationship and ultimately onto the defendant. By the mid-1980s, legal scholars began to argue that the syndrome had the potential to reify stereotypes about women as passive, dependent, and perhaps most damaging of all, less rational and reasonable than men (Schneider 1986). But by that time, the most commonly used strategy among grassroots activists had shifted from direct confrontation, with evidence based upon sociological trends, toward one that bridged discursive differences between activists and the courts. Grassroots activists emphasized reasonable reactions to unreasonable situations by framing their arguments within the discourse of battered woman syndrome.

Despite these efforts, many defendants were represented by attorneys who had little understanding of the dynamics of wife abuse or the psychological response to chronic violence. They were usually not aware of the movement's efforts to disseminate information to trial lawyers. By the mid-1980s, during the Reagan and Bush administrations, the national leadership on domestic violence that had begun during the Carter administration was eliminated and the meager funding provided to organizations such as the Legal Services Corporation's National Center on Women and Family Law was cut even further.[11]

The National Clearinghouse for the Defense of Battered Women
In 1987 the National Clearinghouse for the Defense of Battered Women was founded by Sue Osthoff and Barbara Hart, two activists associated with the battered women's movement in Pennsylvania. It was the first national organization concentrating on the legal defense of battered women charged with criminal activity. From their experiences, Osthoff and Hart understood the need for an organization whose purpose would be to provide "critical assistance, resources, and support to battered women who (i) have killed or assaulted their abusers while attempting to protect themselves from life-threatening violence, (ii) have been coerced into crime by their abusers, or (iii) are charged with 'failing to protect' their children from their batterers' violence."[12]

The Clearinghouse was organized after one of its founders produced a resource packet about how to help battered women who had killed their abusers. When requests for copies of the packet began coming in, it became apparent that there was need for an organization to coordinate and provide resources for battered women, attorneys, and advocates. Within a few years, the Clearinghouse grew into a major national resource and advocacy center,[13] funded by grants[14] and run by a staff of paid employees, volunteers, and interns.[15]

The Clearinghouse has provided technical assistance and resources to thousands of attorneys, expert witnesses, advocates, journalists, and battered women. It has developed a comprehensive resource library and an accompanying annotated bibliography, provided services to incarcerated battered women, and developed resources for groups interested in working with women in prison. In its first three and a half years alone, it provided assistance to 450 women on trial for crimes related to battering.[16] In 1991 the Clearinghouse added clemency to its focus on battered women, reasoning that despite legislation and case law allowing battered women to introduce expert testimony and evidence of past abuse, new laws were not applied retroactively. "Only action by the Governors could provide these convicted women with any relief," stated one member of the organization.[17]

Although awareness of battering has increased in recent years, women charged with crimes because of their victimization are "vigorously prosecuted by the same criminal justice system that often ignored their pleas for assistance *prior* to the incident."[18] Whereas women might receive sympathy or understanding before committing a crime, afterward they are harshly judged, and "as many as eight out of ten battered women charged with killing their abusers are convicted or plead guilty to some charge."[19] Many are sentenced to long prison terms. Defense attorneys are often unfamiliar with the dynamics of crimes resulting from abuse and know little about defense strategies that could help introduce a defendant's life experiences into evidence. Shelter workers and victim advocates are often untrained in helping battered women charged with killing or assaulting an abuser. Although expert witnesses may understand psychological elements of the syndrome, they frequently have little understanding of how it may be used to support a legal defense. In one of its many publications, the National Clearinghouse argues that "Coordinated advocacy efforts are necessary to combat the high conviction and incarceration rates of battered women defendants. Defense team members ... require up-to-date and accurate information on effective strategies. ... The Clearinghouse facilitates necessary collaboration between battered women's advocates, criminal defense attorneys, prison advocates, social scientists and community members . . . to work together in the development of sensitive, effective legal strategies for battered women defendants."[20]

During the 1980s, shelter directors, victim advocates, and other activists recognized that the keys to survival in a hostile political climate were to create networks to share information and coordinate services, and to hold a unified line against efforts to erode the movement's successes. By 1990, state coalitions against domestic violence had formed in all 50 states and the District of Columbia. In addition to facilitating the transfer of information, establishing and coordinating movement policy, and supporting legislation to aid battered women, many state coalitions became involved in organizing for individual and mass clemencies. Their work was aided by the Clearinghouse. Although it was barely two years old at the time, the Clearinghouse provided assistance to aides to Governor Celeste, with the resulting clemencies increasing public awareness and the demand on its resources.[21]

Political Trials and Legal Strategies

From the late 1970s through the 1980s, the primary tactic of the legal defense branch of the battered women's movement was the use of the "political trial." Political trials are those that proceed within a constitutional structure yet serve "the interests of those holding power, whether the power holder is a dominant economic or social group, an individual sovereign, or a ruling party or faction" (Ulmschneider 1995, 123). Here I will argue that such cases also include those whose goal is to demonstrate and challenge biases within the law that serve "the interests of those holding power." Shelters worked to provide emergency housing and other services for battered women while activist attorneys filed class-action lawsuits to compel the police to provide equal protection for battered women (see Jones 1991a; 1991b).

For the battered women who fell through the safety net provided by shelters and police and who resorted to self-defense by killing their abusers, activist attorneys challenged gender biases in self-defense law and devised more effective legal strategies. They did so in a series of political trials that revealed and challenged the androcentric biases in self-defense law, raised public awareness of the cultural contradictions battered women face, and demonstrated that although wife abuse is a problem endured in the "privacy" of the home, it is nonetheless a political issue and a social problem, made worse when battered women defendants are entrapped in violent relationships and denied fair trials when they defend themselves.

Three cases dating from the 1970s are widely recognized as initiating the feminist legal challenge of gender biases in self-defense law. In 1974 Joanne Little, a young African-American woman incarcerated in North Carolina, stabbed a white jailer to death with his knife as he was raping her. Her acquittal was regarded as a victory over racism and was supported by both women's and civil rights groups (Gillespie 1989). The same year in California, Inez Garcia shot and killed a man who had raped her and later threatened to do so again. At trial, Garcia was convicted of second-degree murder. She appealed. The conviction was overturned and a new trial ordered. In 1977, a second jury acquitted her, finding that Garcia had not acted out of revenge for the first rape but in defense against the threatened second rape (Gillespie 1989). The case of *People v. Garcia*[22] set a legal precedent by establishing case law that "extended the interpretation of imminent danger beyond the immediate time period of the assault" (Browne 1987, 172) and recognized the perceptions of danger brought about by the threat of future bodily harm.

In 1977, the conviction of Yvonne Wanrow for second-degree murder and first-degree assault was overturned by the Washington Supreme Court.[23] Wanrow was a Native American who lived with her two children in Spokane County, Washington. Known child molester William Wesler had been released from a mental hospital into her neighborhood. Several months before the homicide, Wesler had molested one of Wanrow's neighbor's children. On the day before the killing, he had attempted to abduct one of Wanrow's children. When this occurred, the neighbor, Shirley Hooper, who was baby-sitting the children, called the police and was told there was nothing they could do until the following Monday morning, when Hooper could sign an arrest warrant. Police advised Hooper to get a baseball bat and "conk him over the head" if Wesler tried to enter her house. The two women decided to spend the night together, and Wanrow brought a pistol with her to Hooper's home. The two women then decided that they were too afraid to spend the night alone. They invited Wanrow's sister and brother-in-law, Angie and Chuck Michel, to stay with them. The four adults stayed up all night, guarding eight children.

Early in the morning, Chuck Michel confronted Wesler, asking him to come to the house to straighten things out. Once in the house,

Wesler, who was intoxicated, was asked to leave. He refused and made comments about a young child who was sleeping on the couch. According to the Supreme Court decision, "Ms. Michel stepped between Wesler and the child. By this time, Hooper was screaming for Wesler to get out. Ms. Wanrow, a 5'4" woman who at the time had a broken leg and was using a crutch, testified that she then went to the front door to enlist the aid of Chuck Michel."[24] When Wanrow turned around, Wesler was behind her. She shot him in a startled reflex action. Wanrow claimed she shot Wesler in self-defense. The issue before the court was the standard of reasonableness of her actions.

After Wanrow was convicted of second-degree murder and first-degree assault with a deadly weapon, feminist attorneys who would later found the Women's Self-Defense Law Project became involved in her case. The Center for Constitutional Rights in New York submitted an amicus curiae brief to the Washington Supreme Court. The brief argued that women have been discriminated against in their access to sports and self-defense training, have been socialized to equate femininity with helplessness, and might reasonably perceive danger in situations that men might not. The only fair standard by which to judge the reasonableness of a woman's actions when defending herself is one that incorporates the woman's perceptions of danger (Gillespie 1989).

That case raised several issues and established a precedent that was employed in subsequent cases. First, the court found that "[w]oman defendant's right to equal protection of the law was violated . . . by persistent use of male gender, that woman's conduct in defending herself [was] measured against that of a reasonable male finding himself in the same circumstances."[25] Second, following *People v. Garcia,* it found that the justification of self-defense should be evaluated in light of all the facts and circumstances known to the defendant, including those known before the killing and not limited to those known at or immediately before the killing. Third, it found that "Until such time as effects of nation's long and unfortunate history of sex discrimination are eradicated, care must be taken to assure that self-defense instructions afford women the right to have their conduct judged in light of individual physical handicaps which are product of sex discrimination and to fail to do so is to deny right of individual woman involved to trial by same rules which are applicable to male defendants."[26]

Feminists defending Yvonne Wanrow accomplished the following goals when the court rendered its decision: they (1) challenged the sexist language of the law and the objective "reasonable man" standard of justifiable homicide; (2) reinforced the expansion of imminence beyond the immediate time of the assault; and (3) allowed for consideration of physical differences between the defendant and the deceased and differences in socialization and self-defense or combat training between the sexes. This case set a precedent to be drawn upon by battered women who argued that they should be permitted to introduce evidence of past abuse and threats of future death or bodily harm in support of their claims of self-defense. It opened the way for educating juries about battered women's state of mind when they kill an abusive partner.

Initially, feminist attorneys focused on how social conditions and physical differences might lead a woman to perceive danger when a man might not; however, in time grassroots activists would focus on the state of mind of the battered woman, with more emphasis on the battering relationship and less on the social context. Expert testimony about battered woman syndrome became the primary strategy by which defense attorneys attempted to help judges and jurors understand the reasonableness of battered defendants' perceptions and actions at the time a crime was committed.

Rules of Evidence, Legal Barriers, and Recognition of Battered Woman Syndrome Unlike the reforms begun under *Little, Garcia,* and *Wanrow,* expert testimony about "battered women" and later "battered woman syndrome" established its place in case law through a circuitous route. In February 1976 Beverly Ibn-Tamas shot and killed her husband, Dr. Yusef Ibn-Tamas, after three and a half years of abuse. The case was tried in September 1976 and Ibn-Tamas was convicted of second-degree murder while armed; however, the judge ordered a new trial based on a technical matter. In July 1977 Ibn-Tamas was convicted of the same crime. Because the judge found mitigating circumstances surrounding the homicide, he sentenced Ibn-Tamas to one to five years in prison. She appealed based on six issues, including the exclusion of expert testimony about "battered women."[27] At trial, the expert witness, Dr. Lenore Walker, had proffered testimony (read into the record but not given before the jury) to explain (1) who can be characterized as "battered women," (2) why the mentality and behavior of such women are at odds with what an ordinary person might expect, and (3) why Ibn-Tamas perceived herself to be in imminent danger at the time of the shooting. Walker's testimony included an explanation of her research on 110 battered women, the cycle of violence, women's shame about the abuse, and their fear of leaving. When asked whether battered women were a recognized diagnostic category within psychology, she replied that they were not (Walker 1989, 269), and her testimony was excluded.

Beverly Ibn-Tamas served a total of 12 months before being paroled (Walker 1987). She was out of prison when the case was remanded for a new trial, based on the reasoning that expert testimony was central to her defense. The appeals court could not find that the conviction should be reversed because it could not tell from the record whether the criteria for the admission of expert testimony had been met.[28] Before what would have been her third trial, attorneys filed briefs in favor of their positions on the admission of expert testimony. At an evidentiary hearing, the judge ruled that he would not reopen the case on the basis of the exclusion of expert testimony because Ibn-Tamas had failed to establish the scientific recognition of the expert's methodology (Walker 1989).[29] Again, Ibn-Tamas appealed.

The appeals court ruled that the trial court was not required to reopen the case, negating the admissibility of expert testimony on battered women in the District of Columbia. Nonetheless, while the case was handed back and forth between the trial court and the appeals court, a period of six years, it was used as precedent in a number of other cases.[30] Interestingly, *Ibn-Tamas* was a case that offered expert testimony about "battered women," was remanded upon appeal, was never reheard, and at which excluded testimony on battered women set a precedent for the recognition of battered woman syndrome, the research for which, according to Walker, was "only in its infancy."[31]

Expert testimony on battered women and battered woman syndrome was excluded because the scientific methodology for research in this area had not been established. Establishing the scientific legitimacy of battered woman syndrome became a goal among some feminists (Rosewater 1988), whereas others warned against the unrestrained use of a psychological syndrome to explain the reasonableness of the actions of battered women (Browne 1987; 1993; Schneider et al. 1978; Schneider 1986). With the increased focus on the syndrome, the movement's strategy shifted from directly challenging gender biases in society and the law to helping judges and jurors understand the reasonableness of a woman's perception of imminent danger and the need to use deadly force. The shift was subtle but important.

The first time that expert testimony on "battered wife syndrome" was introduced and upheld on appeal was in the 1980 case of a New Hampshire man charged with attempted first-degree murder of his wife.[32] The defendant, Donald Baker, entered a plea of not guilty by reason of insanity. The defense featured two psychiatrists who testified that, in their opinion, Baker was legally insane when he tried to kill his wife. The prosecution entered into evidence the testimony of an expert on domestic violence, who testified that "current research does not indicate that mental illness is an important cause of wife-beating [and] . . . wife-beating is not necessarily caused by or reflective of mental illness. In response to a hypothetical question, [the expert] stated that . . . a marriage such as the defendant's would probably fall within the contours of 'battered wife syndrome.' "[33] The prosecution used this testimony to support its theory that the attempted murder was one in a long series of battering events and had no relation to mental illness or insanity. When Baker appealed his conviction, the Supreme Court of New Hampshire ruled that, regarding expert testimony on battered wife syndrome, "the court did not err in permitting the jury to weigh and determine the probative value of the opinion testimony."[34] Baker's conviction was upheld, and the case was subsequently cited by the Supreme Court of Georgia in the case of Josephine Smith.[35]

In 1981 expert testimony on battered woman syndrome, offered in support of self-defense claims of a woman in Georgia and another in Maine who had killed abusive men, was admitted on appeal. Each of the cases cited *Ibn-Tamas,*[36] and one cited *Baker.*[37] In the Georgia case of *Smith v. State,*[38] Josephine Smith was charged with murdering her boyfriend. Smith lived intermittently with her partner, the father of her second child. On the night she shot and killed her boyfriend, she had returned home around 11 P.M. When her partner began to make sexual advances toward her, she told him to stop because she was tired. He responded by shaking her and saying, " 'You don't tell me when to touch you.' "[39] Later, as Smith sat on the floor, curling her hair, her boyfriend kicked her in the back, hit her in the head with his fist, grabbed her by the throat, choked her, and threw her against a door. Josephine Smith ran to a chest of drawers, grabbed her gun, and ran downstairs to call her mother, but her partner had taken the upstairs phone off the hook. As she ran out of the apartment, her boyfriend slammed the door on her foot. "The defendant then fired the gun three times with her eyes closed."[40]

At trial, Smith testified that her partner had beaten her throughout their relationship. She was afraid to quit seeing him because he threatened her. She testified that the beatings increased in frequency when she moved from her mother's home into her own apartment and that after a beating, her partner would apologize. Smith said she did not call the police or tell her friends because she believed him when he said he would stop beating her. She testified that on the night of the shooting, her partner said he was going to do something to her and call her mother to get her. She was afraid he was going to hurt her more than he had previously and she shot him out of fear for her life.

Smith's attorney called a clinical psychologist whose testimony was ruled inadmissible because the judge believed the jurors could draw their own conclusions as to whether the defendant acted out of fear.[41] The expert proffered testimony that it is not uncommon for battered women to fail to report physical abuse to police or their families. She explained that battered women frequently withhold information about abuse from friends and family members out of fear that they might interfere and be injured. The expert also proffered testimony that it is not unusual for battered women who have been abused over a long period of time to remain in such a situation. The expert explained that such women typically have low self-esteem and believe that the man is not going to repeat the abuse when he promises he will not. The psychologist said that battered women become increasingly afraid for their own well-being.[42] In summary, the expert tried to explain why Smith did not leave her boyfriend and described the defendant's psychological reaction to ongoing abuse.

The jury never got to hear the expert's testimony, and Josephine Smith was convicted of voluntary manslaughter. She appealed, and the court of appeals affirmed the trial court's exclusion of the expert testimony. Smith appealed again, and the Georgia Supreme Court ruled that expert testimony was admissible because it did not interfere with the jury's obligation to determine the facts of the case and was beyond the understanding of the average juror. This ruling expanded the ability of experts to testify in the abstract about battered woman syndrome so they could also render an opinion as to whether the defendant acted in self-defense (Walker 1989). The judgment in Josephine Smith's case was reversed, and she was acquitted.

Throughout the 1980s, overcoming evidentiary rules and gaining the admissibility of expert testimony on battered woman syndrome became the primary goal of grassroots activists involved in the legal defense branch of the battered women's movement. This trend continued despite continued warnings by founders and former members of the Women's Self-Defense Law Project against its unrestricted use. Although the Women's Self-Defense Law Project had some impact on the direction self-defense strategies took during the mid- to late 1970s, by the 1980s the goals of the movement were loosely coordinated through friendship networks within the larger battered women's movement and among trial lawyers and expert witnesses. National organizations advocate the use of battered woman syndrome as a self-defense strategy for battered women only on a case-by-case basis. The movement's focus on it appears to have emerged from grassroots efforts.

Following the Smith case, several other states ruled that jurors could not be expected to draw conclusions about a defendant's behavior without hearing expert testimony (Walker 1989).[43] Overcoming evidentiary rules concerning the understanding of the average juror appears to have been the lowest hurdle activists and appellants faced. The second most difficult rule concerned the need for expert testimony to be more probative than prejudicial, or to reveal more about the facts of the case than to prejudice jurors.

In April 1980 Linda Anaya stabbed and killed her partner, Frank Williams. According to the appellate record, Anaya and Williams had lived together in Cumberland County, Maine, for approximately five months, during which Anaya had attempted suicide at least twice. The couple fought regularly. Williams had threatened to kill Anaya by holding a knife to her throat on one occasion and threatened her with a hammer another time.[44] During the time they lived together, Anaya had stabbed Williams in the back once, and Anaya had received bruises and treatment for a concussion. In March 1980 Anaya was treated for face and head injuries caused by Williams, and according to a neighbor, "[l]ife at the apartment was 'like a madhouse.'"[45] During this period, Williams threatened to kill Anaya if she left him. The facts of the events on the evening of the homicide are unclear, except that a neighbor testified that Williams was intoxicated and that there had been a fight. When the police arrived at the scene, "[t]hey found Frank Williams . . . lying on the floor unconscious while defendant stroked his head and talked to him."[46] At a preliminary hearing, Anaya's attorney called psychologist John Bishop to the stand. After an extensive examination, conducted in the absence of the jury, the judge ruled that Bishop was qualified to testify but that the evidence would be excluded as "irrelevant, prejudicial, and confusing to the jury."[47]

Had he been allowed to testify, Bishop would have described psychology's analysis of the behavioral and emotional patterns of battered women, including the cycle of violence and factors leading to male violence. Later in the trial, the defense attempted to introduce evidence that Linda Anaya was a victim of battered woman syndrome. A doctor who had treated her on at least five occasions testified about the extent and nature of her injuries but was not permitted to testify about the syndrome because the court found the evidence to be irrelevant and without foundation. Anaya was convicted of manslaughter and appealed. In 1981, the Supreme Judicial Court of Maine remanded Anaya's case for retrial, finding that the expert testimony was in fact more probative than prejudicial.[48]

During this time, several convictions and decisions to exclude expert testimony were upheld based upon the previous two rules of evidence. Nonetheless, the body of appellate court decisions during the 1980s suggests that the requirement that the methodology of the expert be accepted within a scientific community was the greatest obstacle to legal recognition of battered woman syndrome. Some courts in the early to mid-1980s did recognize the scientific legitimacy of the syndrome.[49] At least one appeals court equated it with the post-traumatic stress disorder experienced by hostages or prisoners of war and made note of the historical legal and cultural acceptance of wife abuse.[50] Nonetheless, it was not until the early 1990s that other courts began to accept the syndrome as a diagnostic category or to recognize the expert status of those who had worked with or studied battered women and who wished to testify on their behalf.[51]

Part of trial court activists' motivation for focusing their efforts on battered woman syndrome was to overcome institutional barriers to helping jurors understand why battered women do not just leave their partners and why their perceptions and subsequent actions should be judged reasonable. They also worked to expand the applicability of the syndrome to explain seemingly bizarre or sadistic behaviors after the homicide.

In 1983 the Illinois Court of Appeals expanded the admissibility of battered woman syndrome expert testimony when it remanded the case of Jeannette Minnis, a battered woman who dismembered her husband after killing him.[52] According to the appellate record, Jeannette Minnis's husband, Movina, had forced her to solicit other women to have "three-way" sexual encounters, during which the other woman was to instruct Jeannette on how to please Movina. When Jeanette failed to bring home a woman, he would beat her. On the day of the killing, Movina brought home a male prostitute, whom he introduced to Jeannette and took into his weight room. Jeannette was sitting on the floor watching television when Movina and the prostitute came into the room. They pinned her down with a barbell and forced her to watch them have intercourse. After that, both men sexually assaulted Jeannette. Then, fearing that she would tell people about the homosexual encounter, Movina tied Jeannette to a doorknob and left. When he returned, he pushed her head into the toilet and threatened to kill her. He forced her to perform fellatio and then took her into the bedroom to rape her. The two struggled on the bed, and Jeannette managed to push Movina onto the floor. She testified that she then went to the corner where she had always been forced to sit while under punishment from Movina. She remained there, fearful that if she moved, he would kill her. After an undetermined amount of time, she went to check on him. Upon touching him, she realized he was dead, then she dragged him into the bathroom. She resolved that no one would ever know what had happened. She dismembered his body, put the parts in garbage bags, and placed them in dumpsters throughout the Decatur, Illinois, area.

At Minnis's trial, evidence of the dismemberment was introduced, and her attorney argued that he had to introduce evidence of battered woman syndrome to help the jury understand such behavior. The court ruled that the homicide was accidental and that evidence of battered woman syndrome would not be admitted, "since it would be relevant only to the perception in the mind of defendant at the time of the killing," and that "[t]he dismemberment is a factor which the jury can and should consider and literally has nothing whatsoever to do nor is it tied in any way with the battered woman syndrome."[53] The Court of Appeals ruled that although expert testimony in support of the claim of self-defense was unnecessary, the exclusion of expert testimony regarding Minnis's state of mind at the time she dismembered her husband deprived her of "her constitutional right to present a defense."[54] The trial court's decision was reversed, and the case was remanded for a new trial.

By the late 1980s, expert testimony and evidence of past abuse and prior threats were routinely admitted in most states, and factors such as stature and training in self-defense were given consideration in determining whether defendants honestly and reasonably believed they were in danger at the time the homicide was committed. Nonetheless, one of the obstacles that has faced battered women defendants, and that continues to be an institutional barrier to their presentation of a full defense, has been the introduction of evidence in support of a claim of self-defense in nonconfrontational homicide cases (Bates 1991). When defendants are permitted to introduce expert testimony and evidence of past abuse, unless the standard of reasonableness is a subjective one, which allows for a consideration of the defendant's perceptions, an acquittal is still improbable because the jury is unlikely to be instructed on perfect self-defense, making it impossible to acquit on the grounds of justifiability without going outside the law.

In most jurisdictions, meeting the standards of perfect self-defense means the homicide was justifiable and the defendant should be acquitted. Meeting those of imperfect self-defense means the homicide is excusable and the defendant should be found guilty of a lower degree of homicide, such as manslaughter. North Dakota is different. In that state the law holds that in cases of justifiable homicide, the defendant shall be acquitted, whereas in excusable homicide, the defendant shall be found culpable for the commission of a crime, but no punishment will be given. Nonetheless, if a person "recklessly believes [but not unreasonably believes] that the use of force upon another is necessary to protect himself [*sic*] against unlawful imminent serious bodily injury *and* the force he uses causes the death of the other, he is guilty of manslaughter, and if a person's belief is negligent in the same regard, he is guilty of negligent homicide."[55] The difference is that to avoid punishment, the defendant must not only show that she honestly and reasonably, or honestly but unreasonably, believed she was in imminent danger. She must also show that her belief was not reckless or negligent. This legal distinction was crucial for at least one North Dakota woman.

Janice Leidholm and her husband, Chester, lived together in a marriage described in a Supreme Court decision as "an unhappy one, filled with a mixture of alcohol abuse, moments of kindness toward one another, and moments of violence."[56] Early on the evening of 6 August 1981, the Leidholms returned home from a party at a gun club in the city of Washburn. They had both been drinking. On their way home, they began to argue. The argument continued after they arrived home. Janice tried to call the sheriff, but Chester prevented her from using the phone by pushing her down. Later, the fight resumed outdoors, where Chester pushed Janice to the ground. After Chester went to sleep, Janice stabbed him to death with a butcher knife. At trial, Janice Leidholm pleaded "self-defense." The jury had to decide whether her perception of danger was "honest and reasonable," "honest but unreasonable," "reckless," "negligent," or nonexistent to determine Janice's level of guilt.

Leidholm's case differed from those of most battered women who kill in nonconfrontational situations. Leidholm was permitted to have an expert testify in support of her claim of self-defense so the jury could better understand her state of mind when she killed her husband. The problem arose when the judge's instructions to the jury included an objective standard of self-defense rather than the subjective one called for by state law. Leidholm was convicted of manslaughter and sentenced to five years in prison, with three years suspended.

Although she was convicted, Leidholm is the first defendant who killed her abuser in a nonconfrontational situation and was permitted to introduce battered woman syndrome expert testimony for whom there is an appellate record. Because of the error the trial court made regarding its instructions to the jury, Leidholm appealed her conviction, which was reversed and remanded for new trial. When the North Dakota Supreme Court issued its decision in May 1983, Leidholm had served most of her two-year sentence. The import of this case lies in the legal recognition of battered woman syndrome expert testimony in support of a claim of self-defense in a nonconfrontational homicide, and in the supreme court's opinion that Leidholm was entitled to be judged according to a subjective standard of reasonableness.

The case of Betty Hudley,[57] a Kansas woman who killed her abusive husband on 13 January 1983, was similar, illustrating that even when evidentiary rules are overcome, decisions based upon other criteria, standards, or rules can prevent the jury from considering all the evidence in support of a battered woman's claim of self-defense. Betty and Carl Hudley were married about 10 years when she killed him. During their marriage, according to the appellate record, "[h]e had knocked out several of her teeth, broken her nose at least five times, and threatened to cut her eyeballs out and her head off. Carl had kicked Betty down the stairs on numerous occasions and had repeatedly broken her ribs. Mrs. Hudley suffered from diabetes and, as part of his abuse, Carl prevented Betty from taking her required dosage of insulin on numerous occasions by hiding it or diluting it with water."[58] After being hospitalized for unknown causes, Betty left Carl and moved into a motel.

"As in typical wife-beating cases, her moving did not eliminate the problem."[59] Carl broke into Betty's room while she was in the shower. He choked and threatened her, then forced her back into the shower, where "he shaved her pubic hair in a rough and violent fashion, nicking and cutting her."[60] He then raped her, after which he continued to threaten her. He threw a dollar bill toward the window and demanded that she go get him cigarettes, threatening her with a beer bottle. She testified at trial that he had beaten her many times in the past with beer bottles. She was afraid and went to her purse and took out a gun, closed her eyes, and shot twice, killing him. There is no mention of expert testimony or battered woman syndrome in the record of her trial; however, Hudley had many witnesses who corroborated her testimony that her husband had beaten her on many occasions and attempted to kill her by tampering with or hiding her insulin.

In the state of Kansas, self-defense law is based upon a perception of "imminent" danger, a term that permits jurors to consider evidence beyond the immediate confrontation leading to the homicide. Instead, the judge at Hudley's trial instructed the jury that "A person is justified in the use of force when . . . he [*sic*] reasonably believes that such conduct is necessary to defend himself or another against such aggressor's *immediate* use of unlawful force"[61] (emphasis in original). This instruction prevented jurors from considering all the evidence of Carl Hudley's past abuse and threats toward his wife. Betty Hudley was convicted of involuntary manslaughter and sentenced to serve two to five years. She appealed on the basis that the instructions to the jury were erroneous. Her case was remanded for a new trial.

Beyond this challenge to the legal standard of self-defense, it is interesting to note that throughout the appellate record, a minority of supreme court justices refer to such issues as women's stature; the similarities among the psychological reactions of battered women, hostages, and prisoners of war; the pervasiveness of wife abuse and its legal justification as far back as "Old Testament times";[62] and the social attitudes, mores, and institutional patterns that condone wife abuse in the United States and entrap women in abusive relationships.[63] Over a 10-year period, particularly in traditional confrontational cases, many appellate and supreme courts recognized that women needed to be able to fully explain the reasons they perceived danger when they killed an abusive mate.

In nonconfrontational situations, however, there has been resistance. Many judges and appellate court justices fear that if the jury is able to consider *all* the evidence in cases in which women kill sleeping husbands, the gendered balance of power will be disrupted, leading to "anarchy" and the categorical legalization of opportunistic killings. When they have been required by case law or statute to admit evidence of past abuse or expert testimony on battered woman syndrome, judges have resisted permitting juries to consider all the evidence by refusing to instruct them on both perfect and imperfect self-defense. This tendency is exemplified in the case of a North Carolina woman who killed her sleeping husband in June 1985.

Judy Ann Laws Norman was married to John Thomas "J. T." Norman for 25 years. According to the appellate record,[64] J. T. Norman was an alcoholic who forced his wife to prostitute herself. If she did not bring home a minimum of $25 each day, he would beat her. He commonly called her names, such as "dog," "bitch," and "whore,"[65] and beat her almost every day with whatever objects were handy. He put out cigarettes on her skin, threw food and drink at her, refused to let her eat for days at a time, threw glasses, ashtrays, and beer bottles at her, and at least once smashed a glass in her face. He commonly forced her to sleep on a concrete floor and to eat pet food out of a bowl. The records state that "Norman often stated to both defendant and to others that he would kill defendant. He also threatened to cut her heart out."[66] He had beaten her continuously for several days before she killed him.

The police were called to the home, where they found Judy bruised and crying. One of them advised her to take out a warrant, and Judy responded that she was afraid J. T. would kill her if she did so. The police left but a short time later were again called to the home because Judy had taken an overdose of sedatives. At that time, her husband interfered with emergency personnel who were trying to treat Judy. He was drunk and made statements such as "If you want to die, you deserve to die. I'll give you more pills" and "Let the bitch die. . . . She ain't nothing but a dog. She don't deserve to live."[67] A officer chased J. T. Norman out of the home but did not arrest him.

At the hospital, Judy Norman was advised to have her husband committed for his alcoholism and to press charges.[68] When released from the hospital, she was advised not to go home. She went to her grandmother's house for the night and returned home the next day. Witnesses testified that her husband beat her all day and threatened to kill her. Judy's mother called the police because J. T. was beating her daughter. The police did not respond. Late in the afternoon, J. T.

wanted to take a nap. When he lay down on the larger of two beds in the bedroom, Judy started to lie down on the smaller bed. Her husband called her a bitch and told her to sleep on the floor like a dog. Judy went next door to her mother's house. There she found a gun. She took the gun home and shot her husband while he slept.

At her trial Judy Ann Norman was permitted to introduce evidence of her husband's abuse and to have experts testify on her behalf. The experts explained that Norman perceived her husband to be omnipotent, and that social agencies, police, and the courts were incapable of protecting her from him. One equated her psychological response to that of prisoners of war.[69] Despite the introduction of evidence of the lengthy history of abuse and expert testimony showing the impact that abuse and the failure of the criminal justice to protect her had on Norman's perceptions, the judge refused to instruct the jury on perfect or imperfect self-defense. Norman was convicted of voluntary manslaughter. She appealed.

The Court of Appeals of North Carolina ruled that Norman was entitled to an instruction of perfect, but not imperfect, self-defense and remanded the case for a new trial. That judgment was stayed pending appeal, and the Supreme Court ruled that Norman was not acting out of perfect or imperfect self-defense when she killed her sleeping husband and that the trial court was not in error in convicting her of voluntary manslaughter and sentencing her to a six-year prison term.[70] In its decision, the court expressed concern that allowing defendants like Norman to have the jury consider their crimes under the conditions applicable to perfect self-defense "would result in a substantial relaxation of the requirement of real or apparent necessity to justify homicide."[71] Their concerns extended further. The court ruled that "The relaxed requirements for perfect self-defense proposed by our Court of Appeals would tend to categorically legalize the opportune killing of abusive husbands by their wives solely on the basis of the wives' testimony concerning their subjective speculation as to the probability of future felonious assaults by their husbands. Homicidal self-help would then become a lawful solution, and perhaps the easiest and most effective solution, to this problem."[72] The court expressed no opinion about the long-term abuse with which Judy Norman lived, except to say that it was never life threatening. It made no comment on the failure of law enforcement or other social services to protect her from her abusive husband. Instead, the court focused on protecting men like J. T. Norman from wives they had terrorized and tortured.

The legal defense branch of the battered women's movement has stirred fear of an "open season" on abusive men in appellate and supreme court justices. Statements like "[H]omicidal self-help would become a lawful solution" indicate the degree to which the law upholds the interests of abusive men, particularly when such rationales are used to prevent jurors from deciding upon a defendant's innocence or guilt. Perhaps the most striking commentary regarding the potential results of considering the context of the relationship and the experiences and perceptions of the defendant was passed down in a state appellate court decision in the case of *State v. Stewart*.[73] In that case, the justices rendered the opinion that "To permit capital punishment to be imposed upon the *subjective* conclusion of the individual that prior acts and conduct of the deceased justified the killing would amount to a *leap into the abyss of anarchy*" (emphasis added).[74]

Peggy Stewart admitted that she shot and killed her sleeping husband, but she showed evidence of his abuse toward her over many years and introduced expert testimony that she "suffered from battered woman syndrome."[75] Drawing upon battered woman syndrome, the trial judge instructed the jury on self-defense, and she was acquitted.[76] Unfortunately for Stewart, Kansas is the only state where the prosecution can appeal an acquittal. The state appealed, arguing that the judge's self-defense instruction to the jury was an error because Stewart had failed to show that "imminent threat or a confrontational circumstance involving an overt act by an aggressor" had occurred.[77] Although Stewart was permitted to introduce expert testimony about battered woman syndrome and her state of mind, the Supreme Court of Kansas, fearing a "leap into the abyss of anarchy," ruled that she was not entitled to an instruction on the basis of self-defense, without which the jury would either have to convict Stewart of some degree of homicide or step outside the law to acquit her.

Limitations of Battered Woman Syndrome in Support of Self-Defense

Cases like those of Peggy Stewart, Judy Ann Norman, and Betty Hudley illustrate some of the limitations of relying on evidence of past abuse or expert testimony on battered woman syndrome. The legal reform that resulted from the trials of women like Josephine Smith and Linda Anaya made it possible for jurors in nonconfrontational cases to hear evidence of past abuse and to be educated about the dynamics of violent relationships so they could understand why these women stayed with their husbands. Hearing the evidence did not guarantee that jurors would be legally able to consider it. To ensure that jurors are able to consider all the evidence presented in court, particularly in nonconfrontational cases, the laws of perfect and imperfect self-defense must be changed.

There are many problems with battered woman syndrome. It has the potential to reinforce stereotypes about battered women as less rational than men who kill (Browne 1993; Schneider 1986). It is difficult to explain why women who exhibit traits of learned helplessness would suddenly take such a drastic step to defend themselves (Callahan 1994). There are institutional barriers to presenting such evidence to the jury in nonconfrontational cases (Bates 1991). Nonetheless, battered woman syndrome has been used to challenge the "reasonable man" standard in states with objective self-defense standards. It has helped to educate juries about the prevalence and dynamics of wife abuse and helped jurors understand the behavior exhibited by women who refused to ask for help or who returned to abusive men.

Although expert witnesses and defense attorneys have focused on the social-psychological aspects of the syndrome, they are not forbidden to discuss cultural, socioeconomic, or legal factors that make it difficult for women to escape such relationships, nor are they prevented from showing the similarities between the psychological profiles of battered women and those of hostages, victims of terror, or prisoners of war. By framing their challenges in psychological terms, activists in the legal defense branch of the movement were able to overcome some of the institutional barriers to the full legal defense of battered women who defended themselves. Once the admissibility of expert testimony on battered woman syndrome was established, the movement could expand its application to crimes committed "under duress," or as a result of threats or physical coercion from abusive men (see Appel 1994), or to defend women from charges of failure to protect their children from abusive mates. Such advances have been hard won and even more difficult to maintain. As recently as 1997, the Arizona Supreme Court reversed a 1984 ruling, stating that evidence of battered woman syndrome could not be used to show that a defendant lacked the mental capacity to protect her child from abuse.[78] The movement must constantly guard against the seemingly inevitable backlash against women's rights.

The work of the legal defense branch of the battered women's movement is far from complete. One of its current challenges includes overcoming the "imminence" requirement in self-defense law to show that defendants reacted honestly and reasonably in killing their partners. Miller (1994) has suggested changing the imminence requirement to one of "unavoidable" danger. Maguigan (1991, 383), however, argues that "the most common impediments to fair trials for battered women are the result not of the structure or content of existing law but of its application by trial judges." She argues that the most needed legal reform consists of rules that require trial judges to consider all evidence of the social context of the crime and to provide jurors with instructions on the relevance of that evidence to defendants' claims of self-defense. She contends that the greatest impediment to a fair trial is error by the trial court judge. Efforts to accomplish the reforms called for by legal scholars like Miller and Maguigan have already begun. Legislators' and judges' recognition and understanding of the need for such reform began with their acceptance of battered woman syndrome. Despite its limitations, the syndrome provided a framework through which authorities could begin to view the world through the eyes of battered women defendants.

Conclusion

The battered women's movement has never advocated that women have a right to, or should, kill abusive men, even in confrontational situations. Rather, it has made every effort to prod the police to arrest abusive men and the courts to take their crimes seriously; it has provided alternatives for battered women in the form of support groups, hot lines, emergency shelter, and transitional housing; and it has worked to influence public attitudes about wife abuse and family violence. Abusive men commonly threaten beatings before committing them. They often stalk partners who leave, submitting them to worse violence or death, forcing many battered women to return to the abuser. Violent men systematically denigrate and isolate women, leaving many of them no alternative but to stay in the relationship. The battered women's movement contends that it is as unreasonable to expect such women to confront their abusers during an assault as it is to expect a hostage or prisoner of war to overpower a terrorist while he or she is awake.

Although innovative defense strategies have been developed and disseminated, feminists in the larger battered women's and prisoners' rights movements have mobilized on behalf of incarcerated battered women. Some created support groups and other opportunities for recovery and empowerment in the prisons; others responded to inmates' organizing efforts. As incarcerated battered women have become organized and empowered, activists outside and within the prison systems have mobilized large-scale clemency campaigns with women convicted of killing someone who abused them. In 1990 the Celeste clemencies set a precedent that would be followed in a number of other states. In chapter 4, I examine the history of the Ohio battered women's movement, its mobilization for clemency, and the resulting release of 26 incarcerated battered women.

Chapter Four

The Ohio Battered
Women's Movement
and the Celeste Clemencies

The Celeste clemencies were the result of feminist activism in Ohio and throughout the nation that originated in the early 1970s. They were the culmination of nearly two decades of effort to understand the dynamics of wife abuse, establish alternatives for battered women, and devise effective defense strategies for women who killed their abusers. In the 1970s, throughout the nation feminists worked to establish emergency shelters for battered women. In the 1980s, while many shelters were being run by mental health professionals, feminists turned their attention toward class-action lawsuits to force the police to protect battered women, toward legislation to enhance programs and protection for such women, and toward legal defense strategies for battered women who killed.

For activists, the 1980s was a decade of slow progress and strong-willed determination to succeed. During that time, many women who killed their abusers were denied the right to introduce evidence of the context of their actions. Despite the growing consciousness of wife abuse, many battered women who sought aid from public institutions were told there was nothing anyone could do. It was those women who, while in prison, came to believe they deserved clemency and mobilized to achieve it. In this chapter I examine the history of the clemencies in Ohio, and in chapter 5 I describe the subsequent efforts in other states where activism for large-scale clemencies has resulted in the review of more than one woman's case.

Feminism, Homicide, Self-Defense
Reform, and Clemency:
A Historical Overview

Prior to 1990 a large-scale clemency of battered women convicted of homicide in Ohio would have been difficult to justify to the public. Before that time,[1] it was impermissible in Ohio for battered women accused of killing abusive partners to present expert testimony regarding battered woman syndrome, and their right to introduce evidence of a history of abuse was left to the discretion of individual judges. In January 1981, in the case of *State v. Thomas,*[2] the Ohio Supreme Court ruled that the admission of expert testimony on behalf of defendant Kathey Thomas, who had murdered her common-law husband, was inadmissible because (1) it was irrelevant to the issue of whether Thomas acted in self-defense at the time of the shooting, (2) the jury was able to understand the issues without an expert's testimony, (3) the syndrome had not been accepted as common scientific knowledge, and (4) testimony by an expert would do more to prejudice the jury than to help get at the facts of the case. In March 1990 that decision was overturned by the same court in the case of *State v. Koss.*[3] In August 1990, H.B. 484 was signed into law by the governor. Both *Koss* and H.B. 484 recognized the scientific legitimacy of battered woman syndrome and the right of defendants to introduce expert testimony at trial.

The passage of H.B. 484 came in the early stages of a national wave of legislation that recognized battered woman syndrome or took into account the history of violence in a relationship and the effects it may have had on the defendant. In 1987 Missouri enacted legislation recognizing battered woman syndrome.[4] In 1989 Louisiana passed a law stating that in cases in which there is a history of violence between an intimate couple, it is not necessary to first show a hostile act on the part of the victim and that expert testimony about the impact of the victim's assaultive behavior on the state of mind of the defendant was admissible.[5] Since 1990, when Ohio H.B. 484 was passed, legislation permitting expert testimony on battered woman syndrome or establishing a standard of reasonableness that includes consideration of a history of abuse has been passed in 13 states: Arizona,[6] California,[7]

Georgia,[8] Kentucky,[9] Maryland,[10] Massachusetts,[11] Nevada,[12] Oklahoma,[13] South Carolina,[14] Texas,[15] Utah,[16] Virginia,[17] Wyoming.[18] Five states—Georgia, Louisiana, Ohio, Texas, and Wyoming—require that the defendant present a claim of self-defense for expert testimony to be admissible. Three states—Louisiana, Maryland, and Oklahoma—require that the defendant legally establish that she is a battered woman before such evidence may be admitted.[19] In 1991, United States Representative Constance Morella (R-MD), introduced a nonbinding resolution expressing Congress's belief that "expert testimony concerning the nature and effect of domestic violence ... should be admissible when offered in a state court by a defendant."[20] Although Ohio was third to establish such legislation and almost the last to enact case law recognizing battered woman syndrome, activists in that state were in a unique position to play a leadership role in the clemency movement once the law was in place.

Although Celeste's decision was clearly unpopular among his detractors, as evidenced by editorials, sheriffs, and prosecuting attorneys accusing him of creating an open season on men,[21] it has served as a precedent in other states where individual and large-scale clemencies have been granted and policies have been altered to grant battered women greater access to the clemency review process. The Celeste clemencies not only marked a breakthrough after nearly two decades of activism in the battered women's movement; they and the legal changes and clemencies that have followed are symbolic of the convergence among feminist, mental health, and legal advocacy perspectives within the movement. The battered women's movement has followed trends similar to those identified in the women's movement (see Echols 1989). A feminist analysis of wife abuse has been influenced by a focus on "female differences," including an emphasis on women's response to battering, their less violent tendencies, and their subordinate position in society.[22]

Early in the national battered women's movement, feminists were suspicious of the inclusion of therapeutic treatment as part of shelter services (Ahrens 1978; 1980; Andler and Sullivan 1980; Ferraro 1983; Johnson 1981; Schechter 1982; Tierney 1979). Despite this early distrust, throughout the 1980s the feminist analysis of wife abuse began to draw together structural, cultural, and psychological components of violent relationships and to encourage a feminist response at all levels. One result was the greater inclusion of feminist therapies and counseling services in feminist shelters. Another was the scientific legitimization and legal acceptance of battered woman syndrome. The emergence of a feminist psychology of wife abuse drew together divergent perspectives, calling for social change and treatment, into an approach that assumes that personal transformation and empowerment are means by which social change might be accomplished.

Microcohorts and Communities in the Battered Women's Movement

Examinations of the Ohio battered women's movement have supported the allegations of those who argued that the movement had been co-opted at the shelter level. Although some social movement organizations have become more concerned with conventional social service goals than with feminist concerns, many shelter providers have tried to balance their efforts to provide services with their desire to effect social change (Schechter 1982; Tierney 1982). For most activists, involvement in the formation of shelters and the trials of women who had killed or assaulted abusive men became "critical turning points" (McAdam 1988, 5) that impacted their worldviews, careers, and activism.

As the movement grew, its diversity derived from the microcohorts and communities of which it was comprised. The concept "microcohort" refers to groups within political generations that emerge at distinct phases of a movement (Whittier 1995). This concept informs an understanding of differences in collectivities that join a movement in different contexts and incorporates the concept of community. A social movement community is "a network of individuals and groups loosely linked through an institutional base, multiple goals and actions, and a collective identity that affirms members' common interests in opposition to dominant groups" (Taylor and Whittier 1992, 107). By drawing upon both concepts, an analysis of similarities and differences among communities and microcohorts is made possible. Both enhance an analysis of informally linked groups within the larger social movement. Microcohorts are unified by shared experiences, social networks, the larger political environment, and available resources (Whittier 1995). Communities are linked together by shared identity (Taylor and Whittier 1992) and a common collective action frame that singles out some existing social condition or aspect of life and defines it as deserving of corrective action (Snow and Benford 1992, 137).

Although members of a particular microcohort may come to the movement at the same time, differences in identity, frame, and community of orientation have the potential to make crucial differences in their activism and to create factions within a movement. Joining a movement at the same time and within the same context does not ensure unity within the microcohort. Members may or may not stand in opposition to dominant groups. Those who do may enhance the movement; those who do not may neutralize or reverse the movement's accomplishments, although they may consider themselves to be an important part of the movement because of the services they offer or their ideas about the direction the movement should take.

The first microcohort of the Ohio battered women's movement was made up of feminists committed to providing an escape route for battered women and working toward social change. In the Cleveland area, where the microcohort that later organized and led the clemency movement originated, there were two overlapping communities. The first was made up of white, upper- and upper-middle-class women who were politically liberal and tended to be the "conscience constituents" (McCarthy and Zald 1977) of other left-wing movements. In the early 1970s, they were politically well connected and held high aspirations for their own careers in politics, law, medicine, psychology, and other areas of public service. Within the women's movement, they were on the cutting edge of feminist activism, organizing groups and establishing services and then moving on to new causes and campaigns.

The second community was made up of middle-class women who were activists in the women's and other left-wing movements. The primary difference between these two groups was socioeconomic status. Whereas the first group provided money and connections, the second group provided in-kind services by organizing community education events and volunteering in the shelter. These two communities, as a unified microcohort, challenged the supremacy of the "family ideal"— the belief that the family is private, that it should be protected from government interference, and that it should be preserved (Pleck 1987). Although these two communities were distinguishable because of social class and the resources they brought to the movement, they adhered to the same collective action frame and worked together, engaging in complementary roles. Together they made up the microcohort I have labeled "founders."

Drawing upon the model of consciousness-raising groups, founders believed that once women realized their experiences were not unique, they would be empowered to change their lives and society. Empowerment would be made possible by providing women with a safe space in which they could "get their lives together" and leave busive relationships. Nationally, as in Ohio, movement founders were responsible for naming and creating public awareness of wife abuse as a social problem. The context in which they created the movement was one of few available resources, a general lack of awareness of the prevalence or complexity of wife abuse, and a shortage of feminist literature on the issue. In Ohio, founders were part of the larger feminist community and organizations that had been established during the early 1970s, including the Rape Crisis Center, Cleveland Women Working, Cleveland Women's Counseling, and the Cuyahoga Women's Political Caucus. Their opportunity structure was enhanced by friendship networks, including many members' acquaintance with government officials and potential sponsors. Their social backgrounds and concomitant connections gave them opportunities that were not available to less privileged activists.

Throughout the history of the Ohio battered women's movement, elite founders have been front-runners. They have played a fundamental role in creating consciousness of women's issues, educating the public about various forms of gender oppression, establishing resources to address social problems, educating and pressuring authorities for change, and gaining access to positions of authority to carry out the feminist agenda. In the mid-1970s, founders established a shelter for battered women in Cleveland and soon turned it over to a new microcohort of activists. Although founders left the shelter, they did not leave the movement.

In the late 1970s the context in which the second microcohort entered the movement was one of greater public awareness and governmental concern over wife abuse, greater availability of funding, and an emergent feminist literature on the issue. In the 1980s, during the Reagan and Bush administrations, this context became more hostile for feminists. As the new microcohort joined the movement, it was faced with the realization that the founders' empowerment model was not adequate to meet the needs of the women they wanted to help. In this climate, they maintained a feminist commitment to empowerment and social change but recognized that women sometimes needed professional services to help them deal with such issues as clinical depression or substance abuse. They were more willing to incorporate feminist counselors into their staff of formerly battered women and paraprofessionals. Although these women modified the strategy of the first group, founders concurred with their approach. For that reason, I call this microcohort "joiners."

Joiners differed from founders in background. They were not as well connected to government officials or potential sponsors as were founders, nor were they as heavily involved as activists or conscience constituents in left-wing movements. Some were trained as administrators and others as counselors, but many received their only training on the job, in the course of volunteer work, or while surviving a violent relationship. They have carried on the movement in a variety of settings, including shelters, hot lines, advocacy programs, and women's prisons. They came from both feminist and nonfeminist backgrounds but shared in common a commitment to social change and the empowerment of battered women. Although many of these activists came to the movement with little feminist consciousness or identity, they gradually adopted the collective action frame that wife abuse is an issue of power. They believed that wife abuse is perpetuated by a patriarchal society and that individual change through empowerment is one strategy for achieving change at the structural level. At the same time, however, they recognized that many women require a great deal of immediate pragmatic assistance and therapy before they can begin empowerment. Whereas founders believed that personal transformation would lead to social change, joiners recognized that some women required therapy before they could begin to understand their oppression as women. As late as 1996, many joiners continued to staff or direct shelters that were initially founded by nonfeminists. In such settings, they have had the impact of incorporating feminist theories and strategies for social change into programs that offer shelter, counseling, and other forms of assistance. They have appropriated nonfeminist shelters for the movement, situating mental health perspectives within a feminist framework.

Like founders, joiners' commitment to social change was based upon a feminist identity. They worked to advance the feminist agenda in all aspects of their lives, even when working in environments hostile to feminism. In addition to being linked by formal networks and informal relationships, this microcohort has been marked by an intellectual connection among women and men who may never have met. A common collective action frame, which emerged and developed through feminist research on wife abuse throughout the 1980s, has made it possible for even isolated activists to be connected with the movement and, in many cases, to make dramatic contributions.

As the issue of wife abuse gained legitimacy, funding sources began to seek out programs to sponsor, showing less interest in giving money to feminist programs and greater attraction to those employing scientifically legitimatized treatment programs carried out by degreed professionals (Ferraro 1983; Johnson 1981). Nonfeminist mental health workers began entering the movement at the same time joiners did. As the third group to enter the movement, they sought money to address issues of "family violence." I call this group "agency maintainers." Although they entered and attempted to co-opt the movement during the same period and within the same political environment as joiners, they represent a separate community, due to differences in their collective identity and collective action frame. Some members of this group self-identify as feminist or profeminist. Nonetheless, their analysis of family violence is based on a presumption of gender equity in the family, with women and men equally capable of violence. This community does not challenge the family ideal. Through this community, batterers have been diverted from courts and potential prison terms into treatment programs and couples counseling. These programs represent efforts to keep couples together and to minimize government involvement in the family. Although they have successfully mobilized public resources, agency maintainers' efforts have had the effect of reprivatizing family violence.

For the Ohio battered women's movement, the 1980s was a decade of struggle, compromise, development, and growth. A feminist analysis of wife abuse was developed that incorporated theories and research from a variety of disciplines. As program directors worked to provide services while maintaining a commitment to social change, the movement advanced through the actions of its founders, most of whom, by the early 1980s, were no longer associated with direct service agencies. Founders went on to constitute the most influential component of the battered women's movement, through their activism as legislators, cabinet members, directors of government agencies, judges, doctors, psychologists, and in Ohio, as the first lady. This microcohort, and the community of feminists that joined them in their efforts to effect social change, have been crucial elements in the advancement of the battered women's movement and its goal of justice for battered women.

Movement Beginnings

Although activism was taking place in other parts of the state (Whittier 1995), the first shelter for battered women in Ohio was founded in

Cleveland. Like national trends, the movement there was an outgrowth of the women's, antirape, and victim advocacy movements and was advanced predominantly by feminists in the newly emergent radical women's movement. These movements were couched within a "social movement industry" (McCarthy and Zald 1977) comprised of activists previously involved in left-wing movements of the 1960s, as well as upper-middle-class professional women seeking to address gender-based injustices. Although they appear to mirror early manifestations of the liberal and radical branches of the women's movement (Carden 1974; Cassell 1977), in Cleveland these two groups overlapped and worked together.

The battered women's movement in Cleveland began in 1973 when two women, who shared a friend who had been brutally raped, learned that although legal assistance was available to perpetrators of crime, no services were available for victims. Both women worked in the Cleveland judicial system. When they learned about the availability of seed money from the newly created Law Enforcement Assistance Administration (LEAA), they wrote a grant to establish a Victim Assistance Unit within the Cleveland prosecutor's office. The unit was funded in 1974 and hired two full-time staff members. Housed in the prosecutor's office, founders and employees of the Victim Assistance Unit quickly became aware of the prevalence of violence against women in intimate settings and of the general acceptance of such violence by public officials. An early worker in the Victim Assistance Unit explained that when the office was first established, the staff was generally unaware of the prevalence or severity of wife abuse. Early feminists assumed that women who had been beaten by their husbands would be assisted by police, prosecutors, and judges. A member of the staff explained how their consciousness was raised and how the job of assisting battered women fell to them. She said,

We had an office . . . downtown. . . . All these women would come in and say that their husbands had beaten them, and the prosecutor that we were next door to, we could hear him say to them, "Well a man has a right to do this." I mean it was really an amazing, amazing education for us. . . . So we talked to him and asked him if he please would send those people over to talk to us. And all of a sudden . . . we started to get all these referrals of domestic violence, and it was totally out of keeping with what we thought we would be doing.[23]

During the 1960s, in an effort to address the problems of drug abuse, unwanted pregnancy, and sexually transmitted diseases among young adults, Free Clinic was established in Cleveland. It was open to people of all ages but used primarily by those unable to pay for medical care. In the early 1970s, a worker at Free Clinic, herself a survivor of wife abuse, recognized that many women patients had been battered. Around the same time, the recently formed Rape Crisis Center began to receive inquiries from women involved in abusive relationships. Based on observations and inquiries for help, workers in these three settings began organizing the feminist community to do something about what they would later refer to as wife abuse.

Founders' goals for the Ohio battered women's movement were to obtain resources to document and redefine the problem of wife abuse. Along with getting police to arrest perpetrators and convincing prosecutors to take such cases, one of the most pressing problems facing activists was providing women with safe space. Their first goal was to secure funding to rent motel rooms for women until the perpetrator could be evicted from the home. This would require a new set of attitudes among police, prosecutors, and judges, so the Victim Assistance Unit began a series of educational programs while talking to people in the feminist community about what they could do about the problem. The result was an ad hoc committee to address the issue of safe space for women seeking to escape violent relationships. Drawing activists from the feminist and new-left communities, it included women from the Rape Crisis Center, Free Clinic, and the Victim Assistance Unit, as well as founders of a newly organized umbrella group of women's movement organizations called WomenSpace. The committee called itself Women Together, the name subsequently given to the shelter they founded.

Early feminists were faced with an increasing demand for help. Still, they had little idea of the problem they were facing or of the types of resources needed to respond to it. That terms like "wife abuse," "battered woman," or even "domestic violence" did not exist made their job that much more difficult. As one founder explained, "It was kind of serendipitous, you know? We had a need, and in the meantime, [another activist] had visited a program in Toronto. . . . We had no concept of a shelter at all. . . . And [she] had seen this thing in Toronto that was a shelter where battered women—and that concept was barely out there then—could go and be safe. . . . Somehow we all got together in the Victim Service Unit and started talking about shelter" (interview, 10 October 1992).

During this time, the Cleveland-based women's movement began to coordinate its efforts under the direction of WomenSpace. Its role in the movement was to help feminist organizations find resources and coordinate their activities. In 1975, as part of its organizing effort, WomenSpace set up a booth at the Ohio International Women's Year (IWY) convention, held in Cleveland in anticipation of the International Women's Year Convention to be held in Houston in 1977. One of the goals of WomenSpace then was to establish a women's center. True to the collectivist ideals of the time, they used the IWY booth to seek input from women regarding their vision of a women's center. One founder, who had kept the organization's records from the IWY booth, said they received approximately 45,000 responses. Responses varied widely and included suggestions for establishing places to disseminate political and economic information, to hold creative writing workshops, or to receive counseling. The issue bringing the greatest response related to safe space for women and their children. A founder involved with this research explained the process: "We had our WomenSpace sign up and came and said, 'Put your wish here on the bulletin board,' and they would write on green slips. . . . This is a compilation of the green slips. Immediate free housing for women and children in crisis, a place of refuge for women that have no other place to go, accommodations for women who have left home, 24 hour refuge, shelter for women and children in need of immediate help, temporary living quarters for women in crisis, sanctuary for battered wives, co-op housing for women" (interview, 10 October 1992). Still, feminists did not fully understand the nature or prevalence of the problem. More difficult was getting potential funders to believe there was need for emergency shelter for women escaping violence in their homes.

Because the problem of wife abuse was highly privatized, activists in the movement faced a dilemma. They needed to document the existence, prevalence, and dynamics of a problem they did not fully comprehend while trying to convince others to support their efforts. They used two tactics to solve their quandary. First they asked that women's organizations keep track of all requests for help they received from battered women. Although unscientific, this approach proved important in documenting the problem to potential funders. Second, they needed to raise public awareness of wife abuse while trying to understand the problem themselves. In May 1975 WomenSpace, which at the time was playing a major role in helping Women Together secure funding, sponsored the Battered Woman Forum, a "speak-out" held at a local YWCA. The first of many, the speak-out provided a space in which women who had been beaten by intimate partners could tell their stories. One of the founders explained the process: "The whole concept was that women who had been battered got up and said, This happened to me. I'm not ashamed of it. I want other women to know so that they will come forward and know that we're trying to establish ways to help each other" (interview, 21 July 1992). This tactic played to the larger strategy of empowerment, by helping women "reclaim" their experiences and identities, overcome their shame, and understand their experiences within the larger social context. Because speak-outs were staged as media events and covered by the press, they worked to advance the movement's strategy of raising public awareness of the issues.

By 1976, when it was opening its own office, WomenSpace played a major role in addressing the needs of battered women and their children. Along with Women Together, which it was helping with funding, WomenSpace established a hot line. Activists recruited Cleveland Women's Counseling to arrange shelter for battered women and their children in private homes and rented a room at the YWCA where women could be housed temporarily in emergency situations. WomenSpace activists were central in helping Women Together get off the ground, and once it was funded, WomenSpace relinquished control of the shelter.

A stable source of funding is essential in the creation and operation of a shelter. By mid-1976 a grant proposal had been written and submitted, but it had not yet been formally reviewed. Nonetheless, when WomenSpace member Dagmar Celeste offered to rent her vacant house to Women Together, the organizing committee mounted a campaign to seek donations from women's community members to fund the shelter until the foundation money was allocated. On 1 December, the shelter opened its doors. That it opened without a secure funding source attests to the grassroots nature of the feminist community. Before Dagmar Celeste's offer, founders worried that even if the shelter were funded, they would be unable to find a landlord willing to rent to them or a neighborhood open to the idea of a home for battered women. When the Celestes offered their house, founders knew it was necessary to raise the funds to rent it since nothing else might be available. One of the founders explained their dilemma, saying,

The problem was that we had informally been told that we were going to get the grant, but it would be four months before the money actually would be there. . . . I went to a friend of mine and . . . she said, "Well I would be willing to make a commitment of $50 a month for four months to help you keep that house, and I'm sure other people would, too. Why don't you ask?" So I started asking . . . everybody I could think of. By the end of the day I had enough money committed to cover the mortgage, to cover the utilities, and even to pay somebody part time to staff the place (interview, 7 October 1992).

In addition to asking everyone they could think of, Women Together advertised in the *WomenSpace Newsletter,* asking for donations and volunteers.[24] The privileged positions of many founders in the larger women's movement made it possible to get funding and to open the shelter before formal funding was secured. Well-connected founders were able to make informal contacts with potential funding sources to convince decision makers of the need for shelter and the group's ability to provide reliable services. In addition, feminists in WomenSpace who had expertise provided training and assistance with grant writing, making reliable funding possible.

Women Together envisioned that the shelter would be staffed by nonprofessional women and that access to professional services would be provided through referrals. Its self-help orientation is reflected in the following quote from an undated *WomenSpace Newsletter:*[25] "The emphasis will be on providing a breathing space for each woman to reassess her situation and herself, on helping her to develop and utilize her own strengths for her life, and on encouraging women to support each other both during and after their stay at Women Together."[26] When the shelter opened, it had a full-time paid staff of three: a coordinator, an advocate, and a resident manager. The shelter was run by feminist volunteers.[27] As it grew, feminists remained committed to hiring formerly battered women, based on a belief in self-help and empowerment and that only someone who had survived the experience could fully understand what a battered woman was going through. This practice provided formerly battered women with jobs and residents with role models.

In 1978 activists lobbied for a bill that would enhance the ability of the police to arrest violent marital partners and permit married persons to get restraining orders without first filing for divorce. On 27 March 1979 Women Together saw their work succeed with the passage of H.B. 835, which outlined civil and criminal procedures for such cases. The same year, in an effort to ensure reliable funding to replace foundation support, activists successfully advocated the passage of S.R. 46, which increased taxes on marriage licenses, the proceeds of which would be used to fund shelters.

A Transition in the Movement: Feminism and Therapy

By the early 1980s, most movement founders had left Women Together to pursue their activism through their careers. Before and after founders left, joiners came to the movement in search of jobs. Most were hired as shelter advocates to help residents get jobs, social and legal services, and housing. Like the founders, joiners came to the movement with strong feminist beliefs, but unlike their predecessors, most of whom never worked in the shelter, joiners' analysis of the problem was modified by direct contact with residents. They were overwhelmed by the demands of feeding, housing, clothing, and otherwise providing for women and their children, and they became aware that safe space and legal protections were only the first steps in providing for the needs of battered women and their children.

Although there was some pressure from potential funding sources, the primary motivation to professionalize services was based upon an understanding of the dynamics of abusive relationships and women's response to repeated violence. Joiners were faced with the task of improving services for battered women while avoiding a shift to a purely mental health perspective. In the greater Cleveland area, as throughout the United States, some shelters were successful; others were not. Women Together compromised on such issues as shelter organization, the role of formerly battered women on the staff, and the requirements and responsibilities of residents. One joiner explained the tension between the roles of social movement organization and the social service agency Women Together had become. She said,

We started out like every other shelter . . . you know, providing a place for women to stay. . . . We didn't have the staff to do much beyond that. . . . I don't think that we ever thought that was enough. . . . I also think that the needs of the women that we dealt with were really extensive. So if I had a woman who came into shelter who was chemically dependent and who wasn't dealing with her chemical dependency, chances were pretty good she wasn't going to be able to accomplish any of the other things she wanted to be able to accomplish . . . because her focus was going to be on her use. So to some degree I think we did have to kind of change our priorities.[28]

The provision of counseling and other professional services was perceived, among joiners, as a means of helping women work through problems that might prevent them from leaving abusive relationships. In a society and in situations unsympathetic to the direct expression of the anger that results from abuse, women often direct their rage inward, developing feelings of alienation, sometimes creating the appearance of helplessness, or acting in complicity with the abuser as a means of ensuring long-term survival (Grahamet al. 1994; 1988; Rosewater 1988; Walker 1979; 1987). Psychological profiles of battered women indicate that they tend to experience a "reactive behavior set to being a victim of violence, which includes anger, confusion, fearfulness, weakness, and a sense of pessimism" (Rosewater 1988, 211).

In the mid-1970s, the literature on women's reactions to violence was only beginning to be published. At that time, joiners were learning firsthand that battered women needed more than shelter and were often not ready to be empowered, in the feminist sense. Instead, the issues counselors worked on with women included overcoming clinical depression or substance abuse, correcting the belief that battering was deserved, learning to perceive the batterer in a realistic light and to direct and express anger appropriately, and overcoming insecurity about being able to confront the abuser or leave the relationship.

Joiners believed that battering could cause behaviors that, outside the context of abuse, might be perceived as abnormal. They did not believe seemingly abnormal behaviors were the result of personality disorders or character defects. Nonetheless, because battered women were often combative, uncooperative, depressed, or generally unmotivated, and because the demand for shelter always exceeded the ability to meet needs, services sometimes took on a punitive character, designed to exclude all but the most motivated "clients" (see Ferraro 1983). During this phase, the meaning of empowerment shifted, as did the relationship between battered women and the movement. The same person last quoted talked about the period when Women Together began to implement a hierarchical structure and professional services:

It became a requirement in the shelter that you couldn't just come and stay. . . . You needed to be busy during the day. You needed to be out in the community . . . getting your life together, so to speak. So you needed to be going on welfare, and . . . looking for housing, and all those things. I think [these requirements are] a perception of what empowerment means. And I think that that's where we were coming from. We wanted the women in the shelter to start feeling like they had some power over their lives, and so what we would do is we would encourage them to start taking some action to change the situation that they were in. I think in some instances we probably jumped the gun. . . . I think that shelters, depending on how they function, are very controlling places.

Where co-optation has occurred, it has not tended to result from sponsors' demands for hierarchies and professionalization. In many shelters, a hierarchical organization was put in place while providing for self-governance by battered women. Additionally, many shelters actively sought and worked to develop feminist therapies to address the immediate needs of women and ensure their longer-term empowerment. Rather than being influenced by outsiders, transformation by shelters away from feminism has traditionally been a form of ideological co-optation in which direct-service providers lose sight of the feminist collective action frame and adopt a victim-blaming approach to services. The tendency away from feminism is, in part, the result of professional training, particularly in individual-oriented fields, such as psychology and social work, and is prevalent where feminist networks are weak or workers are isolated from a feminist community (see Schechter 1982). During the 1980s, some shelters offered professional services while maintaining a social change orientation. Others lost sight of feminist principles and became concerned with individual change in its own right. It was the latter group of shelters, not the movement itself, that was co-opted.

Joiners approached the provision of therapeutic services as one means to eliminate violence against women. If battered women needed counselors to help them understand the dynamics of abusive relationships and achieve their goals, joiners saw the provision of such services as a "right to treatment." Their willingness to do whatever was necessary to provide services to battered women and their children was not perceived by founders as a violation of original movement goals. Rather, it was a response to an understanding of a complex problem. One founder explained,

I mean, in those days we really . . . had no idea how to provide services in a feminist way. Talk about an issue where women were decimated! I mean, these were wrecks. . . . Emotionally, I mean they were, you know, depressed, they couldn't get out of bed, they wouldn't change the diapers on their own kids, they would get into battles with you. . . . Then at that point, the Women Together organization . . . began to discover a lot of things, including the battering syndrome. . . . And in the process we began to learn some of the lessons we needed to learn in terms of how to provide any kind of services to these people (interview, 26 June 1991).

Initially, movement founders resisted analyses of wife abuse that included an examination of the psychological profiles of battered

women. This may have been a reaction to the social scientific literature of the time, which focused on masochism as the cause for abuse,
but it was undoubtedly influenced by radical feminism's focus on cultural and structural influences on women's lives. The inclusion of a focus on mental health issues among battered women emerged with direct experience with women trying to escape and survive abusive
relationships, the development of a feminist literature on the social
psychology of violent relationships, and the transition away from radical feminism and toward cultural feminism.

Movement Maturation

In shelters that were co-opted during the 1980s, the turmoil of transition was particularly painful for joiners who were driven away; however, rather than relinquishing the movement to nonfeminist professionals and therapists, they sought other opportunities to continue
their work, primarily in other shelters, the victim rights movement,
and batterers' treatment centers.

For the Ohio battered women's movement, the 1980s was a period
of experimentation and growth, despite a fiscally and politically hostile
context. Joiners throughout the state worked to define what they
meant by empowerment and to balance professional services with a
feminist model of organization. Although some shelters maintained a
commitment to social change, for many, simply existing and empowering individual women were all the changes they could offer. Others
were able to work for change exclusively on the local level and primarily around issues that directly affected them. The difficulty in working
toward social change while doing what essentially amounted to running a social service agency and keeping it funded was that resources
were quickly exhausted trying to keep pace with the demands of daily
operation. Time was the resource shelter workers lacked most, so social change was advocated on a purely pragmatic basis. Although they
desired an opportunity to network with other shelters, particularly
those oriented toward social change, shelter workers ended up feeling
isolated and overwhelmed with work.

During the 1980s a statewide network of family violence organizations became one avenue through which shelters might advocate for
change; however, by the late 1980s many shelter directors concluded
that the network had become so ideologically diverse as to make it difficult to focus on social change on behalf of battered women. The di-

rector of a former member shelter explained, "Action Ohio had been so diluted that there were lots of people in decision-making positions that weren't dealing on a day-to-day basis with victims. And there were many of us who believed that we really needed to come together and make sure that domestic violence service providers, being primarily shelters, really had a real voice, a voice that was speaking for [shelters]" (interview, 6 May 1992). By 1988, many shelters in Ohio were ready to come together to form a feminist network focused exclusively on effecting social change. That year, many shelters left Action Ohio and formed a coalition of direct-service providers, the Ohio Domestic Violence Network (ODVN). The motivation for forming ODVN was the belief that there is strength in numbers.

After deciding organizational issues and formulating a mission statement, ODVN launched into advocacy for change on behalf of battered women. Their first goal was to gain passage of H.B. 484, the law in Ohio that ultimately granted legislative recognition to battered woman syndrome and the right of defendants to introduce expert testimony. This community was only indirectly aware of the clemency efforts in the state and they never directly joined forces with founders,[29] but it was at this point in laying the foundation for the clemency decision that the work of these two microcohorts overlapped most. The work of these two groups was aided by the work of feminists in state agencies and by a community of incarcerated activists and the volunteers who supported them. It was this conjoining of efforts that laid the groundwork for the Celeste clemencies. The governor could have legally granted clemency to whomever he chose, as long as those cases had first been reviewed by the Adult Parole Authority. Still, legal recognition of battered woman syndrome established the public relations framework for his decision. To gain that recognition, the legal precedent that was based on events that began in the late 1970s had to be reversed.

Activism Enters the Judicial System

From the beginning, the battered women's movement in general, and Women Together in particular, placed great emphasis on public education and social change. Although Women Together's challenges to institutionalized sexism were common, their most public action, and certainly the one with the most notable impact, occurred in 1978 when Kathey Thomas shot and killed her common-law husband. The case of

State v. Thomas involved a young African-American woman who had lived in Cleveland for 10 years with her abusive partner, Reuben Daniels. Thomas was a recipient of Aid to Families with Dependent Children (AFDC) but had temporarily given her child to her mother to protect him from Daniels's violence. On 12 January 1978, during an argument, Thomas picked up Daniels's gun and shot him twice. Aside from appearing to be a "welfare cheat," Thomas abused drugs and alcohol. When she killed Daniels, the two had been using drugs and Thomas was not being beaten. These factors made her a less than "ideal" victim. Nonetheless, Thomas's case appealed to feminists who were triply motivated to participate. They wanted the public to understand why Thomas, or any woman being battered, would stay with yet ultimately kill a man who had repeatedly beaten her. They saw Thomas's case as an opportunity to participate in the movement to challenge gender biases in self-defense law. And they wanted to show that the home is not separate from civic or political life and that it is an arena in which women are dominated by men.

Thomas's lawyer shared a house with activists in the battered women's community and members of other left-wing movements. Feminists and other activists formed an ad hoc committee to support Thomas. Their efforts focused on educating the public about social and political issues involved in wife abuse. One founder explained their response to the case: "We were all into the same kind of political attitudes. It was an exciting time. . . . We thought we could change the world. . . . So we formed this committee with the purpose of doing a lot of community education because we thought if the community understood better the issues, there would be a better chance that [Kathey] would have at least a fighting chance in court."[30] The group called itself the Goldflower Committee. Although it was shortsighted on the impact public education would have on Thomas's case, it focused specifically on her trial.

The larger issue being raised by such defendants was the gender bias in the reasonableness standard of self-defense law (see Gillespie 1989). A licensed psychologist on the WomenSpace board, a psychologist on the Women Together board, and an alternative expert witness were willing to testify. The court disallowed the testimony, and Thomas was convicted of murder. Her case was upheld by the Ohio Supreme Court in 1981 and became case law, barring the admission of battered woman syndrome expert testimony in that state for the next nine years.

The organization and tactics of the Goldflower Committee are exemplary of founders' commitment to social change at three levels: empowerment of the individual, changes in the dominant belief system regarding wife abuse, and structural change, in this instance in the legal system. By befriending Kathey Thomas, they demonstrated the support of the women's community and helped her understand the patriarchal context in which the years of abuse and subsequent homicide took place.

While the Goldflower Committee worked on the *Thomas* case, Women Together and the Rape Crisis Center sponsored a speak-out for women who had defended themselves against violence. By sponsoring the speak-out and recruiting Yvonne Wanrow to moderate it, the feminist community worked to raise public awareness of the inequity in the reasonableness standard and the need for an understanding of the state of mind of the defendant at the time of the crime. In doing so, the Cleveland movement drew upon and placed itself within the national trend of challenging gender biases in self-defense law through political trials, discussed in chapter 3.

Thomas's case, and others like it, demanded that the courts recognize the cultural acceptance of wife abuse, the social support given to men who beat their female partners, and the gender biases in self-defense law (see Fiora-Gormally 1978; Gillespie 1989). In Ohio, the *Thomas* case, like cases in other states, instigated legal discourse about whether the state of mind of the defendant should be considered at trial, and challenged the notion that women who defend themselves are irrational, insane, or of diminished capacity.

The question most commonly raised by jurors, prosecutors, judges, and others involved in addressing the issues of battered women is "Why didn't she just leave, rather than killing or trying to murder the abuser?" (Gillespie 1989). Addressing that question requires an understanding of the gender biases in social institutions and dominant ideologies, an examination of the assumptions regarding the sanctity of private life, and an assessment of differences in the socialization of children. It is at this level that the philosophical connections among grassroots activists, national leaders of the battered women's movement, and the larger women's movement become most apparent.

Research has shown that girls are socialized to be more passive and dependent than are boys and to look to others for protection (Davis 1984; Hansen and Hansen 1988; Mayes and Valentine 1979;

Zern 1984). In sports and recreation, girls have historically been exposed to fewer opportunities to develop physically or to learn self-defense skills (Bird and Williams 1980; Jones 1980; Theberge 1989; Wilmore 1974). Whether from fairy tales, the movies, or role models, young girls are socialized to believe they will one day marry and have children and be dependent upon a husband for protection and support. Further, research has shown a pattern of "cooling out" girls from subjects, such as science and mathematics, required for entry into many demanding and well-paying positions (Ernest 1976; Hall and Sandler 1982; Kelly 1984; Lummis and Stevenson 1990). Where women enter into traditionally male occupations, discrimination plays a crucial role in limiting their upward mobility (Dubnos 1985; Frank 1988). Despite women's increasing participation in the labor force, they have been ghettoized into a few low-paying positions, and when they enter traditionally male occupations, they tend to earn less than men (U.S. Department of Labor Women's Bureau 1993).

Making it on one's own goes against women's socialization and the cultural expectations they experience and is made difficult by their lower wages and concentration in jobs with little opportunity for upward mobility. Nonetheless, many would argue that money is certainly no reason to stay with an abusive mate. It is necessary to look still further. Religions of the Jewish and Christian heritages have depicted women as "help mates" to men, to be protected as long as they behave properly but vilified if they step outside established decorum (Reineke 1989; Richardson 1988). Many battered women report going to their religious advisers and being told to pray for guidance, become better wives, and go home and help their husbands find religion (Walker 1979). Dominant ideology about women's inferiority to men is pervasive in American society. It affects women's aspirations and the opportunities offered them. Gender biases, combined with the belief that the family is private and that government should not interfere, have been shown to affect the willingness of police to respond or arrest in cases of domestic violence as well as prosecutors' and judges' ideas about how cases of wife abuse should be handled (Browne 1987; Dobash and Dobash 1979; Gelles and Straus 1988; Gillespie 1989; Martin 1981; Walker 1979; 1987). Feminists contend that women's pleas for help have not been taken seriously.

Research has shown that some men use violence as a form of control over their partners and that when challenged by separation, they become enraged (Browne 1987). Fifty percent of women who leave abusive partners are further terrorized, and over half of all female homicide victims have been murdered by abusive former mates (Browne 1987; Moore 1979). The victimization rate of women separated from their husbands is 25 times higher than that of married women (U.S. Department of Justice 1995). Abusive men frequently threaten their partners or family members with worse violence or death if they make an effort to leave. Leaving does not end the violence; on the contrary, it may make it worse.

Throughout the United States, from the late 1970s through the 1990s, the struggle over legal recognition of battered woman syndrome was one aspect of the larger movement to change the system to protect battered women and end violence against women and their children. The battered women's movement has been one of the most successful movements in United States history. Since the early 1970s, the movement has established more than one thousand shelters and at least as many hot lines (Jones 1994). Activists have lobbied for legislation to fund shelters and criminalize family violence, demanded tougher arrest laws and sentencing guidelines, filed class-action law suits on behalf of victims, established victim advocacy programs, set up treatment programs for batterers, produced films and documentaries and a scientific literature about wife abuse, educated judicial officials, developed legal strategies to defend battered women who have killed abusive partners, and set up prison support groups for battered women (Jones 1994). As part of the national movement, the Ohio battered women's movement engaged in all of the above strategies, often at the local level and less frequently at the state level. Activists interested in legal reform were integrated into the larger movement through informal communities; they were kept apprised of national trends through national organizations and networks.

In the wake of the *Thomas* decision, direct-service providers continued to provide shelter, raise public awareness, and work to improve and coordinate the response of the police and judicial system in their particular localities. Movement founders began to secure positions in all three branches of state government, in which they mounted a feminist campaign that helped to achieve many statewide reforms. They worked both within and outside governmental institutions and agencies, pressuring formal decision makers and working to raise public awareness of the issues.

Two of the activists involved in Thomas's trial were psychologists. Following similar legal strategies throughout the country, they had volunteered to serve as expert witnesses but were prohibited from doing so. Although they identified problems in the preparation and handling of Thomas's case, they also thought that nonadmission of expert testimony was rooted in misogynist assumptions about women's inability to tell the truth and a deep-seated fear of women's anger. One of the activists involved in the trial described judicial attitudes: "One of the things that came up was . . . 'You're giving women a license to kill. Any woman will now say she was battered.' It also says something about the bias that exists around feminists, that somehow you'd come to court and lie through your teeth" (interview, 30 May 1992). This recognition of the insidious misogyny pervasive in the legal system made founders more determined than ever to change things by building their careers and lives around these issues. The founder just quoted decided to leave Women Together and challenge the judicial system. She earned her doctorate and became one of the most active expert witnesses on behalf of battered women in the state. Nationally, she was part of a community of activist lawyers, expert witnesses, and victims'-rights advocates working to improve defense strategies for women who killed or assaulted others while defending themselves from violence.

Through trial court activism and the establishment of case law, feminists challenged and reformed the law in most states. Their efforts in court were supported and enhanced by activists more focused on public education, which helped to create a social climate conducive to the actions of activist lawyers and psychologists and to educate judges about the need for activism from the bench. Where courts were unwilling to take an activist stance by recognizing emergent social scientific findings or stepping outside the law to address the requirements of groups whose needs were not represented, other activists worked through the legislative and administrative branches of government to effect change.

Entry Into the Political Process

Many movement founders launched political careers that brought some of them into legislatures, where they continued to work on behalf of battered women. One woman explained her metamorphosis from grassroots activist to activist legislator. She said, "I left [Women-Space] at the end of November in 1979. . . . I went to be on the staff of ERA America. . . . I was in every state when [the ERA] was defeated. . . . That's when I decided to run for the legislature. I said, 'I can do this better than these turkeys. This is not a problem' " (interview, 3 September 1991). The women who ran for office tended to come from families that had been active in politics, although not as elected officials, and to have been actively involved in campaigns. Their careers were encouraged and supported by local and statewide left-wing and feminist communities and organizations. In the evolution of their involvement in politics, from grassroots organizing to institutionalized politics, they tended to see holding office as a form of activism. When asked if she thought her early activism differed from her job as a legislator, the woman just quoted replied, "I think it's all part of a continuum. You know, you need to have people fighting on the inside and fighting on the outside. People are just in different positions to do different things at different points in their lives. But in order to make the changes that we need, we need to have people pushing hard from all the different angles." In the legislature, movement founders acted on behalf of specific battered women, sponsored and cosponsored legislation, and worked to raise their male colleagues' consciousness regarding women's and battered women's concerns.

In the 1980s and 1990s, women were underrepresented in the Ohio legislature. As a result, feminists were often targeted by women outside their districts as representatives who might be more sensitive to their problems. The few feminists in the legislature then came to represent women throughout the state, in addition to their own constituents. Rather than trying to address everyone's needs, feminists adopted the tactic of educating their colleagues about women's issues. The following story was offered by the woman just quoted as an example of the strategies used to encourage others to become more aware of women's issues: "I had this one woman who called me who was trying to figure out how she could get prenatal care. . . . So I put her in touch with her representative, who came back to me and said, 'This is crazy!' . . . And it was when we were trying to do a piece in the legislature [on the issue]. So I got this great ally out of it. I mean, the lady got what she needed, and I got some male person who was in the legislature who understood what I was talking about." Creating allies in the legislature and the courts, among the police, in the prison, and in the administrative branch of government has been a central feminist strategy in most of the states where mass clemencies have been achieved, and it is one that has been overlooked in the literature on the battered women's movement. By establishing careers in positions of authority, Ohio feminists appropriated the legislative branch of state government to achieve their goals. Their work was supported by feminists outside the government as well as within it.

One day in 1988, Ohio Representative Joe Koziura (D-Lorain) was listening to a radio talk show when he heard Lynn Rosewater, a movement founder who had become an expert witness, talking about the fact that Ohio did not allow expert testimony regarding battered woman syndrome. After hearing her speak, he went to Jane Campbell, one of the founders then in the legislature, and learned that what he had heard was true. When he said he was "going to fix it," Campbell offered her assistance but let him take the lead. Her decision gained the movement another feminist ally, whom direct-service providers felt comfortable calling upon when they needed assistance. In May 1989[31] Koziura introduced H.B 484, which was ultimately signed into law in August 1990. Despite the fact that legal recognition of battered woman syndrome and the right of battered women to introduce expert testimony was established in *State v. Koss* in March 1990, Koziura and feminists in the legislature and throughout the state wanted to establish legislative recognition to prevent the case from being overturned at a later date. Within the legislature, Koziura's greatest support came from the founders of the women's and battered women's movements, who had established their careers there. Throughout the state, it came from direct-service providers and a community of trial court activists whose efforts were coordinated by the newly formed Ohio Domestic Violence Network (ODVN). An opportunity structure in which such legislation might pass and ultimately have its greatest impact was being laid by movement founders in the executive branch of government, the cabinet, and various state agencies.

In 1982 Richard Celeste was elected governor by a decisive majority. His success was due, in part, to the recession and high unemployment that had hit the state, particularly in the "rust belt," and to anti-Republican sentiment. Voters were liberal on economic, but not social, issues. To fight against further erosion of jobs and school closings, voters elected Democrats to office across the board. In 1986 Celeste ran for reelection against James Rhodes, a shopworn candidate who had already served four terms as governor (in two, two-term periods). Ohio's economy was on the rebound, and voters reelected Celeste to office by a decisive margin. In neither campaign was he elected on social issues, nor did he stress them. While he had the legal authority to grant clemency to anyone whose application had been reviewed by the Adult Parole Authority, he lacked a political mandate on left-wing or feminist social issues. He had received the backing of feminists and left-wing activists advocating for social change, but his staff understood the political risks of being too socially progressive, and they worked to protect him from such demands.[32]

The governor and first lady treated the administration like a partnership. When the governor took office in 1983, he provided Dagmar Celeste with a staff and office space in the state house and depended upon her to get involved with many of the issues affecting Ohio citizens. After the 1982 election, Dagmar Celeste called together feminist friends, including many who had been involved in WomenSpace and Women Together, to help her create an agenda, which she and feminists throughout the state worked to implement over the next eight years. The first lady explained, "I brought together about 20 women in my life for a retreat and basically asked them to develop an agenda for me, as first lady. . . . And we basically came up with a four-tiered agenda. . . . And I worked for the eight years that I had . . . on these four areas. They were recovery, . . . women, . . . education, and peace. Now, the interesting thing about . . . domestic violence, it touches on all four."[33] Some of the women who helped to establish the agenda went on to serve in the "First Lady's Unit," but more served in cabinet- and subcabinet-level positions as directors of government agencies and in other positions. During Celeste's two terms in office, the governor regarded the first lady as a source of leadership. Through their partnership, they worked toward numerous feminist goals, including day care and pay equity for state employees, greater access to employment opportunities for women, a prison system that offered more opportunities for education and recovery, the issues of incarcerated women, greater awareness of women's issues in mental health and addiction, and clemency. Although the governor was sympathetic to feminist concerns, his level of understanding was enhanced by the work of Dagmar Celeste and her staff. Like legislators and expert witnesses, she worked to educate the governor and his staff about feminist issues and to create allies within his administration. The governor described the first lady's efforts:

[Dagmar] had things she was interested in and a large number of requests coming from around the state to be involved in issues that were important to her, and usually important to me. Her issues weren't issues I didn't care about, I mean, that she had to impose on me. It was helpful to me that she could take an interest in some things, and I could count on her doing a lot of the getting educated and understanding what was happening around Ohio and being able to share that with me in the same way I would count on a cabinet member or someone else to help me (interview, 13 August 1992).

In the second term, their efforts to address women's issues became more focused and better organized when, by executive order, the Governor's Interagency Council on Women's Issues was formed. Its mandate was as follows: (1) survey state agencies to determine their efforts to address women's needs for public policy and budget priorities; (2) assess the needs of women, with a special focus on minority women; (3) review each agency's programs and its impact on women; (4) identify successful agency efforts that might be replicated and develop new strategies to improve the government's responsiveness to women's issues; (5) monitor legislation affecting women and identify opportunities for state agency involvement; and (6) coordinate discussions between the governor and women's organizational leadership.[34] The council was guided by a "Feminist Policy Criteria," a statement that provided guidance on the creation and implementation of policy. Some of the principles embodied in the "Criteria" statement were that "the policy does away with the gendered public-private distinction," it "does not reinforce [the] notion that government beneficiaries are incapable, dependent and stupid versus that goverment [sic] professionals are competent and rational," and "the policy gives people more control over their own lives."[35] The result of the executive order to create the council was a formal feminist network representing governmental departments and agencies, which provided a forum in which feminists could exchange information and ideas and coordinate their efforts. It also established formalized direct access to the governor and the legislature, which increased feminists' influence throughout the state.

With backing from the Interagency Council, as the second term progressed, the First Lady's Unit increased pressure on members of the governor's staff who thought certain issues "too controversial" for the governor to address. Although one might not normally look within the government for evidence of activism, the role of the First Lady's Unit, the Interagency Council, and the partnership between the first lady and the governor should not be underestimated when seeking to understand the clemency decisions, which were part of a larger feminist agenda. Said the governor, "We had, within the Bureau of Employment Services,[36] a Women's Division . . . and they were strong advocates. . . . And of course, Dagmar was the strongest advocate of all. I mean, no one was better than she was on this issue. . . . We had a Women's Council within state government, who worked on an agenda for women. . . . In my view, I was an enormous beneficiary of women in the political process" (interview, 13 August 1992).

With this network of feminists, Dagmar worked on her four agenda items. Although she worked closely with the governor, at times she worked independently to become educated and informed about various issues. When she became interested in an issue, she was quickly targeted as a source of access to the governor. For example, early in the first term, the first lady began visiting the Ohio Reformatory for Women (ORW) in Marysville. She was interested in the issues of women on death row, but it became apparent to her that a great proportion of women in prison had, at some time in their lives, been victims of family violence and that many required programs and services to recover from abuse. To address their needs, she advocated that existing programs be expanded and that more support and recovery groups be created. But given the increasing prison population and the overcrowding the Ohio Department of Rehabilitation and Correction (ODRC) faced, pressures to expand services were stymied by a lack of space and the ODRC's priority of security issues over recovery.

During the 1980s, religious volunteers at ORW and other prisons in the state advocated for the expansion of recovery services and the creation of a chapel. In 1989, one of them identified a source of money that could be used to fund these goals. He discovered that the system of telephones that had been established to allow inmates to make collect telephone calls had generated a "$3,000,000 windfall" and urged that the money be diverted toward programs that would facilitate spirituality, education, and recovery.[37] An aide to the first lady suggested that she ask the governor to include such a provision in that year's budgetary bill.[38] Dagmar Celeste advocated the chapel's construction and the expansion of recovery services at ORW. Subsequently the governor directed his aides to look into the low priority given recovery services in Ohio prisons and to find ways to expand them, in at least "one or two institutions, like Marysville."[39] The governor's aides concurred that recovery services needed to be expanded but advised against using the telephone money to do so. One result of the activism behind this issue was that in 1990 four new programs for victims of family violence were created. These groups served a role similar to the consciousness-raising groups of the early women's movement.

They were central in assisting battered women in understanding the dynamics of wife abuse, issues of power and control, and the injustice of their incarceration. The empowerment the women achieved by talking with other survivors was crucial in helping them work for their own clemencies.

Women serving life sentences were not eligible to participate in recovery groups or most other prison programs. In 1984 a group of women, under the sponsorship of Rebecca Cardine, a prison employee, formed a support group for women serving life sentences. They called themselves the LIFE Group, LIFE being an acronym for Looking Inward for Excellence. One of the women granted clemency, a former LIFE Group member, explained the group's mission: "It was made up of all women that were doing life and it was sort of like a big support system within itself, because . . . when you're doing life, you had nothing there. All the programs are made up for people with short time. You know, it's about getting you educated or whatever 'cause you're moving on to society. And we were not going back. . . . And so they needed something to kind of get through."[40]

The LIFE Group served as a support system for women who had no access to other services. As it evolved, it also became a center of activism regarding the issues of incarcerated women. The leader just quoted explained: "The LIFE Group got into big issues of what happens in the institution, discussing what we could do about it, how we could write letters to make it better." Because many women serving life sentences had killed abusive partners or father figures, domestic violence and the clemency decisions became important issues for the group. The LIFE Group and the prison domestic violence groups that were formed early in 1990 became important organizational linkages in the clemency process. To understand that connection, we return to an examination of the relationship between the governor's and first lady's staffs.

Throughout his two terms in office, Celeste actively endorsed and was grateful for his wife's work. He made symbolic gestures to show his support, such as housing her office next to his own and giving his chief of staff a mandate to cooperate with the first lady and her staff. Nonetheless, as is often the case when wives of elected officials demonstrate strength and have agendas of their own, resentment was aroused among the governor's staff. The relationship that evolved between the administration and the First Lady's Unit was one in which the latter would initiate ideas by bringing them to the governor's at-

tention. Issues might be raised privately by the first lady, but more frequently they were discussed during one of the regularly scheduled
meetings attended by Dagmar Celeste, the governor, his chief of staff,
and appropriate members of their staffs. If an issue or problem Dagmar Celeste raised required action by the governor's staff, the project
was assigned to one of his staff members; however, when ideas originated with the First Lady's Unit, they were frequently handled with
less urgency. Such was the case with the clemency decisions.

Mobilization for Clemency

Neither the governor nor the first lady recalled precisely when the
idea of a large-scale clemency review was raised, but both agreed that
the idea was hers. She recalled reading about a governor in another
state considering clemencies in 1984 or 1985. Once the idea was
raised, the project was given to an aide to the governor to research.
The aide found nothing, and between 1985 and 1989 the idea of
clemency languished.

During that time, Dagmar Celeste remained active in the prison, visiting women on death row and promoting greater opportunities for recovery. During the summer of 1989, with only a year and a half left in the
term, the First Lady's Unit began to pressure the governor's staff to proceed with the clemency review process. The first issue to be addressed
was the governor's legal authority in granting clemency. According to
Ohio law, clemency reviews could be initiated by application from an inmate to the Adult Parole Authority, at the direction of the governor, or
upon the Adult Parole Authority's own initiative. Before the governor
could grant clemency, the Adult Parole Authority had to thoroughly investigate the case. Nonetheless, the governor was free to reject the recommendation of the Authority once its review was completed.[41]

In November 1989, at the urging of the first lady, the governor ordered the establishment of clemency application and review processes.
In January 1990 he ordered the Department of Rehabilitation and Correction to determine the number of women incarcerated for crimes related to battering and to document the existence of battered woman
syndrome among Ohio's female inmate population.[42] Linda Ammons,
an aide to Governor Celeste, was charged with overseeing the
clemency project. She was unfamiliar with issues relating to wife
abuse, and requested time to study the issue. She read the feminist literature on battered women who kill, contacted activists in other states

who were working on legislation or activism to promote large-scale clemency reviews, and corresponded with a founder of the Women's Self-Defense Law Project[43] and with the National Clearinghouse for the Defense of Battered Women. Ammons accompanied the first lady to the prison to meet with members of the LIFE Group and other support groups. At these meetings, the women told their stories and answered questions about their trials, the sentences they were serving, and their inability to adequately defend themselves at trial. The women's insights and their ability to share them with outsiders were enhanced by the work of a group of volunteers that had befriended the LIFE Group.

Two years after the formation of LIFE, a group of individuals sensitive to the issues of family violence began to visit ORW on a monthly basis. The group was comprised of a Marionist brother who knew a woman serving a life sentence for killing her abusive husband, a Catholic sister, a formerly incarcerated woman who had been serving a life sentence until she was granted clemency by a former governor, and a shelter volunteer active in supporting incarcerated women through correspondence. Calling themselves the Friendship LIFE Group, they visited and brought in speakers in whom the women expressed an interest.

When H.B. 484 (recognizing battered woman syndrome) was introduced in 1989, the Friendship LIFE Group arranged for Joe Koziura, Jane Campbell, and another cosponsor of the bill to speak to the group. This interaction was educational for the women and helped to transform and politicize the "battered woman" identity many LIFE members held. A former member and clemency recipient explained,

Well, I guess that when house bill 484 first was introduced . . . [a Friendship LIFE Group member] knew the people who wrote the bill. And I said . . . "It'd be really nice if we could have them visit and tell us about the bill, so we'll know exactly what it means and what it is saying and how it relates to us." . . . Because . . . you know what the word domestic violence is. And so after it all goes down and it happens and it's over, you know that you were a victim, but you're being punished for being a victim. This was how we explained it. "Well, you know, we were a victim of the abuse from our husbands or boyfriends, so we're still going to be a victim still, because the state is going to punish us for being a victim." . . . And then we unfolded and got into the bill to find out what it was saying and how it pertained to us and our situation (interview, 17 August 1992).

As their consciousness about their experiences was raised, members of LIFE began talking to other women in the prison. Their understanding of the issues, together with the information being shared in the domestic violence groups, had an empowering effect on many. When research for the clemency decisions was conducted, staff members drew upon the insight and understanding of the women in these groups to assist with the process.

Institutional research for the clemency decisions began with the work of Rebecca Cardine, who was charged with looking through the files of all women incarcerated for violent crimes. In February 1989, she sent a summary of her findings to a member of a committee assembled to research wife abuse and its relation to women's crime. She found 97 cases.[44] Applications were distributed to the women included in the summary. Members of the LIFE Group began talking with women throughout the prison and urging anyone who believed she fit the profile to come forward. Subsequently, 18 cases were added to the initial group and 115 cases were sent to the governor.

The LIFE Group and other support groups were central in helping women overcome denial, understand wife abuse, remember incidents of battering, and recall where documentation of their experiences might be found. In the process of learning about H.B. 484, talking with other women, and preparing their clemency applications, they began to understand that they were oppressed as women and that they had much in common with other battered women. Many came to a greater understanding of the social and cultural foundations of their oppression and began working to address the inequities that led to their imprisonment.

Once the clemency applications were filed, members of the LIFE Group encouraged women to write follow-up letters to the governor or Representative Koziura (who had no official role in the clemencies but who was perceived as a powerful ally) regarding events they had forgotten to include in their applications or to express dissatisfaction with the short time they were able to spend before the Parole Board to explain their cases. Although limited in the extent of their activism, these women were not passive recipients of mercy. They were activists engaging in resistance and actively working to educate themselves. One member of the group, a clemency recipient, explained what the group did: "We were sending out for articles and . . . we would share it. When you're in the institution, you get to be kind of secret. . . . They get stuff and they hoard it because they think this is the magic key, and so they'll work the magic key and maybe they'll let you use it later. But as we started to get information, we would put packets of stuff together, illegally xerox stuff and kind of under the cover, 'Read this, you know, this is good reading' " (interview, 17 August 1992).

In addition to empowering themselves through education, the LIFE Group monitored Parole Board hearings and mobilized a letter-writing campaign to make certain the governor had all the relevant facts in their cases and to outline what they believed were unfair practices. The same woman just quoted continued,

Some of the women came out of the board feeling real upset, as if their story was no good. . . . And we were sort of taking inventory about how many minutes did you stay in that [hearing] room when you went? Some women said three minutes, four minutes. Well, how could you tell a life story in three or four minutes? . . . We started watching. . . . And we were timing them. . . . And I wrote a letter to Joe Koziura and . . . I wrote a letter to Celeste about people being in the Parole Board room 5 to 11 minutes and how can they tell their story. . . . So my advice to [the other women] was, "If you can think of anything that you did not mention, send it to Governor Celeste," because we knew that no matter what that Parole Board decided, he was still going to get the stuff and read it. And that's exactly what happened. Women started sending stuff, and we know that it went in the files.

In Ohio, a social movement community comprised of program directors and other staff members, inmates, and volunteers coalesced within ORW. With the help of Dagmar Celeste and other outside activists, the community conducted media events, such as their meeting with 1990 Miss America Marjorie Vincent and the taping of a segment of the television program *48 Hours* on battered woman syndrome, self-defense law, and the role of clemency in serving the cause of justice for battered women.

While waiting for clemency applications to be reviewed, the Friendship LIFE Group sponsored a workshop on domestic violence. It brought in members of the battered women's community from shelters and other direct-service organizations as well as formerly battered women who had received clemency. Kathey Thomas, who had served her sentence and been released from prison, was the keynote speaker. She talked about her experiences as a survivor of wife abuse. Her story has been particularly empowering for battered women who have killed abusive mates. At the workshop she served as an example of someone who had successfully survived a violent relationship and her time in prison. She took control of her life and later went on to work in the prison system, training women to gain access to traditionally male occupations.

While cases for review were being identified, ODRC completed the research ordered by the governor. The first study found that of the 421 inmates then incarcerated for violent offenses, 203 were directly related to "victimization by domestic violence."[45] The second study was conducted by a feminist researcher. In gathering her data, this researcher encountered no resistance. She attributed ODRC's cooperation to the first lady's influence and the opportunity structure it created. She explained, "[Being able to conduct my end of the research] in itself was a miracle, really, because people in Corrections are very reluctant to let [people] . . . futz around, let alone to futz around with the knowledge that this might lead to somebody getting out. But it came down from the governor's office that they were to cooperate, so it paved the way."[46] Working with domestic violence counselors, the researcher drew a sample of 30 women for her study, which consisted of tape-recorded interviews in which women were asked to recall the events of their relationships and crimes.

The prison administration cooperated, but nonfeminist members of the research department at ODRC were not supportive of the study's findings. A senior researcher challenged the findings, arguing that because the women's stories had not been corroborated by their written records, the study researcher should include a statement regarding the limitations of the study's validity. She countered that because people assume that incarcerated and battered women lie and exaggerate, such a statement would ruin the study's integrity. She refused to include the statement, instead drawing on the feminist literature on battered women who kill to demonstrate that battered women tend to underreport incidents of violence rather than exaggerate them (see Browne 1987). Whether working alone or in groups, activists found themselves sustained by their identity and integrity as "good feminists" and by the feminist community that existed in government, the prison, and throughout the state.

The report was submitted to the governor and used to illustrate the impact wife abuse had on women's lives and the relationship of battered woman syndrome to their crimes. It was used as a resource to train corrections personnel, defense attorneys, and members of the Adult Parole Authority about the syndrome and was reported upon at a lecture entitled "Criminal Defense Practicum on Post-Partum Depression and the Battered Woman Syndrome as Defenses to Criminal Liability," organized by the First Lady's Unit and held at the governor's residence in June 1990.

The Decisions

Two people were involved in reviewing each application for clemency, the governor and Linda Ammons, the aide assigned to implement the process. The governor, however, was responsible for all decisions. Once the requests for clemency were forwarded by the Adult Parole Authority, consideration of the cases depended upon full understanding of a highly complex issue. That understanding was enhanced by the work of feminists in national organizations, other states, Ohio government, the courts, the corrections system, and by feminist legal scholars and the clemency applicants themselves.

After reviewing the cases, the governor and his aide endeavored to document and verify alleged incidents. They used five criteria in evaluating each case. First, they had to be convinced that the woman had been battered to a degree that a jury hearing about the abuse and expert testimony about battered woman syndrome would have decided differently. Second, they looked for evidence that the woman had come to terms with the syndrome, such as participation in a domestic violence group or another recovery group. Third, they looked at the woman's behavior in prison, and fourth at her prior criminal record. The governor was not willing to grant clemency to women who had histories of disruptive behavior in prison or who had been convicted of previous violent crimes. Finally, he looked at the length of time served, believing that no woman should be released until she had served at least two years (interview, 13 August 1992). As the governor explained, "I established a minimum of two years, because I felt, in any case, these people were involved in a violent act where some punishment might well have been adjudged by a jury but not the punishment that was handed down, because these women hadn't been able to defend themselves effectively" (interview, 13 August 1992). After extensive review, in December 1990 25 women were granted clemency. In 10 cases, the governor overrode the recommendation of the Adult Parole Authority. Six of those women were eligible for immediate release, and it appears that they were released on the day they were notified of the decisions. Fifteen were scheduled for release after a final visit with the Adult Parole Authority. These women left prison the following April. Four were left to serve the remainder of the mandatory two-year term and were then released. The governor sent 34 cases back to the Parole Authority for further documentation. When Republican George Voinovich became governor in January 1991, the political environment changed, and none of these women was granted clemency.

The governor did not attempt to identify women with battered woman syndrome or to formally apply the syndrome to his decisions. Nonetheless, the *Koss* decision and the passage of H.B. 484 gave him a public relations framework for reviewing the cases. His rationale that juries would have made different decisions had they heard about the abuse and then learned about battered woman syndrome from an expert placed his decisions within a framework of equal justice and fairness and recognition that the actions of women who kill are often based on different, but equally rational, perceptions than are those of men.

Conclusion

Before the Celeste clemencies, a national campaign to assist incarcerated survivors of domestic abuse had mobilized. It consisted of a number of statewide organizations and social movement communities and one active national organization. These organizations and the activist members of less formal movement communities were important sources of information for the governor's staff. Since the Celeste clemencies, these organizations have drawn upon the strategies used in Ohio and other states where women have had their sentences commuted or reduced to inform the mobilization and tactics used in other states. Ohio activists were not the first to promote the idea of clemency, but their success set a precedent for other states, convincing activists and governors that granting clemency to large numbers of battered women is politically feasible and morally just. Its strategy of individual empowerment, career activism, and public education has been used in other states where clemency efforts have been mobilized.

Since its founding in 1987, the National Clearinghouse for the Defense of Battered Women has played a central role in gathering and disseminating information about defense strategies and individual and large-scale appeals for clemency. Since the Celeste clemencies, it has provided information about how to form prison support groups for battered women and has encouraged and supported the formation of such groups.[47] It has also formulated tactics to create media events to educate the public.[48] This model of organizing for clemency, with some variation, has been successfully used in at least five other states, which I discuss in chapter 5. In 1991 the National Clearinghouse began distribution of a clemency manual, written by legal activists.[49] That organization reports that between 1978 and 1996, 103 battered women from 23 states have been granted clemency,[50] and that organizing for large-scale clemencies is under way in at least 26 states in addition to those in which efforts have been successful.

The Ohio battered women's movement is indicative of three trends that are evident in other states, as will be shown in chapter 5. First, the battered women's movement has not been co-opted, as has so frequently been argued in the literature. Although many shelters in Ohio and the United States have likely adopted a mental health model of treatment, the data indicate that, despite a decade or more of struggle, many shelters have developed feminist models of therapy and remained committed to social change and the empowerment of battered women. Because they exist to provide an avenue of escape to women who would otherwise not be able to leave their abusers, shelters are an important source of social change. That direct-service providers and other activists found the resources to work toward legal reform in an era of increasing fiscal and ideological hostility indicates the movement's commitment to feminism.

Second, many feminists who founded shelters and other social movement organizations, such as the Women's Self-Defense Law Project, left these organizations but continued their activism through their careers. It has often been assumed that social movements exist outside government and that once activists take positions as authorities, they run the risk of being co-opted. This may be true of non–identity-based movements, but it has not been true of the battered women's movement. Its activists worked in the courts as defense attorneys, victim advocates, and expert witnesses and infiltrated the legislative and executive branches of state government, most of its agencies, and the prison system, in which they were able to establish a social movement network coordinated through the Interagency Council on Women's Issues. Their efforts to change public policy and educate decision makers were enhanced by, and later informed, the efforts of legal scholars and national battered women's organizations. Although the movement for clemency in Ohio was statewide, it has been in tune with national trends, beginning with the formation of the shelter, the attempt to introduce expert testimony in the *Thomas* trial, the invitation to Yvonne Wanrow to moderate a speak-out on wife abuse, the fight to secure legal recognition of battered woman syndrome, and organization of the first large-scale clemency for women incarcerated for defending themselves.

Third, the battered women's movement has moved into the state prison system and worked to raise the consciousness of and empower

incarcerated battered women. In Ohio, as in other states that have organized for clemency, empowerment and activism of incarcerated battered women have played major roles in educating authorities and the
public about wife abuse and the gender biases inherent in self-defense
law.

In this chapter, I have documented the history and strategy of the
Ohio battered women's movement as it related to larger trends within
the battered women's movement and was ultimately responsible for
advocating for the first large-scale clemency for incarcerated battered
women in the country. In the next chapter, I examine the mobilization
for clemency in six states where campaigns have achieved some level
of success. I identify the similarities and differences among organizing
strategies and analyze the barriers to full success in California, which
has organized a very efficient and highly supportive project that has,
however, failed to yield desired results.

Chapter Five

Clemency after Celeste

Since the Celeste clemencies, there have been mass clemency reviews in California, Illinois, Kentucky, Massachusetts, and Maryland. Florida reformed its clemency review process, providing greater access to the system for women incarcerated for killing men who abused them. While Governor Celeste was reviewing clemency petitions, Governor William Schaefer contacted activists in Maryland and asked them to help him identify women who had been battered and were incarcerated for assault or murder of an abusive intimate partner.[1] In February 1991 Governor Schaefer granted clemency to eight women. Later that year, he granted early parole to two more women. In California in 1992, with the help of activists, 34 incarcerated battered women filed clemency petitions. After strong pressure from activists in that state, Governor Pete Wilson reviewed nine cases. He commuted two sentences by releasing one woman and reducing the sentence of another. As of early 1998, he had not reviewed most of the remaining cases before him.[2] In Massachusetts in February 1992, with the help of activists, eight women submitted clemency petitions to Governor William Weld. In 1993 the governor granted clemency to four women, and in 1994 he granted clemency to two women and denied two others.[3] In December 1991, Florida governor Lawton Chiles revised that state's clemency application procedures so that women who had killed a spouse and could show evidence they had been battered could apply for clemency without a waiver from the governor and two cabinet members.[4] Since January 1992, 26 clemency petitions have been filed, with 9 women being granted some type of clemency and 11 cases pending as of January 1997. In 1994, 12 women in Illinois, again with the help of activists, submitted clemency petitions to Governor Jim Edgar, who reviewed them and granted clemency to four women and denied eight. In July 1995 the Illinois Clemency Project for Battered Women submitted an additional 18 petitions. Governor Edgar reduced one sentence and denied the other 17 petitions. In early 1996 eight more women filed petitions, which had not been acted upon by the end of 1997. Most recently, on his last day in office, outgoing Kentucky governor Brereton Jones, who had been lobbied by activists and inmates in that state, granted clemency to nine incarcerated battered women so they could have early parole reviews and pardoned a woman who had been released from prison. Early in 1996 all the women granted an early hearing were released on parole. A tenth woman, who was eligible for a hearing without special consideration from the governor, was also released on parole.

Approximately half of all incarcerated women have been physically abused at some time in their lives, and 36 percent have been sexually abused, although not all were imprisoned for crimes related to abuse (Correctional Association of New York 1991). Whether all these women are entitled to clemency depends on the facts of each woman's case and the judgment of parole boards and individual governors. Whether their cases should even be reviewed is a matter of political opinion, with some arguing that clemency review sidesteps the judicial process and negates the decisions of the jurors who convicted these women. In this chapter I describe the clemency organizing efforts in Maryland, Illinois, California, Massachusetts, Florida, and Kentucky and identify strategic trends, barriers to success, and potential problems in the quest for clemency.

Maryland

During the 1980s, activist attorneys in Maryland tried but failed to establish case law guaranteeing the admission of expert testimony on battered woman syndrome.[5] Faced with this obstacle, the legal defense branch of the Maryland battered women's movement formally organized in 1989. It formulated a new strategy to obtain justice for women who had defended themselves. At that time, a coalition of private- and public-interest attorneys and other activists formed the Domestic Violence Taskforce as an official entity within the Public Justice Center. It originally consisted of attorneys from major law firms and the Office of the Public Defender, students and professors from the University of Maryland Law School, and others with legal training. "From its inception, the focus of the Taskforce was to effectuate legal reform in areas of law directly affecting women who had experienced abuse from a partner," writes attorney Judith Wolfer.[6] Despite this outlook, few of the initial Taskforce members worked in the area of wife abuse, so they contacted members of the House of Ruth, a domestic violence organization in Baltimore, to help them understand the problems facing battered women.[7] That same year, Maryland's Special Joint Committee on Gender Bias in the Courts, a mutual effort of the Maryland bar and the judiciary, issued a document entitled "Report on Gender Bias," which found that such bias still existed in Maryland courts (Murphy 1993). Together with the House of Ruth, the Taskforce developed a tripartite strategy to reform the law and remedy some of its consequences.[8]

The first step in its strategy was public education. The Taskforce produced a powerful video, *A Plea for Justice,* featuring four Maryland women imprisoned for killing or assaulting their abusers. The objective of the video was to allow victims to tell their stories to a wide audience, thereby creating an intellectual and emotional understanding of battered woman syndrome and battered women's experiences. Activists hoped the video would lead to social change in many sectors (Murphy 1993). Aside from the *48 Hours* segment that portrayed some of the Ohio clemency applicants' cases, *A Plea for Justice* was the first video of its kind (Murphy 1993). The target audience for the video included the governor, who had the power to grant clemency without consulting the Parole Commission.[9] In 1990, the Taskforce premiered the video for a Baltimore audience, which included the mayor, the state attorney for the city of Baltimore, state legislators, judges, the warden of the women's prison, and members of the Parole Commission, among other high-ranking officials.[10] The video received extensive media coverage. By drawing upon battered woman syndrome to explain the experiences of the featured women, it established the framework within which the problem would come to be understood in Maryland.

The second step in the movement's strategy was to pass legislation recognizing battered woman syndrome as evidence in homicide cases. It was first introduced in 1990, where it was attacked as a "license to kill" by opponents. In the 1991 legislative session, supporters of the bill used *A Plea for Justice* to argue the need for the legislation. Finally, in April 1991, the *Battered Spouse Syndrome Bill* passed in the Maryland legislature by an almost unanimous vote.[11] It took effect 1 July 1991, after Governor Schaefer had already granted clemency to eight women.[12]

The third step in the Taskforce's strategy was to obtain clemency for women incarcerated for crimes against abusive partners. Because the governor had never indicated that he was interested in domestic violence, the Taskforce reasoned that its greatest chance of success would come from a class petition to the Maryland Parole Commission. After extensive discussion and consideration of the issues, the Taskforce decided to include in its petition only women who had experienced abuse from their partners and whose crimes were directly related to that abuse. According to a newsletter article explaining the clemency process, "Potentially eligible incarcerated women were identified by law students and professors from the University of Maryland Law School. . . . Identified women were sent a letter explaining the purpose of the project and inquiring if the woman wished to be interviewed."[13] Approximately 30 women chose to be interviewed. A comprehensive interview protocol was established, and interview teams, consisting of attorneys, domestic violence advocates, and law students, were trained on the relevant issues. Women were interviewed in 1989 and 1990, and their stories were corroborated by institutional records, court files, and trial transcripts. The interviews were then discussed among the entire Taskforce. Eight women, whose cases were judged most likely to succeed, were chosen for petition to the Parole Commission.[14]

After *A Plea for Justice* was completed, Governor Schaefer was one of the first legal decision makers targeted to see it. After viewing the film, he went with U.S. Congresswoman Constance Morella to meet with women convicted for defending themselves (interview, 18 March 1994). He met with inmates for over two hours, listening to their stories, and afterward told how his consciousness of the issues had been raised by the experience (Murphy 1993). Later, testifying before a congressional subcommittee considering battered woman syndrome legislation and improved domestic violence training for judges, Schaefer said, "I never focused on the issue of domestic violence until two years ago. I had no interest in it at all and I started off unsympathetic. After hearing the women's stories I decided they should be given a chance to say how they were treated."[15]

After meeting with the inmates, in December 1990, Governor Schaefer contacted the House of Ruth to ask staff to identify battered women who had been convicted of assault or murder of an abusive intimate partner and to report on their opinion regarding the appropriateness of clemency for these women.[16] In addition to understanding and having great sympathy for the women he met, Schaefer was intrigued by the Celeste clemencies and wanted to investigate the possibility of similar action in Maryland. As a member of the Taskforce explained, "Our lucky opening had appeared and we were prepared to race through it."[17]

After receiving the governor's directive, the Taskforce gathered information on 18 additional women, adding 4 to their initial list of 8 women to be sent to the governor. On 23 January 1991 the Taskforce, together with the House of Ruth, submitted a 250-page confidential report to the governor recommending the release of 12 women.[18] On 19 February 1991 Governor Schaefer commuted the sentences of eight women. In a follow-up supplemental report, the Taskforce addressed the concerns of the cabinet in not recommending clemency for the remaining four women. In July 1991, the governor granted early parole to two.

After the initial clemencies were announced, the House of Ruth assumed responsibility for preparing the women for release. Some had nowhere to go. None was prepared to face her deceased partner's family or the awaiting media barrage. The House of Ruth designed a retreat for clemency recipients, at which reentry issues were discussed. It ran a 12-week group counseling program and helped with housing, job placement, and legal problems, at significant expense to itself.

The Taskforce's report was conservative. It included only women its members judged to have a high probability of being granted clemency. Nonetheless, members later learned that "by making our selection of women in the report, we enhanced the credibility of the report and the likelihood that any women would be released."[19] Some women chosen for review were political risks for the governor, including one who killed her abusive husband, a police officer, and another who had a history of drug and alcohol problems. By working with women on their transition from prison to private life, the House of Ruth hoped to reduce the risk to Governor Schaefer and improve the chances other women in Maryland and throughout the country might have for clemency.

As Jane Murphy (1993) has convincingly argued, the inmates' stories, which they told directly to Governor Schaefer or to other officials and the public through the video, played a central role in advancing the clemency process and changing the law in Maryland. Despite some important differences, including the absence of an activist presence inside the administration, the clemencies in Maryland are markedly similar to those in Ohio. But as we will see in Illinois, the voices of inmates are not always a necessary condition to clemency, and in California they have certainly not been sufficient.

Illinois

The Illinois Clemency Project for Battered Women, founded in 1993, is a group of lawyers, activists, formerly incarcerated women, and law students that has been filing clemency petitions on behalf of incarcerated battered women since 1994.[20] The Illinois Clemency Project grew out of the efforts of feminist law professor Mary Becker and two defense attorneys, Shelley Bannister and Margaret Byrne, who specialized "in representing women who are trying to use the legal system to end their oppression" (interview, 8 October 1996). Before founding the Clemency Project, Bannister and Byrne had represented four women who were granted clemency individually. Inspired by the Celeste clemencies, they believed the citizens of Illinois would support an organized effort. They joined with feminist law professors Cynthia Bowman from Northwestern University and Morrison Torrey from DePaul University and called together volunteer attorneys, students from the five law schools in the greater Chicago area, battered women's advocates, and others interested in the issue to form the Illinois Clemency Project. Members of the Project spent little time forming an organization. Once it was organized, the Project successfully applied for several small grants. It also established itself as an agency of a nonprofit, Chicago-based legal advocacy group for battered women called Lifespan, which accepted donations on behalf of the Project.

The work and goals of the Project took precedence over the establishment of a stable organization. As one founder explained, "We're just a totally volunteer . . . organization that basically exists in our consciousness and nowhere else" (interview, 8 October 1996). Even two years after the Illinois Clemency Project was founded, it had no offices of its own, operating out of the director's law office. Once a rudimentary organization was established, activists had to agree upon the criteria an inmate needed to meet to be helped by the Clemency Project. According to a member of the group, they established the following policy: "The woman has to have killed or injured or have been convicted of solicitation to kill an abuser and . . . we have to be able to show that the abuse was not adequately considered, either at trial or at sentencing. And the woman has to have a pattern of abuse that we can verify somehow through either other people or hospital records or police records" (interview, 8 October 1996). They solicited women who wished to consider applying for clemency by sending a statement about the Clemency Project to inmates and prison counselors whom Project members knew, asking them to spread the word. They also advertised in a prisoners'-rights organization newsletter and contacted public defenders throughout the state.

At the same time, they began training law students about wife abuse. Law students learned interviewing methods that empowered inmates to understand the clemency review process so they could make important decisions about going forward and about information they wanted included in their clemency petitions. The inclusion of law students had the obvious benefit of providing a cadre of free workers for the Project and educated a new generation of attorneys who would become prosecutors, defense attorneys, and judges. By educating lawyers early in their professional training, the Illinois Clemency Project helped to disseminate the movement's collective action frame widely into legal institutions.

In Illinois, as in Ohio, the governor has legal authority to grant clemency after the inmate's petition has been reviewed by the state Prisoner Review Board, which is made up of appointees of the governor. The board meets quarterly. The clemency petition must include the inmate's biography, any criminal history, her reasons why clemency should be granted, and her version of the offense. Petitioners may present brief oral arguments or have witnesses testify before the board, although the inmate is not brought to the hearing by the prison. Opponents are also given an opportunity to testify. After the hearing, the board reviews the petition and the prison counselor's assessment of the case and submits a confidential recommendation to the governor, who is free to disagree with the recommendation (interview, 8 October 1996).

In 1994 the Project filed 12 petitions. Interestingly, 1994 was an election year, and activists in the Project were not optimistic that Governor Edgar would grant clemency to any of the women. But as one of the Project's leaders reasoned, "The governor was running against a liberal woman [Dawn Clark Netsch], and he may have been trying to appeal to women voters."[21] In May 1994, the governor granted clemency to four applicants (interview, 8 October 1996).

In the first round of clemency applications, the Project made no effort to frame the petitions in terms of battered woman syndrome. Because its admissibility had been established in case law, the syndrome was less of an issue in Illinois than in states where it had been barred. Activists in that state wanted to avoid it, believing that framing women's decisions to kill in terms of a psychological profile would fail to explain their behaviors. Even if the syndrome did provide an explanation, it would play into stereotypes and myths about women and madness. In the first round of clemency petitions, the Clemency Project framed applications in terms of structural barriers preventing women from escaping violent relationships or fully defending themselves at trial. Specifically, in some cases they argued that prior to 1983, when the Illinois Domestic Violence Act was passed, orders of protection were unavailable to battered women. If a woman was being battered in the 1970s or early 1980s, she had probably already learned that the legal system would do nothing to protect her from abuse. Even if her crime was committed after protective orders were available, that she had been previously denied protection was important in understanding why she stayed with her partner. In other cases, the Clemency Project argued that women were not permitted to introduce expert testimony or, in some cases, even to tell jurors about the abuse that led to the crime. In some cases, the women had not been adequately represented at trial. Some defense attorneys hardly even interviewed the women. Others did not fully investigate or present the abuse at trial.

When Governor Edgar granted the four clemencies in May 1994, he justified them in terms of battered woman syndrome and the (erroneous) "fact" that women in Illinois had been legally prohibited from introducing expert testimony at trial. In July 1995 the Clemency Project submitted 18 more petitions. The governor denied 17 and reduced one woman's sentence from 29 years to 15 (interview, 8 October 1996). As a result of the way the governor framed the issue in the first round of petitions, the Clemency Project made a decision to interview inmates interested in another round of clemency applications and, in appropriate cases, to include evidence about the syndrome. In 1996 they submitted eight petitions, but as of the close of that year, the governor had not acted on any (interview, 8 October 1996).

Affected by national leadership and the feminist literature warning against the unrestricted use of battered woman syndrome, members of the Clemency Project were uneasy about their decision to include it in their clemency petitions, even when evidence of it existed. The lead attorney on many of the cases explained, "We felt kind of conflicted about that. We don't feel that this whole syndrome thing is a very helpful idea when it comes to women's search for equality. And also, to use a psychiatric term in order to describe a woman . . . making this very powerful decision to kill . . . often it didn't really help explain it all. But we have, to some degree, relented. . . . You know, we've jumped on the syndrome bandwagon, to a degree, where we felt like it was appropriate; that is, in cases where there is evidence the woman suffers psychological injury from the trauma" (interview, 8 October 1996). Regarding the governor's failure to act on any of the 1996 petitions by October of that year, the same attorney said,

I don't think any governor will let somebody out of prison shortly before a [national] election. You know . . . it's one of the things we definitely have learned, is these decisions by the governors of this state, and probably by the governors of any state, are very political decisions. They have political implications and the one thing . . . every politician knows is that . . . voters are against crime and one way to generally earn points with voters is to make sure that they understand that you're tough on crime. And to let somebody convicted of murder out of prison does seem to sound like you're not tough on crime. On the other hand, the movement among battered women and their advocates is a popular movement with widespread support, and women voters can be a powerful public block.

Despite their desire to present clemency petitions within an equality-based feminist framework, activists in Illinois made a pragmatic decision to align their presentations with those accepted by the governor. The governor decided against 17 of 18 women in the second round of petitions, after the 1994 election. By early 1997, he had not acted on the third round, even after the national elections. This may indicate that the 1994 clemencies were more the result of the political opportunity created when Governor Edgar ran against a "liberal woman" than the way in which the petitions were framed. By granting four clemencies, he was unlikely to lose support from conservative constituents, most of whom would never vote for a liberal woman; but he could draw votes from his opponent by taking a controversial stand on a feminist issue.

California

When the clemency movement in California began to organize, case law in that state was based upon the trial of a woman who was convicted for shooting her husband to death while he slept. The defendant, Brenda Aris, testified at her trial that her husband had threatened not to let her live until morning.[22] After being convicted of second-degree murder, Aris appealed on five grounds, including the following: (1) the trial court's exclusion of expert testimony that she was a battered woman and how that affected her mental condition at the time of the killing; (2) its refusal to instruct the jury on perfect self-defense; and (3) the judge's refusal to instruct the jury on the meaning of imminence as it relates to imperfect self-defense. The Court of Appeals ruled that the trial court properly instructed the jury on the meaning of imminence in its instructions to the jury. It further ruled that the court erred in excluding expert testimony on battered woman syndrome but that the error was harmless. It reasoned that Aris had not acted in perfect or imperfect self-defense because danger was not imminent when she killed her husband. Thus battered woman syndrome was allowable only in cases in which the defendant could show she was in imminent danger when she killed her abuser.

Activism for clemency in California began as an inmate-initiated movement that was later joined by attorneys and activists from throughout California. Women who are convicted of homicide in California are usually sent to one of two prisons. The California Institution for Women at Frontera is in southern California, about an hour away from Los Angeles; the second is in northern California, in Chowchilla, about three hours from San Francisco. California inmates, particularly those in Frontera, played a central role in advocating clemency, working with the media, educating the public about battered women's issues, and mobilizing support from feminists and left-wing activists throughout the state.

In 1988 Brenda Clubine had been in prison at the California Institution for Women in Frontera for 5 years of a 15-years-to-life sentence for killing her husband. After a three-year effort, she began a support group for incarcerated battered women. It started with 10 members, and within five years had 45 regular participants.[23] In March 1991, the group—Women against Abuse—wrote a letter to Governor Pete Wilson, who had taken office three months earlier, asking him to review the cases of battered women incarcerated for killing their abusers and to consider commuting their sentences. The letter was signed by 34 women. Governor Wilson declined their request to review all women in prison for killing abusers but said he would consider the letter an application for clemency from the 34 women who had signed it. By doing so, he withdrew any control women might have had over their stories and corroborating evidence. He retained government control over their files. The letter attracted the attention of activists throughout the state.[24]

In August 1991 the California Coalition for Battered Women in Prison was mobilized by leaders from a consortium of progressive legal and community groups. Some of the more prominent leaders and their organizations when the movement was founded were Ellen Barry of Legal Services for Prisoners with Children, Ken Theisen and Ariella Hyman of the San Francisco Neighborhood Legal Assistance Foundation, Rebecca Isaacs of Battered Women's Alternatives, Eli Rosenblatt of the Prison Action/Activist Resource Center, and Sheila Kuehl of the Southern California Women's Law Center, who was elected to the state legislature in 1996. In addition, the California Alliance against Domestic Violence was involved in the coalition, as were several private attorneys, including Kathryn Beck, Christine Cordoza, Jane Kroesche, Linda Starr, and Susan Stokes. Santa Clara Professor of Law Cookie Ridolfi mobilized and supervised law students in a movement legal clinic. After the initial organizing meetings, Minouche Kandel became involved with Legal Services for Prisoners with Children and wrote a grant to fund her own salary so she could devote her time to the coalition on a full-time basis. Aside from Kandel's position, the coalition had no funding source and relied entirely on its member organizations, private attorneys, and other activists for resources.

At their earliest meetings, activists decided they would prepare clemency petitions for women who had killed a batterer. After discussions with Sue Osthoff at the National Clearinghouse for the Defense of Battered Women and some debate over the issue, they decided to avoid choosing between "good" and "bad" cases. They would assist any woman who had killed her batterer, without regard to the specifics of the case, and would not promote some cases as more deserving than others. One activist explained, "There was a lot of discussion around it, and there was a pretty strong feeling that we did not want to get into a situation of picking good cases, sort of cherry picking and presenting those first. Because we didn't want to be in that position of saying, 'Well, you're a good candidate; you're a bad battered woman.' "[25]

From a team of more than 100 attorneys, many of whom were in private practice, the California Coalition assigned a lawyer to each woman who wished to pursue clemency review. Each woman was interviewed by her attorney, who then began gathering evidence and preparing the clemency petition.[26] The California Coalition met regularly to discuss the cases and to prepare strategy to pressure the governor to review the cases. Coalition activists envisioned organizing a mass clemency campaign in which a class of women would have their cases brought before the governor.

California activists have had to overcome more obstacles than those in any other state. California is larger than the other states where clemency movements have succeeded. It has relatively more and more powerful right-wing movements with which to contend. As in Florida, women are dispersed among several prisons, making movement cohesion more problematic. The California Coalition was divided between two cities. There were important cultural differences between the more conservative climate of Los Angeles and the more progressive culture of San Francisco. Because of these differences, as well as diverse approaches among activists from social movement organizations, public legal aid programs, and private law firms, slight variations existed in the collective action frame.

While the coalition agreed on the types of cases to accept and how to frame its legal arguments, it had difficulty reaching consensus on whether inmates should speak out and how they should be given voice. Private attorneys tended to prefer to have their clients keep low profiles. Activists advocated building public support and working through the media. Those who preferred the latter were somewhat limited in the strategies in which they could engage. Although their efforts were earnest, without the coordinated public presentation of issues involving inmates, their attorneys, and all other movement activists, they were constrained in building public support. In the end, cases tended to be handled individually, with decisions made by private attorneys rather than by Women against Abuse and the California Coalition as a unified entity.

In 1991, while the clemency petitions were being prepared, the California Legislature passed Assembly Bill 785, ensuring the right to introduce expert testimony on battered woman syndrome. Several legislators expressed interest in meeting with incarcerated battered women. In September 1991, eight members of Women against Abuse testified before legislators at the California Institution for Women at Frontera. The women told of the abuse they had endured, their efforts to escape or seek help, and the desperation they felt when they finally defended themselves. At those hearings, Linda Ammons, a former aide to Ohio Governor Celeste, testified that battered woman syndrome is a form of post-traumatic stress disorder, similar to that experienced by hostages and concentration camp prisoners.[27]

The head of the state legislature's Women's Caucus, Representative Jackie Speier, played a prominent role in organizing the women's testimony and introducing legislation on domestic violence and battered women. The California Coalition worked in partnership with legislators and made strong, successful efforts to pass bills that would help battered women. But they overlooked the importance of establishing contacts inside the Wilson administration.[28]

Although some California activists resisted the use of battered woman syndrome, the enactment of expert testimony legislation in 1992 created a legal rationale for clemency reviews for women convicted before their right to introduce such expert testimony was assured. As in other states, changes in the law made the incarceration of victims of crime seem even more unjust, particularly given the new recognition of the barriers to escape. But battered woman syndrome was not the only argument made in clemency petitions. The case was made for the incompetence of some women's attorneys and that many women did not receive fair trials because they were refused the right to introduce evidence or because they were denied proper jury instructions. From March through October 1992, following the enactment of expert testimony legislation, the California Coalition filed clemency petitions on behalf of 34 women who were incarcerated for crimes against their abusers.[29] (This was not the same group of women who had signed the original letter, although there was some overlap.)

According to California law, the governor has the authority to grant clemency, except in cases involving impeachment, after applications have been reviewed by the Board of Prison Terms.[30] There is no established application protocol. In July 1992, A. B. 2401 was signed by Governor Wilson. It required all commissioners and deputy commissioners of the Board of Prison Terms who conduct parole hearings to receive training on domestic violence and battered woman syndrome.

Despite apparent support for criminalizing wife abuse, Governor Wilson moved slowly on the clemency petitions. In May 1993, he announced that he had reviewed 16 cases. Only six of those petitions had been submitted by the California Coalition. The remainder included members of Women against Abuse who had signed the letter sent to him in March 1992.[31] In this "mass" review, he reduced the sentences of two petitioners, Frances Caccavale and Brenda Aris. Caccavale had lived with her abusive husband for over 40 years before she stabbed him as he was beating her. Caccavale was 78 years old. Wilson explained that he had reduced her sentence to time served because she was old and sick, not because she had been battered. Brenda Aris's sentence was reduced from 15-to-life to 12-to-life so that she would be eligible to go before the parole board earlier. She was paroled in February 1997, becoming only the second woman to be released as a result of five years of efforts in California.

Between May 1993 and the end of the year, Wilson reviewed three petitions submitted to him by the California Coalition. He decided against each case. The women's attorneys advised them to avoid speaking to the press about their cases. As of early 1997, he had failed to review the remaining cases and refused to meet with coalition members or individual attorneys or to hold hearings on the women's cases. Of the cases he has reviewed, he said he looked through the records for evidence that the woman could have left the situation. As one activist said, "That same old question! Why don't they leave? And so he either doesn't get it or if he gets it, he's pretending he doesn't get it in that he's still asking the wrong question, because obviously that's not the question you ask in these cases. You ask at the time when they killed this person, were they in fear for their lives" (interview, 14 February 1997).

Sensing that efforts with the governor might stall, activists in the California Coalition, working with legislators, attempted to provide legal relief for incarcerated battered women. In early 1993, A. B. 2295 was introduced. It proposed to give individuals convicted before expert testimony legislation took effect a chance to have their original trials reviewed (Baker 1994). A.B. 2295 passed the Senate by a vote of 24–5, and the assembly by a vote of 68–3. Despite this overwhelming support, Governor Wilson vetoed it in October 1993 (Baker 1994).

In 1994, in an effort to bring public attention to the issue, as well as to raise funds for the organization, the California Coalition hosted a benefit screening of the Academy award–winning documentary *Defending Our Lives,* produced by activists in Massachusetts.[32] It was during this year that coalition members made their greatest effort to use the media to sway the governor and public opinion. In March, two years after they had submitted the petitions, they held a press conference at the State Building in San Francisco, as they had done the previous year. They submitted petitions in support of the women's release. Feminists wrote op-ed articles. They talked with the press. They argued that clemency for battered women was a national trend. High-profile attorneys appeared on television talk shows and news magazines, explaining why battered women deserve to have their cases reviewed. Efforts to educate the public and influence the governor came from the clemency applicants themselves. They gave interviews to the local and national media, talking with journalists in person or by telephone. They appeared on television documentaries on battered women who have killed abusers and even posted their stories on the World Wide Web.

There was a risk in media exposure. The publicity the media bring to a case can make or break it. If the media decide a woman's case does not merit clemency review, they may depict her as a killer who is "working the system" to gain freedom. Being "trashed" in the media is emotionally and mentally difficult to endure. As of early 1997 Governor Pete Wilson had failed to review the remaining 23 petitions before him. (One woman died while waiting to have her petition reviewed, and another was paroled.) One of the attorneys who had worked with the California Coalition until it unofficially went out of existence sometime in 1995 or 1996 commented that she thought the California movement had failed, in part, because "[w]e didn't pay enough attention to the politics of it, how incredibly political it was" (interview, 14 February 1997).

Unlike Governors Celeste and Schaefer, Pete Wilson was elected to office on a staunchly anticrime platform, which made the political climate all the more difficult for clemency activists. Unlike Governors Edgar of Illinois, Schaefer of Maryland, and Weld of Massachusetts, who were all conservative on economic issues and moderate to liberal on social issues, Wilson's conservatism extends to most social issues. Even if he were to grant clemency to all the applicants before him, it is unlikely he would win votes from feminist or left-wing groups. Further, by granting clemency, Wilson would run the risk of appearing soft on crime to some of his anticrime constituent groups. Although he would be unlikely to lose their votes, his support base is firmly centered among social and fiscal conservatives. To "get to" the governor on this issue, it would be necessary for activists to establish contacts with members of the administration who could raise his consciousness about the issues and to frame them in terms with which he might be sympathetic. His intractability on this issue, however, is undoubtedly related to his politically weak position in the state, as well as his aspirations for higher office, issues that will be more fully explained in chapter 6. These are conditions over which the California Coalition and Women against Abuse could be expected to exercise no control. It is important, however, that activists in that state maintain an "abeyance structure," or enough movement organization that they may mobilize more easily when the opportunity structure becomes less hostile to its goals (see Rupp and Taylor 1990).

Massachusetts

The organizing that took place in Massachusetts was similar to that in California in that it originated with women in prison and then spread outward. Nonetheless, there were important differences. Massachusetts changed its rules governing clemency before the review took place, establishing the first structural change surrounding this issue in the nation.[33] Legislation providing additional protection for battered women was passed prior to the clemency campaign. Another bill was signed into law in 1994, after the governor had granted clemency to eight women. This bill allowed the introduction of evidence of past abuse and expert testimony on abusive relationships and the impact of battering on perceptions of the imminence of danger.[34] Expert testimony had previously been allowable at the discretion of individual judges, a rule that was overturned by the Supreme Judicial Court the same year the evidentiary bill was passed.[35] Governors Wilson and Weld were both staunchly anticrime and pro–death penalty and had demonstrated no sensitivity to incarcerated battered women's issues.

Unlike in California, the movement in Massachusetts developed a strong working relationship with the press. Massachusetts activists effectively used the newspapers to raise public consciousness of domestic homicides and put pressure on the governor to address the problems encountered by women trying to escape violent partners. They worked in the prison, through the media, with the legislature, and with sympathetic aides to Governor Weld to persuade him that battered women are a class of crime victims whom the legal system has failed to protect. They argued that if the women incarcerated at the Massachusetts Correctional Facility at Framingham had not defended their lives, they may well have been dead.

Weld cut funding for Massachusetts shelters in 1991. But after pressure from activists and media support of incarcerated battered women, he decided that battered women in prison were victims of crime and deserved to have their cases reviewed.[36] His decision to grant clemency was made easier by the support of the state's numerous left-wing-movement organizations and its relative lack of right-wing mobilization, but Weld's consciousness about incarcerated battered women was most strongly impacted by the Massachusetts battered women's movement.

In 1989, Stacey Kabat, who had been running substance abuse and domestic violence programs at the Massachusetts Correctional Facility, formed a support and empowerment group specifically for women who were in prison for "defending their lives." The group was called Battered Women Fighting Back! (BWFB!).[37] At the time, Kabat was employed by an organization called Social Justice for Women, and BWFB! was sponsored by Massachusetts Correctional Legal Services, an office that provides legal assistance to inmates and their families for issues related to incarceration.[38] The eight women who joined BWFB! established three goals: (1) to free Massachusetts women imprisoned for defending their lives; (2) to reform self-defense statutes, train the judiciary regarding wife abuse, and educate the public about the severity of domestic violence; and (3) to establish the Massachusetts Advocacy and Defense Network for Battered Women, which would create a legal network on behalf of battered women, provide support services for battered women, and activate an emergency network of formerly battered women and supporters to respond to the issue.[39] As one activist put it, "We were going to work toward . . . freedom and . . . make sure that this would never happen to anybody else again" (interview, 6 February 1997). The clemency goal was established when Kabat learned of the Ohio and Maryland decisions.

Like inmates in Ohio and California, members of BWFB! began to believe they had been triply victimized and deserved to have their sentences commuted. Recognizing that BWFB! would need the help of activists outside the prison, in 1991 Kabat worked with other human rights and feminist activists to organize the Task Force on Battered Women and Self-Defense. The Task Force worked for the goals established by BWFB!

The Task Force was made up of over 100 volunteers, divided into two "teams." The legal team included approximately 35 lawyers, law students, activists, and paralegals.[40] As part of the effort, Harvard law students wrote a manual about commutation, entitled "Commutation for Women Who Defended Themselves against Abusive Partners: An Advocacy Manual and Guide to Legal Issues,"[41] and attorneys with the Task Force, working with other activists, began working with BWFB!

to draft clemency petitions on behalf of the group's members. The media team included activists who worked to educate the media on domestic violence issues and gain their support. They used the media to create public consciousness that battered homicide victims and women who defend themselves were members of a single class. They began a count of the homicides in which women were allegedly killed by intimate partners. They met with local and regional editors of the *Boston Globe* and the *Boston Herald* and convinced them to run homicides of women on their front pages. They worked with local journalists, helping them contact members of BWFB! so that stories accurately depicting the issues were run in the state's major newspapers. BWFB! members joined the media campaign by sharing their stories with reporters and with a crew that came in to film what would become an Academy Award winning documentary, *Defending Our Lives*. When activists wrote editorials for newspapers or did public speaking, they opened their remarks by citing the number of women killed by intimate partners in Massachusetts that year. In addition to the clemencies and media work, members of both teams lobbied the Women's Legislative Caucus for legislation that would enhance legal protections for battered women and ensure their right to fully defend themselves at trial.

Activists made every effort to publicize that 1991 was deadly for battered women in Massachusetts. On average that year, a woman was killed every 18 days, with a current or former intimate partner suspected or charged with the homicide.[42] As one activist explained, "It was real clear that we had to prove that they could've been six feet under just as easy as this person that they had killed. That it was self-defense that we were dealing with here. . . . We wanted to see that the public awareness was heightened to the point that people didn't say . . . why didn't she leave. [We wanted that question] eradicated from the Massachusetts vocabulary . . . [,] that the first thing they'd say was, 'Was she defending her life?' " (interview, 6 February 1997).

In 1991 Task Force members lobbied the Women's Legislative Caucus regarding the need for better protection for battered women and met with at least one aide to the governor to talk about domestic violence and incarcerated battered women. Later that year, legislation was passed to provide improved legal protections for battered adults. Perhaps as a result of the lobbying, the media campaign, or the "groundswell of public support" for battered women, the governor issued a memo to the Advisory Board of Pardons, revising the Commutation Guidelines.[43] Applicants who could demonstrate "a history of abuse suffered by the petitioner at the hands of the victim which significantly contributed to or brought about the offense" could apply for clemency.[44] The revisions established the first structural change in the nation that provided greater access to the clemency review process for battered women. As one Massachusetts activist excitedly asked, "It's basically welcoming us to bring petitions to him, right?" (interview, 6 February 1997).

In Massachusetts the governor does not have sole authority to grant clemency but may deny it, even if the Advisory Board of Pardons recommends clemency. The application for clemency is a three-step process. First, an inmate must petition the Advisory Board of Pardons for a hearing, which it may either grant or deny. Second, if the Board of Pardons grants a hearing, it decides whether to recommend clemency to the governor. Finally, the case goes to the governor, who reviews it and decides whether to grant clemency (interview, 22 March 1994).

On 14 February 1992 the Task Force held a press conference in Boston and submitted eight clemency petitions to Lieutenant Governor Paul Cellucci. In an op-ed article before the petitions were submitted, Stacey Kabat wrote that because of recent legal reforms improving protections for battered women, those who were imprisoned before adequate protections were available should be afforded the opportunity to have their cases reviewed.[45] At the press conference, women lined the two marble staircases coming down into the main entrance of the State House, reading the names of all battered homicide victims from the previous year. An activist present at the presentation commented that "There wasn't a dry eye in the place. The lieutenant governor, I swear to God! He didn't know what hit him" (interview, 6 February 1997). After the press conference Cellucci addressed critics who argued that opening the clemency review process to battered women who had killed their abusers was inconsistent with the Weld administration's anticrime policies. Cellucci was quoted in the *Boston Globe* as saying, "I think fundamentally it's a question of punishing those who commit acts of domestic violence. . . . I think for too long in this state we've kind of treated it as a family matter. You know, the person who commits these crimes needs help . . . but we need to punish them as well."[46] Activists' efforts to frame the issues in terms the governor could agree with had succeeded.

The clemency petitions were not decided all at once. In April 1993 one sentence was commuted; in July 1993 another was reduced to time served; and in November 1993 a sentence was commuted and another inmate was granted early parole. In March 1994, the Advisory Board of Pardons reviewed the remaining four cases, recommending clemency for two women and denying the others. Weld followed the recommendations of the Advisory Board of Pardons and granted clemency to six of the eight petitioners. One of the petitions denied was that of a woman whose case was under appeal. She was later acquitted at the trial court level. One of the so-called Framingham Eight continues to serve her sentence and will not be eligible for parole until 2000.[47]

In January 1994, after these clemencies were granted, Governor Weld signed legislation that allowed evidence that the defendant had been abused and expert testimony regarding the common pattern in abusive relationships in support of claims of self-defense, duress, or coercion. The defendant could offer evidence to show the nature and effects of abuse as well as typical responses to it, including how those effects relate to perceptions of imminent danger and evidence indicating whether the defendant displayed characteristics common to victims of abuse.[48] Task Force activists, working through contacts in the governor's administration and the legislature, had lobbied for the new law as part of their efforts to prevent battered women from being convicted for defending their lives. At least two former members of BWFB! have continued their activism, working with the battered women's movement outside prison. Shannon Booker and Lisa Grimshaw have continued to speak out on battered women's issues. They talk about their experiences and how the legal system discriminated against them by not allowing them to defend themselves at trial. They have lobbied for domestic violence legislation and have continued to fight for the rights of battered women, even while they have endeavored to reestablish relationships with children and recover from the trauma they experienced.

Florida

The Florida clemencies differ from the others discussed in this book because mass clemency was never a stated goal of activists in that state. Instead, Florida activists envisioned reforming the administrative rules governing clemency so that the system would be more accessible to incarcerated women whose crimes were related to battering. In addition, they wanted to work with groups of inmates and help individual women file clemency petitions, prepare for review, and make a smooth transition to life after prison. In the first years of their efforts, some Florida activists envisioned using individual clemencies as a way to challenge stereotypes about women who kill and educating the public about domestic violence and reform laws of self-defense. After a period of reorganization, during 1994 and 1995, the Florida movement focused on clemency for its own sake, hoping to file as many petitions as possible before the end of the Chiles administration in 1998, when the rules of clemency would be subject to the interpretation of a new governor.[49]

According to Florida's clemency rules, the governor has sole authority to deny a clemency request for any reason and to grant clemency, with the approval of three cabinet members. Stringent rules apply, however, to the application for clemency. Before anyone may apply for a pardon, at least 10 years must have lapsed since the completion of all sentences and conditions of supervision. To apply for a commutation, a waiver must first be granted by the governor and two cabinet members, upon the recommendation of the Parole Commission. Once a waiver is issued, the application goes before the clemency board, made up of the governor and members of the cabinet.[50]

The stated goals of the Florida clemency movement were to create greater clemency opportunities for battered women incarcerated for killing abusive spouses, change the legal criteria for self-defense, and educate those in the legal profession about the psychological responses many women have to ongoing violence and abuse.[51] As a result of their activism, the first step of the clemency procedure was changed for women who had killed an abusive spouse and could show they were battered. Previously an inmate needed the recommendation of the Parole Commission and the consent of the governor and two cabinet members to apply for clemency. After the reform, if a woman could show evidence that she had been abused, she was entitled to submit a request to the Parole Commission for a waiver of the first step. If the commission could verify that the applicant's claims met the required criteria, it would then refer the request to a newly created panel of domestic violence experts, who would review it to determine whether the applicant "suffered from the Battered Woman Syndrome at the time of the commission of the crime for which the applicant is incarcerated."[52] The Parole Commission would then use the information provided by the panel in its recommendation to the Clemency Board, made up of the governor and the cabinet, and the case would be reviewed for clemency.

The political struggles over battered woman syndrome began in Florida in 1977, when Joyce Hawthorne, a woman who was married for 17 years to a man who beat and sexually abused her, shot and killed her husband when he threatened to kill her and her children.[53] Hawthorne had learned earlier that day that her husband had sexually molested one of her children. At her first trial, Hawthorne was convicted of first-degree murder. She appealed, based on errors police made investigating her case (Walker 1989). The case was remanded for a new trial, at which Hawthorne attempted to introduce expert testimony in support of a claim of self-defense in the death of her husband. She was convicted of second-degree murder and appealed again, on the basis of the trial court's exclusion of expert testimony on battered woman syndrome. The Court of Appeals found that expert testimony "would provide the jury with an interpretation of the facts not ordinarily available to them" and remanded the case so the trial court could determine whether the witness was qualified to testify as an expert.[54] Hawthorne was convicted at her third trial, but on appeal, her conviction was overturned based on misconduct by the prosecuting attorney (Walker 1989), and she was finally exonerated of all charges against her. In the wake of *Hawthorne,* the admission of expert testimony on battered woman syndrome was left to the discretion of individual judges. The syndrome was finally recognized in 1993, when the Court of Appeals recognized it as a matter of law in *Rogers v. State.*[55]

Activism to gain justice for battered women convicted of killing abusive partners began before *Rogers.* In 1990, Candice Slaughter, a survivor of wife abuse, founded the Women in Prison Committee (WIP), a project of the Florida Coalition against Domestic Violence. WIP was formed when a battered woman in the Florida prison system wrote to Slaughter asking for help in getting a waiver so she could apply for clemency. WIP's first action was a news conference held on the day after Christmas 1990 in front of one of Florida's four women's prisons, where it demanded clemency for that particular inmate "and any of the women who are in prison for acting in self-defense" (interview, 25 February 1994). They organized petition drives and letter writing campaigns, which, according to activists, the governor ignored. WIP decided to target the governor and the cabinet through a media campaign and to meet with members of their staffs (interview, 25 February 1994).

In September 1991, members of WIP were invited to a dinner at the governor's mansion, the purpose of which was to create partnerships between foundations and the government. At that dinner, WIP leaders spoke with one of the governor's aides, who understood and was sympathetic to domestic violence issues. The aide suggested that WIP send a proposal on how the clemency rules should be revised, promising that the administration would consider their suggestions. WIP members visited and talked with battered or formerly incarcerated women throughout Florida. Two weeks after the dinner at the governor's mansion, they delivered their proposal. Afterward, members of WIP, together with Linda Osmundson, president of the Florida Domestic Violence Coalition, met with the governor's aides to discuss the proposal and how the new process would work (interview, 25 February 1994). Three months later the governor adopted the revised policy,[56] which became effective 1 January 1992.[57]

In late 1992 or early 1993, Gwen Spivey, a Tallahassee appellate lawyer, tried to organize a *pro bono* (free of charge) project to help battered women inmates apply for clemency under the new guidelines.[58] WIP met with inmate support groups to explain the new process and encourage applications, but they were resistant to attorneys gaining control of the movement. Spivey's project never fully mobilized.[59] Between January 1992 and September 1993, 15 women applied for clemency under the new rules.[60] The first hearing was held in December 1992, and despite negative testimony from the prosecutor who had tried the case,[61] the first clemency under the new rules was granted in May 1993.[62] A second woman was released in July 1993,[63] and a third woman was sent to work release in November 1993.[64] Only the first two women granted clemency were immediately released from prison. Those who followed were required to go through a work release program before being granted freedom, a policy to which WIP leaders agreed (interview, 28 January 1997).

During 1994, an election year in Florida, only one woman filed for clemency, and she came forward without the help of WIP. During that year, responsibility for filing clemency petitions for incarcerated battered women passed to the Florida Battered Women's Clemency Project, a small organization funded by the Florida Bar Association. During its first year, it was underfunded and staffed by two part-time attorneys who were inexperienced with clemency (interview, 28 January 1997). In January 1996, the Clemency Project was provided enough funding to hire two full-time attorneys and a full-time staff member who did both clerical work and advocacy. Its leader was Jennifer Greenberg, a specialist in death penalty cases, who had experience with clemency. In addition to paid staff, the Clemency Project also enlisted the service of volunteer activists. In a year's time, they filed 10 clemency petitions and, by January 1997, had received waivers for two women to go forward for clemency review (interview, 29 January 1997).

Despite advice from leaders at the National Clearinghouse for the Defense of Battered Women that they should organize a mass clemency project, WIP activists avoided bringing large numbers of clemency petitions before the governor at one time. Instead they wanted to bring petitions forward individually so that each woman's case could be presented in the most favorable light. One activist explained,

I think [a mass clemency] is extremely foolish for many reasons. The first and foremost reason is that to bring many women forward does not alter the system. The goal of this project is not to get women out of prison. The goal of the project is to change how judges and prosecutors are viewing battered women who kill in self-defense. The vehicle is getting women out of prison. Because it overturns a decision, and that makes people hysterical in the criminal justice system. It gets their attention in a way that we have never been able to get their attention. We have done trainings, we've talked nice, you know. We've taken off our gloves. We're not going to do it anymore (interview, 25 February 1994).

In addition, petitions could be carefully timed to coincide with the political climate. Inmates have always had the option of submitting a clemency petition without the assistance of WIP, and those who began the process on their own and later asked for help were assisted. WIP did not try to control who could apply for a waiver or clemency but did make efforts to present women's cases in the most favorable light and to influence media portrayals of clemency applicants. The same activist explained their caution:

None of this is about fairness. . . . This is about politicians who are nervous by nature, and how do we push them in the direction we want to go. . . . We try to find issues that will create a sense of empathy and sympathy . . . because if they see this as a sympathetic situation, then what they do is translate that into their head, that's how the voters will see it. . . . And we try to create a picture of who this person is, versus how the government presents her as this cold hearted killer. . . . My job is to create media that says, "Here is a woman who's a mother who loved her children" (interview, 25 February 1994).

By framing women's cases so they would appear to be sympathetic and by working with the media, WIP attempted to reduce political repercussions and convince decision makers that clemency would not harm their careers. WIP accompanied women upon their release from prison. They trained women in handling the media, went with them to press conferences, helped them decide which reporters to talk to, and provided support during the months after their release. WIP believed that by portraying women favorably and then helping them succeed in their transition to life after prison, they would reduce the political repercussions politicians feared and create opportunities for other women to be granted clemency. When cases were less sympathetic and included a history of drug abuse, prostitution, or prior convictions, WIP advocated that women be placed in a work-release program before being released.

In its effort to reduce political risk and to guarantee a high rate of success for petitioners, WIP avoided bringing cases forward during politically inopportune times. Some activists felt strongly that it was "morally wrong" to encourage women to apply for clemency when chances of a favorable review were diminished. During the 1994 gubernatorial race between Lawton Chiles and Jeb Bush, WIP made a decision not to initiate any new petitions. A WIP activist explained, "We can't guarantee anybody's going to get out. But what we can guarantee at this point is that everybody's running for governor and that people are busy and they are not going to stick their neck out in an election year for women that the public sees as a murderer" (interview, 25 February 1994). Beyond their reluctance to bring cases forward during an election year, however, WIP had no intention of bringing petitions forward en masse even when Chiles was reelected.

Although it was responsible for achieving the revision of Florida's rules of clemency, WIP proceeded conservatively. They did not consider that if Chiles were not reelected, no cases would be before him at the end of 1994. Many governors are more likely to grant clemencies at the end of their administrations. The "gloves came off" in 1996 when responsibility for filing clemency moved to the fully staffed Battered Women's Clemency Project. It was then that efforts to file a large number of clemency petitions and gain immediate release for all women resumed.

The strategy of the Clemency Project was to file petitions on behalf of women who had already served many years of their sentences, together with the "least complicated" cases—or cases in which prior convictions, drug offenses, or other issues would not hinder women's chances for a positive review. The Clemency Project began working to submit a large number of petitions to Governor Chiles during his last year in office, when activist attorneys hoped he would be willing to consider some of the more controversial cases.

WIP filed 16 petitions in 1992 and 1993 and achieved nine clemencies (interview, 29 January 1997), but it was relatively timid in bringing cases forward and advocating strongly on behalf of petitioners. Perhaps because it is staffed by paid attorneys rather than nonlegal, volunteer activists, the Clemency Project has been much more aggressive in identifying women, researching their cases, and filing petitions. Clemency Project attorneys would not turn down an offer of work release, but they believe that there is a balance between reducing the political risk for politicians and getting the justice women deserve, even if their cases are "complicated." An activist with the Clemency Project explained, "As defense lawyer, I look at these cases and ... I say, you know, 'This woman should have the prison gate opened and be given a check for a million dollars and an apology.' So I have real strong feelings ... there has to be a balance between making it politically comfortable, but further punishment and incarceration. ... they can do that to us, or to our clients if they want to, but as a defense lawyer, it's not what I'm asking for" (interview, 29 January 1997)

Activists with the Clemency Project have worked informally with WIP. Each believes it is important to support women after they are released from prison to help them recover from the trauma they have experienced and to reduce the political risk to Governor Chiles and other governors throughout the nation. Funding for the Clemency Project is due to continue through 1998, when Chiles will leave office and the rules of clemency may be changed by a new governor. Until that time, attorneys for the Clemency Project intend to gain the release of as many women as possible.

Kentucky

The battered women's movement in Kentucky followed a trend away from framing legislation or clemencies in terms of battered woman syndrome and toward changing self-defense law. The trend away from battered woman syndrome first manifested in a mass clemency campaign in Illinois in 1992. Although Illinois activists later framed some of the clemencies in terms of the syndrome, they did so only because they thought it was something the governor understood. Similarly, legislation passed in Massachusetts in 1994 avoided reference to the syndrome, whereas in California, where the climate has been hostile to imprisoned battered women, efforts to frame the issues in those terms have continued.

When the battered women's clemency movement became organized in Kentucky, it did so in an atmosphere in which the meaning of battered woman syndrome had been a source of controversy in the courts and only recently resolved. In 1987 the Kentucky Court of Appeals ruled that battered woman syndrome was a mental condition and that only a psychiatrist or a clinical psychologist could offer expert testimony about it.[65] This ruling curtailed the access of women, particularly those living in poverty or in rural areas, to other types of experts (such as shelter workers or nurses) with whom they may have had contact or who could be more easily brought in to testify. It illustrates some of the problems identified by feminist legal scholars who have warned against using the syndrome or other defense strategies that draw upon women's impaired mental state (e.g., Browne 1993; Schneider 1986; 1996; Schneider et al. 1978). In a 1990 decision, the Supreme Court of Kentucky overturned the 1987 court of appeals ruling, finding that "Battered woman syndrome is not a mental condition and, thus, expert testimony on battered wife syndrome need not come from [a] psychiatrist or clinical psychologist."[66] In effect, the supreme court ruled that an expert who testifies about the syndrome may explain it more broadly, to include a discussion of the social context of the violent relationship as well as the psychological response to living with ongoing abuse.

In 1992 activists in Kentucky made a complete break with battered woman syndrome when they lobbied for the passage of H.B. 256, which was signed into law the same year. The legislation redefined the meaning of imminence, saying, " 'Imminent' means impending danger, and, in the context of domestic violence and abuse . . . belief that danger is imminent can be inferred from a past pattern of repeated serious abuse."[67] Despite the expansive definition of battered woman syndrome handed down by the state Supreme Court in 1990, the legislation included a section guaranteeing the admissibility of evidence showing that the defendant was battered by the person she is charged with killing or assaulting.[68]

By law in Kentucky, violent offenders who use a gun in committing a crime are not eligible for probation or conditional discharge. Those convicted of a capital offense and sentenced to life cannot be released on parole until they serve at least 12 years. All violent felony-level offenders are required to serve at least half of their original sentences before they are eligible for parole. H.B. 256 amended the law so that these requirements no longer apply to a person who was battered by the person they killed or assaulted.[69] In an effort to remedy the situations of women who had entered guilty pleas or were prevented from showing evidence at trial that they had been battered, the legislation established their right to file a motion with the courts in which they were tried, so the judges who had originally sentenced them could verify that they were battered. The entire act was made retroactive to crimes committed after 15 July 1986. This law had the potential to provide relief to incarcerated battered women, but after it was passed it was rarely used. The activists I spoke with explained that judges did not fully understand why they were required to re-hear cases and, therefore, that they were not amenable to holding new trials for women they had already sent to prison.[70]

Prior to the passage of this legislation, Kentucky attorneys who had defended or otherwise become interested in the cases of women incarcerated for killing abusers worked to gain their client's release by filing individual clemency petitions. In December 1991, outgoing governor Wallace Wilkinson pardoned a woman who had already been released from prison and denied clemency to two other battered women whose cases he considered at the same time.[71] Until 1995, when Governor Brereton Jones left office, that was the extent of activists' success in that state. During and before the Jones administration, Kentucky governors could not serve two consecutive terms. Few have run for national office after their administrations ended.

In January 1992, shortly after Governor Jones was sworn in, he appointed Marsha Weinstein executive director of the Commission on Women. She had been active in children's and women's issues for years and first met Jones in 1988 during an unsuccessful campaign for state representative. When she started her job as executive director, she found a file in her desk on clemency, which included articles on the Ohio clemencies. As a result, she thought about trying to get some battered women out of prison at the end of the Jones administration.

Between June 1993 and March 1997, the chair of the Parole Board in Kentucky was Helen Howard-Hughes, who had served as executive director of the Women's Commission in the late 1970s and early 1980s. While at the Women's Commission, Howard-Hughes had received a federal grant to study domestic violence in the state at a time when the first shelters were being established and legislation drafted. Feminists in Kentucky government worked hard to get Howard-Hughes appointed as chair of the Parole Board. After Howard-Hughes was appointed to the position, Weinstein suggested to her that they should try to do something to get battered women out of prison. Howard-Hughes agreed to look into it.

At that time, Weinstein had no idea what the proper procedure was to initiate such a project and had no understanding of the difference between pardons, commutations, or clemencies. Weinstein approached an aide to the governor, suggesting that she was "investigating" the "possibility" of getting pardons for battered women in prison. The aide said that it was the governor's policy not to pardon anyone who had been out of prison less than 10 years. Undeterred, Weinstein began to identify feminist allies in the women's prison and the administration and to cultivate good relations with the media. Her strategy was to bypass aides to the governor who opposed her and to gain favor with the press, through which she would build public support for incarcerated battered women.

Chandra McElroy worked at the Kentucky Correctional Institution for Women at Peewee Valley, where she ran a support group for battered women who had killed or assaulted their abusers. McElroy founded a group called "BOSH," an acronym for Battered Offenders Self-Help. In 1994 she contacted Weinstein, inviting her to the prison to talk to the group about domestic violence. Weinstein knew that Howard-Hughes had promised to review women inmates' files to identify women who had been battered and incarcerated for homicide or assault, but she did not talk about the possibility of a clemency to McElroy or BOSH members. Instead, she took with her Sherry Currens, executive director of the Kentucky Domestic Violence Association, and the two talked with the group about wife abuse and related issues. As they were leaving, one of the BOSH members said that she felt that no one cared about them and that as battered inmates, they had no voice. Weinstein suggested to the group that they make a quilt, portraying their experiences and expressing their feelings.

As Howard-Hughes conducted her investigation into the cases of the approximately 300 women incarcerated at Peewee Valley, she identified 105 cases that involved murder, manslaughter, reckless homicide, and first-degree assault. Of those cases, 27 involved domestic violence.[72] At that time, Public Advocate Allison Connelly became aware of the reviews Howard-Hughes was conducting and assigned public defenders in her office to look for women whose cases might have been overlooked and to prepare clemency petitions for those who were eligible, according to the criteria established by H.B. 256 (interview, 22 and 29 January 1997). Connelly, Howard-Hughes, and Weinstein had been appointed by Governor Jones,[73] and all held strong feminist convictions regarding the injustice of incarcerating victims of domestic violence (interview, 22 January 1997). As insiders in the administration, they played a key role in promoting and accomplishing the clemencies. They were supported by the National Clearinghouse, which sent them information on how other states had organized for clemency, and by Sherry Currens, who drafted a "Clemency Plan," which helped to keep everyone in the network on track. The Clemency Plan included the following: meetings with the Parole Board to determine who might be eligible for clemency and what evidence the board might be willing to consider in petitions to be filed; a meeting with the governor's office to determine whether the governor would consider a clemency review; the role the public advocate's office had agreed to play in the preparation of petitions; the role Chandra McElroy would play in providing additional support to women in prison regarding domestic violence issues; and the scheduling of testimony in favor of a domestic violence bill before the legislature during this period.[74] While Weinstein worked in the governor's office and with the media, Howard-Hughes worked with the Parole Board, McElroy worked in the prison, Connelly oversaw the clemency applications, and Currens—an outsider to the administration—coordinated the activity of this social movement community.

In the summer of 1995, Howard-Hughes invited Currens to conduct domestic violence training for members of the Parole Board. After that, the board reviewed the files identified by Connelly and Howard-Hughes, finding justification for early parole in 14 cases. Five of those women were eligible for a hearing with the Parole Board, but because of the law requiring violent offenders to serve half their sentences before being eligible for parole, a hearing was impossible for nine of those women unless that requirement was commuted.[75] The nine had submitted petitions to the Parole Board, which then recommended to the governor that he commute part of the women's sentences.[76] Inmates and career activists began a campaign to build public support and neutralize criticism surrounding the clemencies. They had to do little to convince the governor that clemency was necessary in those nine cases. In addition to the nine submitted to the Parole Board, advocates worked behind the scenes to secure the release of four additional women who were not bound by the 50 percent rule but whose crimes were related to battering.[77] The governor did not grant clemency in those cases. One of the four women was released on parole during the Patton administration, which took office in December 1995. The remaining three were still in prison as of early 1997.

Like incarcerated women in other states, inmates in Kentucky played an active role in educating the public about domestic violence and the law and advocating for their release. The tactic that received the most media attention when the clemencies were announced was the quilt the women made representing their experiences with violence. On 26 August 1995, which was, not coincidentally, the 75th anniversary of suffrage for American women, Governor Jones saw the quilt at the state fair. According to one activist, he was deeply moved by it and said, "We've got to do something to get these women out" (interview, 29 January 1997). The process had already been set in motion.

The women's activism included much more than quilt making. Initially, it required reclaiming their experiences as battered women who deserved to be released from prison. They had to learn to be able to talk about their experiences. Women started haltingly with each other, eventually learning to express and deal with their feelings. As they were empowered, they were able to talk more openly about their lives, articulate the ways society failed to protect them from abuse, and explain how the judicial system judged them by an unfair standard. Each of the women wrote her story, some including documentation and pictures, which were sent to the governor to help him understand what they had lived through. They wrote letters and talked to the media whenever the opportunity presented itself. With the help of public advocates, they told their stories in a video seen by some members of the Parole Board. Without the work done in their support groups, it is doubtful that many of them would have been willing or able to talk so openly about their experiences or to articulate the injustices they had experienced. As one journalist explained in reference to the film, "All the women's comments are notable for one thing: They have found a voice for their feelings, a voice they evidently didn't have, or couldn't find, when they killed or injured their alleged abusers."[78]

In 1995, on behalf of the nine clemency applicants, the Parole Board recommended to Governor Jones that he commute the requirement that they serve half their sentences so they would be eligible for early review. On 11 December 1995 he granted clemency to those nine women, also pardoning a woman who had already been released from prison,[79] and on 4 January 1996 the board granted parole to all nine women and an additional one who did not need clemency to go before the board.

The clemencies in Kentucky were made possible by a network of feminists working from inside the system, within the Jones administration, the women's prison, and the public advocate's office. Their work was made easier by journalists who understood the issues and worked to portray them fairly, as well as by positive editorials published before the clemencies.[80] It was informed by the work of clemency organizers who had gone before, by the National Clearinghouse, and by the statewide network, whose leaders created an action plan and coordinated activists' work. Finally, it was made possible by a governor who has been described as being "tender hearted" and "supportive of women's issues."

Conclusion

Activists in the six states that have attempted or achieved multiple clemencies have used a number of tactics to achieve success. The strategy, which has varied from state to state, has been to establish support groups in prison, where battered women begin to understand their experiences and reclaim their identities. In most states, those women have actively pursued clemency. Outside activists, working with incarcerated women, have played a central role in every state. In some states, those activists were part of a social movement organization; in others, they were government officials loosely organized in a feminist community. In most states, the women's ability to tell their stories—through writing, the media, videos, or needlework—was central to educating authorities, raising their consciousness, and pressuring them to do something about the injustice of incarcerating victims of abuse whom society failed to protect. In most states, efforts were made to frame the demand for clemency in terms that adhered to newly created law or that otherwise created sympathy for victims. In every state, the success or failure of clemency was dependent upon the political-opportunity structure. Inmates and activists can do everything right, but if authorities will not listen or if they have too much to lose by granting clemency, activists have little choice but to reframe their demands and work to elect more sympathetic officials.

Chapter Six

Identity, Strategy, and Feminist Tactics in the Clemency Movement

Popular analysis has labeled the 1980s and 1990s a "post-feminist" era. Accordingly, during the 1980s, longtime activists left behind their feminist commitments, and younger women "were uninterested in feminism and the women's movement even as they reaped the benefits of women's expanded access to education and careers" (Whittier 1995, 2). As Whittier has shown in the larger women's movement, and as I have shown in the clemency movement, feminism has evolved rather than faded. Movement founders have strategically moved into jobs where they have advanced feminist goals, and joiners have worked with them through traditional social movement organizations. Analysts who argue that the 1980s and 1990s are a postfeminist era have been looking for activism in places liberal democratic theories suggest it should exist but in few places where it lives.

Assumptions that political protest happens outside of government and that what occurs in the "private" arena has little political impact are well applicable to class-based social movements. Nonetheless, few systematic efforts have been made to determine the extent to which class-based movements have worked through careers, institutional channels, or personal relationships to achieve their goals. Examination of identity-oriented movements requires analysis of the political context and the activism that takes place in all domains, including government and other arenas of institutionalized authority, traditional social movement organizations, careers, personal relationships, social movement networks, and more informal movement communities. It requires an understanding of the ways that activists create democratic public spaces (Cohen 1985) and how those spaces lead to social change.

I have three goals in this chapter. The first is to identify the conditions under which the battered women's clemency movement has been likely to succeed or fail. Such identification is important to activists in other states who are organizing clemency projects as well as to social movements scholars. My second goal is to identify the successful and unsuccessful strategies of this movement. Third, by drawing from resource mobilization, new social movement, and feminist theories, my aim is to develop a theoretical model of identity-oriented social movements. The development of such a model is central to understanding social movements as entities that exist wherever activists live and work.

Theoretical Framework

The clemency movement has helped release over 100 incarcerated battered women, but its success has often been mixed with disappointing failure. Understanding what has lead to success or failure requires examining the movement from a synthetic theoretical perspective, which draws together central concepts from resource mobilization, new social movement, and feminist theories.

Resource mobilization theory is grounded in theories of liberal democracy, which define politics as separate from civic society, personal life, and social movements (Acklesberg 1988; Ferree 1992). With its rigidly defined ideas about social movements, resource mobilization theory is problematic in the examination of women's movements, because it is based upon a liberal democratic tradition of personal and civic life (Ferree 1992). It assumes that activists are outside of institutionalized positions of authority and overlooks the feminist strategy of placing women in key political positions and other careers in which they will work to create social change. Resource mobilization theory excludes the feminist tenet that the personal is political and obviates an examination of acts of "everyday resistance" (Collins 1990). Despite these weaknesses, theorists within the resource mobilization tradition have developed concepts that are useful in examining movements that work within and outside of institutionalized authority. Resource mobilization theory provides a framework for analysis of the mobilization of tangible and intangible resources.

Postmodern, critical, feminist, and new social movement theorists argue that a merging of political and nonpolitical spheres has taken place in postindustrial societies (Acklesberg 1988; Alonso 1992; Bernstein 1985; Elshtain 1981; Foucault 1979; Habermas 1985; Melucci 1980; Morgen and Bookman 1988; Mouffe 1992; Offe 1985; Taylor and Whittier 1992; Touraine 1985). Central to these theories is the idea that the personal arena has political ramifications. Inherent to feminism is the belief that consciousness raising and personal empowerment are at the core of individual liberation and social change (Cassell 1977; Evans 1979; Morgen and Bookman 1988). Any examination of the battered women's clemency movement that is based upon liberal democratic assumptions would necessarily overlook the activism that has taken place in nontraditional arenas and obscure an examination of activists' efforts to create a political and cultural context conducive to movement success (Gagné 1996).

New social movement theory emerged in an effort to understand the structural roots of new "post-materialist" forms of discontent (Cohen 1985; Inglehart 1977; Klandermans and Tarrow 1988; Melucci 1985; Offe 1985; Pizzorno 1978; Touraine 1985). It has focused on a "new class" of professional "knowledge workers" who, because of their higher levels of education, relative affluence, and work-related autonomy, are believed to comprise the activist base of non–class-based social movements in the post-World War II era (Brint 1984; Flacks 1971; Inglehart 1977; 1979; 1986). Grievances are believed to have shifted away from material and class-based concerns of labor unions and socialists to lifestyle concerns, including gender relations in the home and in society at large. Resource mobilization theory has tended to assume that activism is something one does rather than an important aspect of the self. Feminist theory has provided a framework through which to examine everyday resistance but has otherwise provided few concepts through which to analyze activism from a social movements perspective. New social movement theory provides the tools necessary to examine and understand activism in everyday life. Its concepts of collective identity, social movement community, collective consciousness, collective action frames, and identity transformation are central to the examination of identity-oriented movements (Cohen 1985; Epstein 1990; Melucci 1985; 1989; Mueller 1987; Snow and Benford 1988; 1992; Taylor and Whittier 1992; Touraine 1985). Nonetheless, it lacks the conceptual tools necessary to examine the formal organizational features of social movements. The three are compatible, if certain adjustments are made.

By drawing upon the concepts within resource mobilization, feminist, and new social movement theories and by basing them on the feminist assumption that there are no real separations among social movements, government, civic life, careers, and personal life, a new theoretical framework emerges through which it is possible to understand that activism is more than something one does. It is a way of defining the self and the world. It is a way of life.

Factors Associated with Clemency

The battered women's clemency movement has worked at many levels to gain freedom for women incarcerated for defending themselves and to challenge the law that led to their convictions. Activists have worked outside the government, in positions as leaders and members of national, statewide, and local social movement organizations. As insiders and outsiders of institutionalized systems of authority, activists have worked to create change through their jobs as support group facilitators, prison employees, attorneys, victim advocates, shelter workers, aides to the governor, parole board members, legislators, cabinet members, and directors of state agencies. They have worked through their personal relationships to convince those in positions of authority that clemency was right. Clemency activists have created consciousness-raising and empowerment groups, through which incarcerated women's identities were transformed and politicized, and they worked to educate the media and coworkers in the government about wife abuse, gender biases in the law, and feminist issues in general. Inmates and other activists have worked to educate the media and government workers about wife abuse, gender biases in the law, and feminist issues in general. They have established contact between the media and incarcerated battered women, as a way of giving voice to women whose experiences have been institutionally muted.

Political Opportunities

In the battered women's clemency movement, the success of efforts to frame issues in social justice terms was dependent upon the political context of each state and the extent to which governors were willing to open the democratic process. Before we can analyze the other factors and strategies that affected movement success or failure, we must examine the political opportunity structure present in each state at the time mobilization for clemency occurred.

The political process model of resource mobilization theory provides a framework in which to examine social movements in relation to institutional political processes. It allows for an analysis of the relative strength or weakness of political parties and the economy, the salience of social and economic issues in public opinion, the platforms upon which officials ran for office, demographic movements or realignments of power, and the ability of social movements to mobilize support and neutralize opposition (McAdam 1982; Tilly 1978). Even in years when a governor is not up for reelection, she or he may be reluctant to grant clemency, fearing it may hurt the election chances of allies in the legislature or that it may be used negatively in future races.

Illinois In 1994, the year Republican Illinois governor Jim Edgar ran against Dawn Clark Netsch, a liberal state senator from Chicago, Edgar granted clemency to four women. Republicans controlled the state senate but not the house of representatives. Indicators at the time suggested that Illinois was trending strongly Republican. Edgar won 64 percent of the vote. Republicans swept statewide offices and captured control of the house of representatives (Barone and Ujifusa 1995). It is possible to infer that Edgar felt strong enough politically to grant clemencies without fearing repercussions. It was unlikely that his opponent would use the decisions against him in the race for governor, and it had the potential to draw swing voters into his camp. One question remains, however: what made him review the clemency petitions and decide favorably in four cases?

Activists in Illinois never relied on publicizing the stories of clemency applicants, and inmates were too poorly organized to speak through the media. In the context of an election year in which Edgar was virtually assured of winning a second term, it was enough for activists to put the petitions before the governor and count on him to act on them. Once the political opportunity passed, it would take greater levels of activism, contacts with insiders in the Edgar administration, and a forceful presentation of the movement's collective action frame to win clemency for additional women. Illinois activists have not established networks with sympathetic administrative insiders, and their contact with inmates has been primarily limited to interviews rather than discussions in support groups. Efforts to empower inmates have centered around preparation of the clemency petition.

In Illinois, opportunities for battered women to participate in feminist support groups were limited, so activists needed to gain the trust of petitioners and make the application process as empowering as possible. A conundrum was that activists allowed women to talk about experiences they had learned to cope with through repression, only to return them to their cells, with little support network in place. Because of the absence of a strong social movement community within the prison, Project attorneys have been able to accomplish only limited public education. There is no network through which incarcerated battered women can speak out through the press. Instead, attorneys, law students, and other volunteers have gotten moderate media coverage, spoken publicly, and posted synopses of women's stories on the Internet. The inmates themselves, however, have remained relatively muted.

Whereas Illinois activists attempted to interact with inmates who were not organized into movement communities, California activists treated an organized community of inmate activists as individual petitioners. Illinois has been more successful despite the lack of inmate organization and activism, but this may be due more to Edgar's run for office on a platform of welfare reform. Wilson ran on different issues.

California   Governor Pete Wilson has been intractable in his resistance to clemency. Wilson has taken liberal positions on some social issues, such as abortion and gay rights. His support of these issues derives from his belief that government should not interfere in private life, a traditional conservative view. In line with this philosophy, Wilson has always been staunchly anticrime and strongly in favor of the death penalty.

Wilson was first elected governor in 1990 by a narrow margin in a race against San Francisco mayor Diane Feinstein. The following year, he raised taxes, angering members of his own party. In 1992 Democrats retained control of both houses of the state legislature, keeping Wilson in a weak position. In 1994 California was in a recession that had begun in the late 1980s, leaving Wilson politically vulnerable. He ran for reelection against Secretary of State Kathleen Brown, who was against the death penalty and regarded as more socially liberal than Wilson on a number of issues, particularly crime. Wilson campaigned against Brown on a tough anticrime, anti-illegal immigration, and anti-affirmative action platform. Perhaps because of his ability to strike a chord in a state seeking a "moral compass or sense of virtue," Wilson won by a margin of 14 percent (Barone and Ujifusa 1995, 81), a landslide by California standards. The governor had little to gain and much to lose by granting clemency, a decision that ran counter to everything he had stood for.

Activists in California had one advantage over those in Illinois. California inmates at Frontera were a cohesive social movement community even before the California Coalition was founded. The Illinois Clemency Project was founded by attorneys who understood the importance of empowering women and treating them as a class, whereas the California Coalition was founded by activist groups who lost control of clemency petitions to attorneys with corporate backgrounds. Neither state made alliances with administration insiders. Neither succeeded in meeting with the state governor or any of his aides. Still, the political context could be overcome in some states, with an aggressive strategy.

Massachusetts   Massachusetts activists took a political climate not unlike that in California and Illinois and turned it to their advantage. If Governor Jim Edgar's clemencies in an election year are not evidence enough that activists do not need to wait until the last term a governor is in office to seek clemency, Governor William Weld's decisions the year before he ran for reelection and grants of an additional two clemencies the year he was reelected should further support that evidence.

In 1990, when Weld first ran for office, Massachusetts was in a recession. In 1989 the state essentially had gone bankrupt, and in 1990 both the Republican and Democratic parties ran fiscally conservative candidates for office. Weld ran on a platform promising to hold down taxes and government spending. He beat Democrat John Silber by a three percent margin, with strong votes from women and baby boomers (Barone and Ujifusa 1991).

In this traditionally Democratic state, Weld was considered an economic and anticrime conservative as well as a cultural moderate who supported strong families, some feminist issues, and gay rights as a matter of smaller government and a right to privacy. He believed in keeping government out of people's pocketbooks and bedrooms, a policy antagonistic to the battered women's movement, which has depended upon government funding for shelters and state prosecution of perpetrators of domestic violence. In 1991, Weld cut state spending, "not reducing increases from some projected level, but actually cutting spending" in absolute terms (Barone and Ujifusa 1995, 631). In the process, he cut funding for shelters, incensing activists in that state and provoking them to join the movement for clemency.

Despite his 1995 announcement that he would serve as national finance chairperson for Pete Wilson's presidential campaign, Governor Weld did not share the California governor's anticrime attitudes. Weld announced he would not run for reelection and that after his current term, he would retire to private practice (Barone and Ujifusa 1995). In 1996, however, he ran against incumbent U.S. senator John Kerry in an unsuccessful bid for office, indicating Weld's aspirations for higher office. In a state that gave the nation Willie Horton and the fear that furloughed or paroled criminals would wreak havoc on society, Battered Women Fighting Back! was able to convince Weld of the fairness of reviewing eight women's cases for clemency.[1] The organization did so without making alliances with administrative insiders.

In this climate of economic concern in a traditionally Democratic state, a Republican governor could grant clemency to seven women without losing votes, as long as he maintained his fiscal conservatism. Democratic opponents were unlikely to criticize him for the decisions, and Republicans would not castigate him unless he violated the fiscal trust. The movement needed to convince Weld and the public that incarcerated battered women were victims of crime who, unlike so many other battered women, were alive because they had defended their lives. Other activists have used different strategies to convince governors to grant clemency. In Massachusetts, they did so through the media. In Florida, they took an inside track.

Florida   In terms of criminal justice, Florida is one of the most conservative states in the nation. With Florida's population of white southerners and elderly retirees, the state government has often responded to high rates of criminalization with strong punishment. It is possibly the state with the strongest support for capital punishment (Barone and Ujifusa 1995). Despite these trends, since the early 1970s Florida voters have elected liberal Democrats as governor, with the exception of Bob Martinez, elected in 1986. When Governor Martinez pushed through a tax on services, which was later repealed, his popularity sank, opening an opportunity for Lawton Chiles, a moderate Democratic governor. Chiles beat Martinez by a comfortable margin in 1990, having run on a platform calling for government reform and reductions in spending. Governor Chiles has signaled support for clemency for incarcerated battered women but has approached the issue with caution.

In 1992, Chiles's budget called for $1.3 billion in new taxes, and his popularity plummeted, making him politically vulnerable only two years before he would run for reelection. He was able to recover by 1994, when he narrowly defeated Republican Jeb Bush (Barone and Ujifusa 1995). His reelection was due, in part, to his efforts to stop the flow of refugees from Cuba to Florida. Republicans won three lower statewide offices, took control of the state Senate, and increased their strength in the House of Representatives. Not only was Chiles politically weak, his party was vulnerable to further losses in state government in upcoming elections. Although it appears that Chiles sympathizes with incarcerated battered women, he is in a politically vulnerable position, from which he must try to preserve political collateral for members of his party and as much clout for himself as possible until the next election, in 1998.

Within this environment, activists took advantage of newly elected governor Chiles's popularity in 1991 by calling for reform of clemency rules. Not knowing that Chiles would propose a tax increase, which would diminish his political strength, they could not have been expected to move quickly enough to push through a large-scale clemency review by mid-1992. (A mass clemency was not the movement's goal at that time.) Chiles's decline in public opinion polls may have made him circumspect about appearing weak on crime. He granted clemency to two women in 1993, but when activists brought forward a "messier" case, in which the petitioner had been a victim of child sexual abuse and addicted to drugs and alcohol, he asked them to bring him a better case. Activists compromised by agreeing to place her in a work-release program. Leaders of Women in Prison soon agreed that all clemency recipients should be placed in work-release programs before being paroled or unconditionally set free.

The office of governor of Florida is not a powerful position. Appointments and decisions, including those related to clemency, must be approved by members of the cabinet, who are elected separately. Chiles is, therefore, more subject to political pressures than are many of his peers. In bringing clemency petitions before the governor during his last term in office, the Battered Women's Clemency Project will mitigate political fallout for Governor Chiles. He may make conservative decisions in an effort to reduce the harm to party members in a state that is conservative on crime, or because his discretion is limited by members of his cabinet. Unless Florida activists successfully publicize and frame the issues in terms with which voters are likely to be sympathetic, Chiles is not likely to approach the clemency applications as a social moderate. Activists must take advantage of a small political window of opportunity by persuading voters that clemency applicants were victims of crime whom society failed to protect; that domestic violence is a crime that affects everyone, costing money for police, prosecutors, and judges; that incarcerating battered women is a waste of taxpayers' money; and that unless they had defended themselves, the women applying for clemency may well have been murdered. In a political environment that is swinging to the right, activists must present their alternative visions by tapping into public sentiment to build support for the cause of safe families and reduced taxes. In a more traditionally liberal state, such as Maryland, alternative strategies may be practiced.

Maryland   Maryland is a traditionally Democratic state. In 1986 Democrat William Donald Schaefer was elected governor with 82 percent of the vote, the largest percentage ever in a contested gubernatorial race. Schaefer took office in the activist style that had made him popular in his 15 years as mayor of Baltimore. After a rough start with the legislature, his victories built a momentum that carried him into the 1990 election, in which he carried a more modest 60 percent of the vote. Schaefer was an extremely popular governor, and the decline in his margin of victory may have been due to the Reagan cutbacks in federal government during the 1980s. Maryland is home to the Social Security Administration and the National Security Agency. With the Reagan budget cuts, Maryland lost 21,000 government jobs. At the same time, the state added 294,000 jobs in services, trade, and finance, a 38 percent gain, for which Republicans were widely credited. In 1990 the GOP won county executive positions in the three largest Baltimore-area suburban counties, and a large majority of new voters registered Republican (Barone and Ujifusa 1991).

Although the state was trending Republican during Schaefer's second term in office, his clemencies have less to do with statewide politics than with his popularity, his activist style of governing, and his affiliation with a network of Baltimore activists. In 1989, the Maryland Domestic Violence Taskforce was founded. Although it was a statewide social movement organization, the majority of its membership and its organizational base were located in Baltimore. In 1990, upon viewing the Taskforce's video, *A Plea for Justice,* and learning of the Celeste initiative in a large-scale clemency review, Schaefer agreed to meet with incarcerated battered women. He asked leaders of the Baltimore shelter, the House of Ruth, to identify battered women who had been convicted of killing or assaulting an abusive intimate partner. The Taskforce had already done most of the work, and the movement followed on the coattails of Schaefer's political momentum.

This is not to suggest that the movement was not responsible for the clemencies. Activists had done the organizing; educated the public, members of the parole board, and other governmental authorities; worked with women inmates; and performed the tedious work of documenting women's cases. They drew upon Baltimore-based friendship networks and contacts with Representative Constance Morella to convince Schaefer that he should listen to battered inmates tell their stories. Activists recognized a favorable political context and created a niche for themselves within it, and when the window of opportunity presented itself they raced through it.

Kentucky   In Kentucky, the governor has more power than executives in most other states. Between 1888 and the time Governor Paul Patton took office, in 1995, governors were limited to one term in office. Otherwise, they have been relatively free of the constraints of the legislature, which meets only 60 days every two years or when called into special session by the governor. The governor also has the power to revise line items after the budget is passed by the legislature. Democrats have tended to control statewide and national elections, although in recent years that trend has shifted, particularly as national leaders have promoted antismoking health policies in this state that is dependent upon tobacco as one of its key cash crops.

In 1987 Brereton Jones was elected lieutenant governor as a Democrat, serving with Governor Wallace Wilkinson (Barone and Ujifusa 1991; 1993; 1995). In 1991 Democrats controlled both houses of the legislature and all but one statewide office. That year, Jones was elected governor with 65 percent of the vote. Although he has held the two highest positions in Kentucky state government, Jones appears to have no aspirations for higher office. In a state where the governor "stands at the apex of Kentucky politics" (Barone and Ujifusa 1995, 541), where fear of crime is not a major political issue, and where Democrats have tended to dominate, Jones had few restraints on his

decision to grant clemency. His only opposition came from disorga-
nized, anticrime, antifeminist constituents from the rural areas in
which the majority of clemency recipients had resided.

Jones was not elected to office on a profeminist platform, but he did
appoint strong women to key positions in his administration. When
Marsha Weinstein, executive director of the Women's Commission,
learned of the Ohio and Maryland clemencies, she decided something
similar could be done in Kentucky. She drew upon a community of
feminists in Kentucky state government, who worked as advocates for
Kentucky women. Feminists found a way to give voice to incarcerated
battered women, working with the inmate support group BOSH and
with journalists in major urban areas in the state. When Jones encountered their stories, he was free to vote his conscience without fear of
repercussion for himself or for fellow party members, because public
opinion was strongly in favor of the decisions.

Each state has its own unique political-opportunity structure, and it
has been the role of activists to seize upon or create chances for
women's clemency petitions to be seriously considered and reviewed
by individuals who understand the legal, social, and social psychological issues. In some states, activism has been organized primarily, if
not exclusively, outside the executive branch of government. In others, activists have established contacts with administrative insiders or
have been insider activists themselves. The role of volunteers in the
clemency movement has been essential, but unlike many social movements, the majority of its leaders have been paid for their activism.
Some have written grants so they could work as activists, others have
found positions in social service or social movement organizations,
and still others have established careers in government or state agencies so they could use their jobs and positions of authority to advance
feminist issues. The clemency movement has differed from many nonfeminist movements because activists have worked through their careers to transform American society and achieve justice for women.

Creating Alternative Visions of Reality

As previously discussed, within the feminist literature some legal
scholars have argued against the use of battered woman syndrome.
Others have advocated its expansion to include diverse experiences
and reactions (Callahan 1994; Dutton 1993). Strong arguments have

been made in favor of legal reform, including the redefinition of imminent danger (Miller 1994), the inclusion of defense of the psychological self (Ewing 1987), and the creation of a "battered woman defense,"
which would allow a more subjective test of reasonableness in jurisdictions that call for a more objective standard (Miller 1994). In addition to advocacy for legal reform, others have argued that the greatest
barrier to women who defend themselves from abusive men is not the
law itself but the rules of evidence that allow judges to prevent women
from presenting evidence of abuse and to refuse to instruct juries on
perfect and imperfect self-defense (Maguigan 1991).

All of the participants in this debate make important points. Laws
and rules of evidence need to be reformed, judges need to be educated, and the system needs to change if battered women are to receive critically needed services and fair trials when the system fails.
But arguing in favor of change will not automatically bring it about,
particularly in opportunity structures that have become increasingly
conservative. The more radical the change that is advocated, the less
likely it is to be institutionalized, unless activists are willing to promote their agenda items through alternative routes. But rhetorical
compromise has its limits, and activists must avoid sacrificing movement goals to achieve political appeal.

The way issues are presented to the public depends upon the collective action frame of the movement, which varies slightly among
statewide movements. In the clemency movement, framing has two dimensions. The first is the way events, facts, and issues are presented
in clemency petitions, read by governors and parole boards. The second is the way they are offered to the public. Related to these dimensions are the criteria upon which cases are selected for inclusion in a
movement's mobilization for clemency. The way an issue is defined
will determine who is included and excluded and will affect the ways
in which they may be presented to authorities and the public.

In their efforts to establish a feminist vision of reality and present it
to the public and authorities, activists in some states have avoided
framing issues in terms of battered woman syndrome, whereas others
have embraced it as a way to present them in terms authorities and
the public might accept. As large-scale clemencies have been
achieved, statewide movements have tried to avoid framing issues in
terms of battered woman syndrome, primarily because of potential
detrimental side effects. Nonetheless, the precedent set by those who
used the syndrome has made it easier for activists in states that have

subsequently organized for clemency to frame their demands in social justice terms. There has been a gradual movement away from battered woman syndrome, a trend that has been mitigated by pragmatic concerns with the political opportunity structure.

Regardless of where in the overall movement they have begun, state clemency movements have tended to succeed when they packaged their demands in terms with which the public and authorities were likely to agree. The battered women's clemency movement is in the unique position of being able to use both conservative and radical feminist rhetoric and to put demands in terms of either "victims' rights," which has conservative connotations, or "women's rights." As a whole, the clemency movement has created an alternative vision of the world by tendering collective action frames that align with Americans' beliefs in justice, the family ideal, and the protection of innocent victims and that challenge their assumptions that the United States justice system is as fair to women as it is to men. Where clemency movements have succeeded, activists have engaged in a strategy of rhetorical co-optation of right-wing discourse, using conservative terminology to achieve feminist goals.

Particularly with the earliest clemency campaigns, and despite the interest of governors like Celeste and Schaefer, activists recognized the need to be conservative in framing the issues and in choosing women to be released. Despite Dagmar Celeste's privileged position of first lady, she and the governor recognized the political animosity created by her involvement in the Celeste administration. They knew it was important to use conservative discourse to achieve radical action. In Ohio, activists incorporated cultural feminism's emphasis on gender differences and spiritual growth with their goal of social change. As a seminarian, feminist, student of family therapy, and believer in 12-step traditions of recovery, Dagmar Celeste was a spiritual person who believed strongly in recovery as a road to personal and spiritual growth and in personal empowerment as a means to social change. Many members of her staff were followers of the same feminist traditions. But because of the spiritual elements in their beliefs, they were able to co-opt the conservative rhetoric of "spiritual growth," "recovery," and "peaceful families" to present many of their issues in a "pro-family" light rather than in a "pro-woman" frame. Arguing against such issues portrayed opponents as "anti-spiritual growth," "anti-recovery" from addiction, abuse, or dysfunctional families, and perhaps most central, "anti-family."

In Maryland, activists weighed pragmatic concerns against philosophical arguments. They put forth sympathetic cases, believing that women applying for clemency should exemplify legislation they hoped to get passed. Additionally, they hoped that if they acted conservatively they would be more likely to get some women out of prison. In Florida, the concern with a negative backlash, evident in the period immediately following the revision of administrative clemency rules, was so strong that petitions were prepared individually, with a great deal of energy and resources devoted to influencing the media's portrayal of women under review. Activists in these states knew it would take only one clemency recipient to commit a violent offense after release for the entire future of clemencies to be jeopardized.

That women were reviewed and released as a group, initially in Ohio and a year later in Maryland, sufficiently established an alternative vision in the minds of activists in other states. When activists in California, Florida, Illinois, Kentucky, and Massachusetts learned of the Ohio and Maryland clemencies, they realized incarcerated battered women in their states might also get clemency. Once the precedent was set, their frames relied more on anticrime and social justice and less on mental health terms, but those trends were mitigated by perceived political opportunities.

Relying on a social justice frame, Illinois activists won clemency for four women in an election year. Later, when they framed cases in terms they thought the governor accepted, they found their window of opportunity had passed. That Governor Edgar was no longer up for reelection when the second two groups of applicants came forward undoubtedly influenced his decision to reject most of the second group and his failure to review the third group. But activists did little to present their vision of reality to Illinois citizens and therefore sacrificed any public support or moral outrage they may have been able to create.

In California, activists steadfastly avoided screening out "bad" cases and instead chose to assist any woman incarcerated for killing a person who had abused her. In the actual petitions, cases were presented based upon their individual merits rather than within an agreed-upon framework. Publicly, California activists refused to privilege good cases by showcasing them in the media. Instead they talked about how their demands for clemency were part of a growing national movement aimed at bringing justice to battered women. Though made upon meritorious principles, the decision not to present the issues by drawing on the facts of more favorable cases may have cost California activists an opportunity to control public perceptions of their demands or to catch the governor's attention. One activist attorney involved in the movement explained,

It's one of the tricky issues that we encountered. . . . Because the Coalition didn't want to get in the position of championing particular cases, we didn't do a lot to highlight any particular case. . . . I think in the end . . . there were very good reasons why we didn't want to do that, but strategically that sort of maybe prevented certain cases from being resolved. . . . And I think there was this sort of naivete that a lot of us had that these cases are so compelling that all the governor has to do is read them, and of course he'll be moved by them and he'll grant clemency to these women. And in reality, it doesn't matter what the cases were about. It was all a political decision.[2]

California activists attempted clemency in the most difficult political environment of any discussed in this book. It was important for them to take an aggressive, proactive stance in presenting their issues to the public in terms that would both agree with commonly held values and challenge popular misconceptions. Incarcerated battered women are crime victims who have been convicted and sent to prison. The movement attempted to get that message out to the public, and it succeeded in building some support throughout the state, but because of the geographical separations between movement centers, the size of the state, and the strength of right-wing movements, their task was more onerous than those in other states. It is possible that the California Coalition could have made the issue more politically feasible by highlighting individual cases that drew upon right-wing concerns with crime victimization.

One of the benefits of not pitting "good" cases against "bad" ones is that California inmates have been less likely to be hurt by the loss of control of access to information about their cases. One of the consequences has been the loss of opportunity to educate the public about the issues and raise public opinion in favor of the women's release. Another consequence is that women with good cases may have had their petitions denied or ignored because their stories never got to the governor.

California and Massachusetts are commonly compared, primarily because when the clemency movement in each state became organized they were governed by Republican politicians; but there are important differences. California is a large state with very active and powerful right-wing movements. Massachusetts is smaller, and has fewer right-wing movements and a liberal press. In California, activism for clemency was begun by inmates, who did not realize that a letter requesting clemency, which included neither the details of each woman's case nor evidence to support her claims, would be considered an application for clemency. When activists outside the prison organized, the wheels of clemency were already in motion and included cases the California Coalition would have declined to take. Aside from the issue of framing, this outcome speaks to the importance of coordinated activism among movement organizations and communities. In California, 34 women were represented by clemency activists; in Massachusetts there were 8. Framing is not the only factor that has affected the outcome of clemency movements, but it is one that should not be overlooked.

Kentucky and Massachusetts activists have been the most aggressive in framing their demands for clemency in terms of justice for incarcerated battered women. Activists in Kentucky garnered favor with the press, particularly in the state's two major urban areas—Louisville and Lexington—by holding workshops to demonstrate to journalists that women's issues were marginalized or ignored in the press.[3] Even though clemencies were organized and promulgated by administrative insiders, activists never took for granted the potential impact public opinion might have on the governor's decisions or on the outcome of movements in other states. One result of their efforts was that during the summer before Governor Jones announced his clemency decisions, the media published numerous stories and editorials that depicted the clemencies as a matter of delayed justice for victims of crime. Even after his decision was announced, editorials advocated that the "victims deserve[d] more than clemency" and that the newly elected governor, Paul Patton, "would be wise to appoint a task force . . . with the charge to develop a sane and fair policy toward abused women who take violent actions against their abusers."[4] The Kentucky movement succeeded in establishing an alternative understanding of incarcerated battered women.

In Massachusetts activists worked through more traditional social movement organizations without the aid of insiders in the Weld administration. Activists followed principles central to human rights activism to show that incarcerated battered women in prison would have been dead had they not defended themselves. Members of the Massachusetts movement worked to create consciousness of all battered women as a class, some of whom were killed by their abusers and others who would fight for their lives, only to be convicted and sent to prison. The Massachusetts movement worked to create public awareness of the dangers with which battered women live. One activist explained:

We started this media campaign . . . showing that this was not just an individual issue, that it was really a class of people, in the legal sense of the term "class." . . . You're not going to be sympathetic to eight women who've killed their batterers if you don't think they could've been dead. . . . It was self-defense that we were dealing with here and we needed to raise public consciousness. . . . One of the key things in human rights work is that you record factually and accurately and you expose it consistently over time. So that was the goal here, to make sure that the public was starting to get fed information.[5]

Activists worked with newspaper editors to get front-page coverage of homicide reports of women killed by men with a history of abuse. They helped journalists interested in writing factual stories about the women who were seeking clemency. When stories about the "Framingham Eight" were published, according to activists, the public mentally juxtaposed them against the front page stories of women who had died at the hands of abusive men. When activists presented eight clemency petitions to the lieutenant governor, they read aloud the names of women who had been killed that year by abusers in Massachusetts. They created an alternative understanding of battered women as a legal class subject to brutal assault, lack of protection, and homicide if they did not protect themselves and to charges of murder if they did. Two months later, Lieutenant Governor Cellucci declared a public emergency in Massachusetts regarding domestic violence and established a statewide governor's commission on the issue, which he chaired. Within two years, six of the petitioners would be released from prison and one would have her conviction reversed on appeal. Even in this politically hostile environment, with no contacts inside the Weld administration, Battered Women Fighting Back! was able to achieve clemency for seven of eight applicants. Framing was an important part of the victory, but it would not have been as successful if inmates had not been able to speak out articulately and cogently about their experiences.

When studying social movements, many analysts hold to the belief that activism involves such actions as picketing, marching in the streets, chanting, or otherwise demonstrating in public. Although clemency activists have held some public protests, they have tended to focus their efforts on creating democratic spaces (Cohen 1995) in places where women's voices, experiences, and concerns have traditionally been excluded or marginalized, including the government, courts, prisons, and the media. The creation of democratic spaces involves redrawing the boundaries between public and private domains and transforming formerly private realms into social arenas for the creation of collective identity and the development of collective action frames. Those who have failed to create democratic spaces or to present the issues in terms compatible with and challenging to public sentiment have been less successful in gaining the release of women incarcerated for defending themselves from abusive men.

Creating Democratic Spaces

Incarcerated battered women are a relatively impoverished and powerless group. Yet in most of the states we have examined, prison support groups have played a central role in educating authorities and the public and in advocating for clemency. Only the noninmate activists in Illinois attempted large-scale clemency reviews without establishing routinized contact with prison support groups. California was the only state where some attorneys resisted publicizing women's cases, and even there inmates worked actively with the media.

Recent social movement research has focused on the relationship between collective consciousness and collective action, or how inequality in the social structure and dominant meaning system is translated into subjectively experienced discontent (Fantasia 1988; Ferree 1992; Ferree and Miller 1985; Gamson 1992; Klein 1984; McAdam 1988; Morris and Mueller 1992). Identity-oriented social movements challenge contested social identities by creating and acting upon new collective identities (Cohen 1985; Taylor and Whittier 1992; Taylor 1996). In some movements, this transformation occurs within social movement communities, and in others it occurs through social movement organizations, which "provide 'appropriate' vocabularies" for movement participants, who reconstruct their personal identities in ways that link them to the movement (Hunt, Benford, and Snow 1994). The goal of new social movements is cultural change, beginning at the individual level and carrying on to challenge the dominant belief systems that underlie the social structure. As individuals begin to redefine themselves in accordance with the social movement's collective action frame, they renegotiate their identity, including others' response to the new self (Hunt, Benford, and Snow 1994; Margolis 1985).

The feminist agenda has always included personal liberation, but such a transformation was never construed as sufficient to bring about political change. Liberation, or empowerment, as it later came to be called, was one means by which the social system would be challenged (Kauffman 1989). "Empowerment begins when women change their ideas about the causes of their powerlessness, when they recognize the systemic forces that oppress them, and when they act to change the conditions of their lives" (Morgen and Bookman 1988, 4).

Advocacy of structural change is an important feature of the battered women's and clemency movements, but it is only half the feminist equation, which must include the personal experiences of individual women and battered women as a class. Battered women need legal reform, better police protection, opportunities to escape the abuse, and opportunities for recovery. Whether recovery is a personal or political issue has become the focus of debate among feminists and social movement scholars. Some have argued that recovery and the burgeoning self-help movement in the United States represent the depoliticization of feminism, a displacement of protest focused on political and economic change, an admission of personal powerlessness, and a preoccupation with self and identity (see Taylor 1996). Others have argued that self-help has the potential to empower women and politicize identity, which will ultimately lead to social change (Gagné 1996; Haaken 1993; Taylor 1996). In states where large-scale clemencies have been organized, the battered women's movement has used the language of recovery to gain acceptance of consciousness-raising and empowerment groups for incarcerated women. Support groups are the organizational foundation for clemency activism in women's prisons. It has been through this organizational base that the feminist collective action frame has been disseminated among movement beneficiaries. The result has been the transformation of individual identity and the creation of an oppositional collective identity.

Empowerment is not a guaranteed outcome of support-group membership. But in states where large-scale clemencies were advocated, the most important role prison support groups played was the identity transformation, empowerment, and creation of collective identity that took place when incarcerated battered women listened to and talked with women whose experiences mirrored their own. When inmates worked together for legislative reform and clemency, the result was social movement communities within women's prisons.

Many incarcerated battered women were represented at trial by attorneys who had little understanding of the dynamics of abusive relationships or the psychological response to terror. Many were never given an opportunity to discuss their cases privately with their lawyers. Historically, incarcerated battered women have rarely come in contact with advocates who understood and were comfortable working with them. From the courtroom, they have been sent to prison. Part of prison culture is a norm of secrecy surrounding inmates' crimes. Prisoners are advised never to discuss their crimes with other inmates, and employees are admonished never to inquire. In this "don't ask, don't tell" environment, incarcerated battered women, as with all victims of abuse, tend to assume that their experiences and problems are specific to themselves. They tend to internalize the blame for their abuse, the homicide, their conviction, and their separation from family and friends. They often believe they were bad wives, lovers, and mothers, things they were repeatedly told by the abuser. That they are in prison only attests to their failure as women.

As incarcerated battered women were provided opportunities to discuss experiences they thought only they had endured, their consciousness of the larger social and political context of their lives was raised. Their identities were reconstructed in interaction with others and "in accordance with group guidelines" (Snow and Machalek 1984, 175). Support groups that lack an oppositional collective action frame are less likely to result in the politicization of identity and are often the subject of feminist criticism. In feminist support and recovery groups, empowerment and the politicization of identity were the products of interaction in a group guided by an oppositional collective action frame.

Over time, inmates' identities were transformed from that of individual victim to surviving member of a class, some of whom had been killed by their abusers. After participation in recovery, activists and formerly incarcerated women who had been involved in educational or support groups for battered women realized they were not alone in their experiences. One support group leader and clemency activist, who had been abused as a child, explained her empowerment through recovery: "It's hard to describe what it does for your . . . psyche, your consciousness, your whole sense of self. Your whole reality does this . . . major cosmic shift . . . because you realize that all the shit that this batterer has told you for the whole time you've been in their power, and you're still in their power at that point, because even though they might not be physically battering you, . . . they still got a hold over your mind. . . . [Y]ou realize that everything they told you is bullshit. And it all starts to fall down" (interview, 6 February 1997).

As inmates began to understand that they were not alone, their consciousness was raised about the societal roots of their victimization. In the process of empowerment, many inmates reclaimed their identity as battered women. They redefined themselves as survivors deserving justice rather than victims who should be punished. One clemency recipient described the consciousness-raising and sense of belonging she experienced in a prison support group for battered women: "[L]istening to other women [I could see] the control, the isolation, where [the abusers] want to cut you off from the world, that type of thing. . . . I could relate to how [women] felt about that, because I went through that, you know? How they want to control your whole life and they don't want you to have any friends and . . . your whole world's just you and the abuser" (interview, 31 October 1992). Talking with others like themselves about their experiences was central in helping incarcerated women reclaim their definition of self, a central step in the creation of collective identity (see D'Emilio 1983; Herman and Miall 1990).

The importance of the politicization of identity and the creation of collective identity is threefold: first, privately discussing the violent relationship with women who have been through similar experiences helps the victim reinterpret her experiences within the social context and to begin to redefine herself. As the victim redefines herself as a survivor, she realizes her strengths and how society has socialized her to be weak, failed to protect her, blamed her for her own victimization, and judged her according to standards created by and for men. Second, as the public witnesses the reclaiming and public identification with a previously stigmatized status, public awareness is raised, old stereotypes and definitions are challenged, and a once-stigmatized identity is socially renegotiated and redefined. Incarcerated battered women are redefined from vindictive killers to victims of injustices. Third, by publicly discussing and redefining the issues, the private nature of wife abuse and spousal homicide is challenged and transformed from a personal to a social problem deserving of social recompense.

Recovery groups that do not address the structural manner in which battered women have been entrapped in violent relationships or reveal the gender biases in the law may do little to politicize inmates or develop collective identity. The battered women's movement, which has employed feminist ideas about personal politics and empowerment, has taken "private" issues, revealed their public and political nature, and created "democratic public spaces" from which women's voices could be heard. Once empowered, however, incarcerated battered women run the risk of having their experiences defined within established stereotypes.

From prison, incarcerated women worked to educate authorities and the public about the dynamics of battering relationships, battered woman syndrome, and the failure of the police and criminal justice system to protect. They publicly discussed the gender biases in the law that prevented them from receiving fair trials and the injustice of punishing a woman who killed to defend herself or her children. Incarcerated women worked through the media by talking with reporters, writing letters to newspaper editors, and consenting to be filmed for television news magazines and privately produced videotapes. They agreed to discuss their lives and experiences with legislators and governors and their aides, allowing their stories to exemplify injustices in the criminal justice system. Their goals were to educate authorities and the public about wife abuse, to build public sympathy for their cases and others, and to raise public awareness of the injustices they had experienced. One legislator explained how meeting with incarcerated battered women helped him understand why it was necessary to change the law and remedy past inequities. He said, "I wanted to really talk to a real person who's been through this. . . . One woman told me how the windows were nailed shut. When the guy left . . . he took the phone with him and warned her that if she left the house . . . or contacted the authorities, that her children were going to be in serious harm's way. . . . And this had gone on for a decade! So one day, he came home and . . . he was going to abuse her physically, sexually, too. . . . She shot him dead with a shotgun. And she was in her . . . ninth year of incarceration" (interview, 21 October 1991). The stories of incarcerated battered women are exceptionally powerful, particularly when told by the women themselves. They match real lives with theories and put faces on statistics. Even opponents of clemency or legislation to ensure that battered women get fair trials were moved by the systemic injustices that victims of violence face when they heard survivors speak.

To someone who has never been incarcerated or convicted of a crime, talking openly about the facts of one's case to get out of prison may seem an obvious thing to do. For battered women, overcoming denial, shame, guilt, and humiliation is one of the most difficult things they will ever do. Most enter prison believing that they are to blame for being beaten. One woman, whose son-in-law murdered her husband after she complained to her daughter about the severe sexual abuse with which she lived, was sentenced to death when convicted of conspiracy to have him killed. On death row, she admitted to Dagmar Celeste that she "wanted to die" because she was a "bad woman" who had gotten "every-body in trouble." Celeste exclaimed, "It would have been no sweat to ex-ecute that woman. She would have been grateful!"[6] Another clemency recipient, who had been an active participant in the Ohio movement, talked about her difficulty in overcoming silence and shame and cried through most of the interview. She had been out of prison almost two years when she explained, "I've always thought everything was my fault. I don't know, it's probably because he told me it was my fault so much. But I felt like if I had left him that [the homicide] wouldn't have hap-pened. . . . And he always said he wouldn't let me have any peace, and he was right. . . . I still don't have no peace. It's something that I'll always re-member, and I'm always going to think about [crying] no matter what. . . . And I still blame myself" (interview, 31 October 1992). Before women could talk publicly about their lives, they had to find a way to talk with others about their experiences. They had to redefine their lives within a collective framework and reclaim their experiences and identity. Only then would they be able to find a voice that, for many, was tentative and unsure even after they received clemency.

In the earliest clemency movements, before activists understood the importance of educating and working directly with journalists, the media portrayed issues in dualistic terms. Inmates who had applied for clemency were depicted as "good or bad," "deserving or undeserv-ing." Battered woman syndrome was discussed as "a real response to ongoing abuse" or a way for dishonest inmates to "work the system" in an effort to avoid punishment. One clemency recipient expressed her opinion about a television news magazine segment, in which the stories of two clemency applicants were juxtaposed against each other. One was a kindly, religious, middle-aged grandmother who had hired someone to kill her husband. Before his death, she had tried for years to get help from the police, her priest, and others. Everyone had told her there was nothing they could do. When her husband attacked their youngest child with a chain, she resolved to protect her children. The other woman featured in the segment was a young, attractive mother who shot but did not kill her husband. The husband explained that he had never beaten his wife and that she shot him to avoid having to get a divorce. Her children said that they had never seen their father beat their mother and that they were happy she was in prison. One woman I interviewed, who was not portrayed in the video, explained,

That was a hell of a tape. . . . We were fighting for clemency at this time. . . . They took a strong case, they took a weak case. The weak case was denied. The strong case was given, and she got her freedom. She had been in the penitentiary 15 years. . . . The other one was denied, and that was a very difficult thing for her to live through. . . . She felt very down, depressed. It showed her on there as a big liar. It showed where her children had denied her, and that hurt. And God knows that part should've never been allowed to even be taped. . . . Yes, you can show children and we can talk with them, but don't have a child get on there and say, "Hey, Mom, I'm so glad you're in the penitentiary. Enjoy your life there." That about killed her. . . . It showed her in a very guilty type situation. Maybe she wasn't [as bad as she was portrayed], but her husband didn't die, see? (interview, 31 October 1992).

The decision to go public may have been made out of naïveté, but the ability to articulate the experience of battering and to express the injustice of incarceration for self-defense came from participation in support and recovery groups, as well as from support from activists, family, and friends.

Given how the media treated early inmate activists, it is little wonder that some attorneys have hesitated to allow their clients to talk to the press, and it is no surprise that activists in other states have produced their own videos and worked to develop good relations with journalists. Maryland activists produced *A Plea for Justice* to provide a way for incarcerated battered women to represent themselves before authorities and the public. Massachusetts activists played key roles in the production of *Defending Our Lives,* and Kentucky advocates produced a video to be played for members of the parole board and for the governor. By producing their own videotapes and films, activists could maintain control over the way women were portrayed and prevent the juxtaposition of "good" cases against "bad" ones. Aside from these efforts, however, activists realized the only way to maintain any level of control over the way women were portrayed was to work directly with the media.

In Florida, when the first women were released, activists scheduled interviews with journalists they knew understood the issues. They coached clemency recipients on how to work with the media and made efforts to influence the way the press portrayed the women. They did not always succeed in controlling how clemencies were framed, but they were sometimes able to mitigate the impact of negative stories. Activists in California and Massachusetts wrote op-ed articles, and Kentucky and Massachusetts activists began establishing public support for clemency before cases were formally filed. Activists who worked as government officials in Kentucky and as leaders of social movement organizations in Massachusetts always granted interviews when journalists requested them. In this way, they established rapport with the press, and journalists came to them first, knowing they would be granted an interview. Reporters were therefore more open to being educated about wife abuse and legal biases. Through factual coverage of the issues, rather than dualistic depictions so common in the media, incarcerated battered women were given a space in which they could speak out about experiences they once thought private and that they kept locked in secrecy.

Creating democratic public spaces in prisons and working through the media were important strategies in achieving the large-scale clemencies we have examined, but we cannot fully understand how clemencies were brought about without examining the interaction between prison groups and noninmate activists and the importance of treating inmates as a class.

Identity Politics and the Diffusion of Momentum

Not all of the women who applied for clemency in states where activists created democratic public spaces in prisons or in the media gained their freedom. Rates of success and the subsequent impact of clemencies seem to have been affected more by the degree to which noninmate activists treated inmates as a class rather than as individuals than by the mobilization of resources or the presence of well-organized movement groups. The clearest examples of individualized treatment of inmates were in Florida and California.

Florida's Women in Prison (WIP) was not as large or well organized as the groups in California, Illinois, Maryland, or Massachusetts, but it had the support of a statewide coalition and activist attorneys in the state. Unlike in Massachusetts, Illinois, and California, the activist group had the support of governor's aides and ultimately the governor himself. In California, the inmate support group Women against Abuse was well organized, often gaining media attention without the help of the California Coalition for Battered Women in Prison and despite the advice of some attorneys that they should avoid talking with the press. An important difference between California and Florida and the others examined here is that nonattorney activists in Florida and private attorneys in California have tended to treat clemency applicants as individuals, even when they were well organized and thought of themselves as a group.

In Florida, this strategy caused WIP activists to approach clemencies cautiously, to manage women's interactions with the media after they were released, and to agree that they should be placed in work-release programs before being paroled. Only recently, with the organization of the Florida Battered Women's Clemency Project, have activist attorneys begun to treat incarcerated battered women as a class. WIP activists did achieve a change in administrative rules, but the potential impact of that reform was lost when women were brought out of prison one at a time and portrayed as harmless mothers rather than survivors of an unjust legal system.

In California, the efforts of activists who attempted to treat petitioners as a class were undermined by attorneys who advised individual clients not to speak to the press. When Governor Wilson denied clemency to three women in 1993, a potential demonstration of solidarity was sacrificed when women who had already been denied clemency were advised not to speak out against the governor's decisions and about the injustices they and the women waiting for their cases to be reviewed had endured. Wilson was allowed to slide by with the cases he privately denied, and the movement communicated to him that he would be allowed to do so because inmates could be shamed back into silence. Women against Abuse started out with a strong sense of collective identity and community. Despite the efforts of activists who believed the political aspects of the clemency petitions should be emphasized, the momentum that had built as a result of the Ohio and Maryland clemencies was dissipated in California by private attorneys who insisted that petitioners be treated as clients rather than activists and that their problems be held private, rather than challenging the boundaries between public and private.

By contrast, Illinois feminists, whose activists did not work inside the Edgar administration and had no formalized contact with prison support groups, thought of incarcerated battered women as a class. They brought their cases forward as a group and gained freedom for four women in the first round of petitions. That they had no routinized contact with support groups has rendered problematic their efforts to continue the clemency movement in Illinois and suggests that the interaction between inmate and outsider activists is important. In Massachusetts, there were no activists inside the Weld administration, and the governor was initially unsympathetic to battered women. Nonetheless, activists in that state worked to empower battered women through support groups, interacted with them as a class, encouraged them to stand in solidarity with each other, and created opportunities for them to speak out through the media. Collective identity and community were reinforced, and the momentum of the movement was built up rather than defused.

Social Movement Organizations and Collective Communities

Research conducted within a resource mobilization perspective suggests that resources are most easily mobilized when activists work from some type of organizational base and through established networks to bring in new membership (Freeman 1975; Gamson 1975; Morris 1984; Oberschall 1973). There has been some debate in the literature about the potential impact of organizational styles and the ideal level of organization for movement success (Gerlach and Hine 1970; Zald and Garner 1987; Piven and Cloward 1977). The consensus appears to be that different styles of organization are established as a result of the movement's collective action frame, goals, and projected strategies and tactics, and the political context in which it exists. Various styles of movement organization offer advantages and disadvantages, and activists must be aware of the strengths and weaknesses of the forms they adopt and how structure may affect strategy.

Social movement organizations have played important roles in every state where large-scale clemencies have been attempted or achieved. In Ohio and Kentucky, the most influential clemency advocates were loosely organized within state government. They were a community of professional women who networked with each other to identify potential participants, find ways to bypass opposition, and build support among authorities and the public. Resources were drawn primarily from state offices, with necessary legal counsel provided by public defenders and other state employees. These social movement communities had the advantage of having positions of authority and influence and were able to mobilize resources relatively easily.

Even in states where activism originated within state government, formally established social movement organizations played important roles in lobbying for legislation and keeping the movement on task. As early as 1990, when the National Clearinghouse was relatively young, it played a central role in providing information to activists and aides to Governor Celeste. It has continued to play a central supporting role in every state that has worked for clemency. In many states, informally organized "insider" feminist communities have worked in tandem with more formal social movement organizations, which have provided information, coordinated action, and mobilized constituents when a mass base was needed.

In states where activism was initiated from outside the government, feminists organized into "projects" and coalitions. Clemency projects usually drew their core constituents from other social movement organizations, activist bases, and feminist and human rights communities. In such states as Maryland, Illinois, California, and Ohio, resources including paper, postage, photocopying, and salaries usually came from the home offices of volunteer activists. In Illinois, organizations consisted of volunteers and several boxes of files, which were housed in the office of one of the volunteer attorneys. By establishing itself as an organizational entity, the Illinois Clemency Project received grant money and donations through a tax-exempt umbrella organization.

Activists in many states mobilized would-be supporters through networks of feminist and profeminist attorneys and law schools. Pro bono work is an ethically mandated part of the lives of all attorneys and is often required of law students as well. The clemency movement has been able to mobilize resources by offering activist-minded attorneys and law students an opportunity to do interesting work and to participate in a social movement that has the potential to achieve social justice, challenge the law, and change society. In some states, such as California and Maryland, resources have been mobilized by housing clemency projects in the offices of social justice law centers or by giving volunteers access to office space, law books, telephones, and other supplies. In states, such as Illinois, private attorneys house projects in their offices. In many states, including California, Florida, Illinois, and Massachusetts, attorneys and activists have written grants or received funding from state Bar Associations. Shelters have donated resources, sometimes incurring enormous unexpected expenses, such as when activists in Maryland's House of Ruth agreed to provide pre- and postrelease support services for clemency recipients. In most states, there has been an overlap of the types of resources mobilized and the sources from which they were drawn. In every state, whether clemencies were mobilized and achieved by administrative insiders or leadership was provided by outsider activists, social movement organizations provided the means by which resources could be mobilized efficiently and through which the work of a network of activists could be coordinated.

There has not been a successful movement for clemency that has worked without the coordination made possible by some level of organization, but no particular type of organization has been the key to success. The consciousness and collective identity of feminist activists, whether incarcerated or not, and the ability to create an alternative vision of battered women inmates as prisoners of an unjust legal system has been at the heart of movement success. The only resource that appears to be uniformly associated with movements in every state is the ability of activists to advance clemency through their careers. Some feminists hold jobs as activists, others use their careers as a means to advance the goals of the women's movement, and still others struggle to adhere to their feminist values in jobs that are hostile to feminism and human rights. In every state where activists have used their careers to give voice to incarcerated battered women and mobilize that key resource for clemency, movements have succeeded. Because so many activists in the clemency movement have worked as activist employees, it is important to examine activism on the job.

Career Activism

Radical or class-based social movement activists often look upon participation in government-sponsored organizations or "the system" itself as a precursor to the co-optation of the movement (Helfgot 1981). A major distinction between the experiences of men in the new left, for example, and activists in the women's movement is that the former eschewed participation in "the establishment," whereas many feminists look upon career success as one potential means to address economic and power inequities between women and men. Daniels (1991) has examined the work of liberal feminists who made their careers in the organizations of the women's movement, government agencies, legislatures, and other jobs, working to achieve feminist goals. The goal of such career feminists has been to enter well-paying, powerful positions and to help other women do the same (Ferree and Hess 1985).

Career feminism has expanded beyond that described by Ferree and Hess. In the clemency movement, it has entailed a process whereby many founders of the battered women's movement, who tend to be a generation older than joiners, have established political careers in which they could give voice to women's experiences and establish policies reflecting women's perspectives. In Ohio, these women were responsible for establishing a feminist network in state government, which played a direct role in the expansion of recovery opportunities for women inmates, support for clemency, and a number of other reforms in state government.[7] In Maryland, contacts between movement founders and the governor played an important role in his viewing the film *A Plea for Justice*. The career activism of Representative Constance Morella influenced Governor Schaefer's decision to visit the women's prison. In Florida, an aide to the governor played an important role in providing access to the Chiles administration, and in Kentucky Jones's appointees to the Parole Board and the Women's Commission were leaders and key decision makers in the clemency mobilization process.

In addition to playing important roles in clemency movements, feminist founders have been elected to state and federal legislatures. Movement founders have established careers as expert witnesses and legal scholars, helping individual women defend themselves and educating the public and legal professionals through books and articles. Feminists have not taken over state legislatures, the courts, or administrative branches of government. But through their careers, they have infiltrated the system and appropriated the authority and power necessary to give voice to women and battered women in institutions that have historically silenced them.

Those in government jobs have the obvious advantage of being in positions of authority. Nonetheless, such careers require demonstrations of loyalty to the culture of the administration.[8] Activists maintained their commitment to movement goals, sometimes in hostile environments, by establishing feminist networks and seeking support from feminist communities. In Ohio and Kentucky, feminists created opportunities by avoiding members of the governor's staff they knew to be hostile to the movement, establishing rapport with and educating those who were neutral or potentially in favor of clemency, and working directly with those they knew to be favorable to the cause.

Whereas movement founders established political contexts in which clemencies could be considered, it was often a younger generation of women—joiners—who worked in more hostile environments, often outside formal feminist networks, to do the "legwork" for clemency. In such environments, commitment to feminist identity and adherence to the collective action frame helped determine whether a career activist persevered in the face of adversity. Activists were often proud of their feminist identity and saw it as a call to stand up for unempowered women. For example, one young woman, responsible for conducting research in Ohio to determine whether incarcerated women in her state had experienced battered woman syndrome, exclaimed, "I'm definitely the only person there who would've taken the least bit of a feminist take on this! Not to be conceited about it or anything. If another [feminist] had been there, fine. But I was the only one."[9]

Whether by attorneys, legislators, expert witnesses, aides to the governor, agency directors, researchers, prison employees, or support group facilitators, the overwhelming majority of activism in the battered women's clemency movement has been conducted on the job or in conjunction with the requirements of activists' careers or educational programs. Some activists were drawn together and their activism coordinated by formal groups, others worked directly with members of a feminist community, and still others worked alone in hostile environments, sustained by their knowledge of a national movement and their commitment to feminist identity and the collective action frame.

Feminists have achieved some of their most notable achievements through simple acts of "everyday resistance," in which they refuse to accept the dominant culture's definition of proper power and gendered relations and instead act in ways they believe to be appropriate and empowering to women. Support-group facilitators, understanding the importance of touch in communicating empathy and facilitating empowerment, broke institutional rules by hugging and comforting distraught inmates. Some have been fired for such actions, but they have continued their activism from outside prisons by working through feminist organizations, networks, and communities. Prison employees have helped activist inmates by "looking the other way" when they needed to make copies of articles that would help battered women come to grips with their experiences, or by insisting that every woman who wished to submit a clemency petition be given an opportunity to do so. Agency directors, state employees, cabinet members, and governors' aides have helped outside activists make contact with potentially powerful people, including the governor. When they held positions of authority, feminists acted to give voice to and share power with other women, often in ways not required by their jobs. Their acts of everyday resistance were based upon the belief that male domination exists in all social spheres and major institutions and must be dismantled, with more equitable cultural arrangements and institutional practices established. One woman expressed the idea that feminism is pervasive in every aspect of an activist's life. Asked whether there was a clear separation in her mind between her activism, her job, and her personal life, she said, "I think they're all of a piece. I think we have to let our lives speak, basically. . . . I can't imagine compartmentalizing life. I know it's customary for people to do it, but I can't understand it. . . . I think you're the same person and everything you do . . . it's all part of the same thing. Certainly it all flows into everything else. . . . It's one of the delights of being alive to see that kind of thing happen. You're acting from a core of who you are" (interview, 29 July 1992).

Feminists do not respect the boundaries between personal and political life. Activism is something to be carried on at work, in the home, and in all personal relationships. When a spouse is an elected official, adherence to this belief can create democratic spaces for disempowered groups, as well as bring public scorn to the nonelected partner.

Political Partnerships and Everyday Resistance

Although wives of public-office holders have traditionally exerted influence over their husbands, the emergence of partnerships between elected officials and their spouses has permitted unelected individuals to publicly express their views and to take on work that has more than token value. Although feminists have focused on helping women get elected to public office, they have focused less on the potential effect politicians' wives can have on achieving movement goals. It is feasible that the clemency movement could have had its first large-scale success outside Ohio, but the fact that activists in every other state have credited the Celeste clemencies with helping them achieve their goals is not just incidental. It is central to an understanding of the "new" social movement model.

Among politicians in the United States, a precarious separation between their personal and public lives has always been expected. Basing their opinions on liberal, nonfeminist assumptions about the division that should exist between public and private domains, citizens often resent the privileged access family members have to office holders, particularly if relatives' opinions challenge established power relations. Citizens commonly expect that divisions between public and private will be symbolically maintained, but when spouses or other family members challenge the status quo, the public may vilify the nonelected member and demand that separate domains be upheld.

As women continue to establish independent careers, it will become more likely that male politicians will marry women with political opinions, agendas, goals, and aspirations of their own. Working to elect feminists to public office is one way the women's and battered women's movements have achieved their goals. But elected officials are often constrained in ways that their spouses and family members are not. Partnership politics increases the probability that social movements will gain entrée to arenas of official decision making. The election of profeminist men who share power with their wives is a potential source of access to arenas of power and authority for women's movements.

In Ohio, Governor Celeste lent institutional support to his partnership with the first lady by providing her with a staff and offices in the state house. He empowered her to work toward feminist goals by actively seeking her input, instructing his staff to work with her, and including her in high-level meetings. The governor valued her contributions. Nonetheless, although she kept a low profile during all but the last several months of the governor's second term, Dagmar Celeste's influence did not come without resentment and resistance from the public, the governor's staff, and other public servants. Governor Celeste explained, "The staff of the governor serves the governor and thinks that anything else that intrudes is just that . . . unwarranted intrusion. That's family, that's first lady, whatever it might be. . . . 'Here we are doing the business of the state; why do we need to worry about something that the first lady's interested in?' And so I think it's fair to say that there was never a wonderfully smooth relationship between the first lady's staff and the governor's office staff."[10] Despite resistance, the governor insisted that the first lady's concerns be addressed through official channels, creating countless democratic public spaces for Ohio women.

The spouse of an elected official has freedoms not available to public office holders, who must adhere to myriad policies, laws, and public expectations. Dagmar Celeste compared the role of first lady to the wife in a strategic game. She said,

> I've often viewed the role of first lady as the queen in a chess game. . . . The whole . . . game is built on protecting the king. . . . And what's interesting in chess . . . is that the queen has a lot more mobility than anybody else. . . . She can move up. He can't move at all! . . . Chess is not a feminist game, because there's no point in having a queen, except to protect the king. . . . I would make coalitions with people who didn't serve [the governor's] interests, if they served a feminist interest. And eventually he would come to see that they served his interest, because if he wanted to be what he said he wanted to be, as a progressive feminist politician, eventually it came to serve his interests (interview, 26 June 1991).

If the "queen" had adhered to liberal principles and separated her life from that of the "king," her movement and ability to achieve change would have been reduced to that of players outside the court, such as the pawns.

A Proposed Model of "New" Social Movements

To the extent that new social movements are based upon identity-oriented political strategies, they will follow a model similar to the one exemplified by the battered women's clemency movement. The clemency movement has roots in the women's and battered women's movements, which were established to challenge gendered power relations in social institutions and cultural belief systems. The clemency movement has used a number of different strategies, tailored to the political opportunities in each state.

The movement has adhered to a strategy of "self-limiting radicalism" (Cohen 1985), through which activists have challenged divisions between public and private and created democratic public spaces accessible to marginalized groups, and especially to incarcerated battered women. Activism has been carried out on the job, through volunteer work, in personal relationships, and in careers as public-office holders and appointed officials. One of the most interesting dynamics in this movement is the informal partnership that has evolved between movement founders and joiners, or as Whittier (1995) might put it, between "feminist generations."

Relatively older women, who have had time to establish careers, have played key roles in introducing legislation, challenging case law, and advocating for clemency as part of their politically appointed positions. Many movement founders were in politically elite positions in which they could exert the authority necessary to start the clemency process and create opportunities for women's voices to be heard. Not all movement founders established political careers or occupied elite statuses. But the central factor affecting the model this movement would assume is that when feminists found themselves in influential or authoritative positions, they challenged public and private boundaries, both by discussing issues once believed to be personal or private and by using their positions to demand justice and social change. Feminism is about social mobility for women, but women who occupy their achieved status without empowering others have failed the feminist test.

In the younger generation of movement joiners, women have worked through less powerful and influential positions. Most movement joiners have found feminist communities and networks that support them in their work on behalf of women, but even when they have been isolated, their loyalty to feminist goals has been sustained by their commitment to the feminist identity and collective action frame. In some states, there was no formal relationship between founders and joiners; in others, alliances were established as needs and opportunities presented themselves.

National social movement organizations, such as the National Clearinghouse for the Defense of Battered Women and the National Coalition against Domestic Violence, have played important roles in the emergence of a collective action frame, the dissemination of important information, and the loose coordination of activities. While national organizations and statewide coalitions, task forces, and projects have played important roles in this movement, the glue that has held it together and made it cohesive has been the collective action frame. Because it is an emergent product of feminists at every level of movement involvement, it is both a product of feminist identity and a source of empowerment for movement beneficiaries. The movement's collective action frame has been developed at local, state, and national meetings; through feminist sections of national professional organizations; and in direct-service organizations. It has been discussed in the courts and upheld through the acts of attorneys and victim advocates who demand a feminist interpretation of the law and justice for women who defend themselves. It has been debated and disseminated through women's studies programs, the feminist press, social science, and feminist jurisprudence. Organizations, networks, and resources are important, but as an Illinois activist put it, the movement "exists in our consciousness." That consciousness is perpetuated and dispersed through organizational and community interaction and through the democratic spaces feminists have created in prisons, the media, the courts, government, and other institutions.

If, as I have argued, we are not currently in a postfeminist era, what is to prevent the demise of feminism, particularly as the social and political climate continues its rightward trajectory? As feminist joiners have promoted the clemency movement, they and the founder generation have been careful to make room for a generation of new "recruits." These women and men have been introduced to the movement and its beliefs through the opportunities they have been given to work directly with incarcerated battered women. Clemency project volunteers have been recruited from law schools and universities. There is no way to predict whether they will become core members of the battered women's or clemency movement. But because of the training they have received thanks to the movement, there is a greater chance they will enter their careers with a raised and informed consciousness about wife abuse and battered women who kill. If they are willing to engage in acts of everyday resistance to insist on the legitimacy of their beliefs, a new generation will be born. If they carry on the feminist collective action frame in their jobs, the movement's goals may become institutionalized.

Conclusion

To understand the battered women's clemency movement, we have drawn upon key concepts of resource mobilization, feminist, and new social movement theories. By setting aside the liberal democratic assumptions of resource mobilization theory and drawing upon the feminist tenet that the personal is political, we have been able to examine activism in a variety of settings, including traditional social movement organizations, feminist communities, careers, prison support and recovery groups, and personal relationships. In the course of examining the battered women's clemency movement and the incarnations in which activism has existed, a new model of social movements has emerged. That "new" model differs from the older, class-based models of social movements because of the centrality of identity to activism. Identity-based activists are not reluctant to venture into systems they want to change. They often look upon such career moves as opportunities to advance the movement's agenda. To the extent that movements continue to be identity-oriented, we are likely to continue to see such activism. And to the extent that activists carry on their protests and acts of everyday resistance inside the domain of authority, we are likely to witness the empowerment of muted groups and the institutionalization of policies, procedures, and laws that represent their perspectives and experiences.

In the last chapter of this book, I have chosen to return to the women who have received clemency. Although this book has centered on the experiences of battered women who have killed and on the social policies and structures that entrapped them in violent relationships, it has been easy to lose sight of whom this movement is about. In chapter 7, I give voice to 11 clemency recipients by allowing them to discuss their lives with abusive men, their attempts to defend themselves or protect their children, their experiences in prison, and the efforts they have made to reclaim and reestablish their lives since being released. Aside from the obvious value of listening to and learning from these women, an examination of their experiences during and after prison, where many of them were empowered and transformed, provides important insight to the everyday successes and the dissemination of identity-based movements.

Chapter Seven

The Dissemination
of Identity-Based Movements

In studying any social movement, it is easy for academics to lose sight of the conditions activists are struggling to rectify. To fully examine the clemency movement in this study, it has been necessary to make activists and strategies the primary subjects and to focus on clemency recipients only secondarily. In this chapter, I hope to come full circle in our examination of the battered women's clemency movement.

I have two goals in this chapter. The first is to examine the effects of prison-based social movement organizations, feminist collective action frames, identity transformation, and empowerment on the lives of clemency recipients, both while they were in prison and since they have been released. In this chapter I will show that prison-based support groups were the organizational linkage through which the movement's collective action frame was disseminated to and internalized by many women who would apply for clemency. Through consciousness-raising and internalization of the collective action frame, women's identities—how they thought of themselves and interacted with others—were transformed. Via this transformation, the movement was disseminated to its beneficiary group. Once empowered, these women became important activists in the clemency movement. They played an integral, grassroots role in furthering the battered women's movement's goal of eliminating violence toward women. Like other identity-based movements, the battered women's movement will succeed only to the extent that women are willing and able to resist violence and oppression in all facets of their lives.

My second goal is to give voice to the incarcerated women who fought for and won clemency. The clemency recipients I interviewed for this study had experiences similar to those of the women whose cases were examined in chapter 3. In prison, most of these women participated in support and education groups, in which they were empowered to resist violence in their lives. Most of the women in my sample have avoided violence and abuse since their release from prison. But their resistance has been an ongoing struggle.

Clemency is a laudable and necessary goal of any movement seeking justice for battered women. It is not a panacea. As a result of the violence in their lives, these women lost their jobs and homes. Most with children missed raising them to adulthood. Since being released, they have had to start over in a society that does not easily forgive convicted felons. In Ohio, little was done to provide systematic support for these women, making their adjustment to the outside world more difficult than it has been in such states as Maryland and Florida, which have provided transitional support. Some clemency recipients have faltered; at least one failed to successfully adjust to life after prison. But all have demonstrated a resiliency that suggests they are, above all else, survivors.

The Women in This Chapter

In the course of conducting research for this chapter, I attempted to interview all 26 women who were granted clemency by Governor Celeste. That was not possible. One woman was reincarcerated approximately one year after her release, when she became involved with an abusive man and was arrested for selling drugs. Another woman died of breast cancer, which was diagnosed in prison. At least two clemency recipients had lived in homeless shelters: one had since gotten an apartment and agreed to be interviewed; the other did not respond to my efforts to contact her, and I was told by other clemency recipients that she did not want to be bothered by the media or social scientists. One woman had been reunited with her children and was having difficulty living on the welfare check and food stamps to which she was entitled. As a convicted felon, she had difficulty finding a job and was not eligible to live in public housing. In my efforts to contact her, I was informed by the Ohio Department of Rehabilitation and Correction that she had been charged with welfare fraud. There were five others whom I could not locate and five more who declined to be interviewed when I did reach them. One woman would not grant a formal interview, but we conversed over the telephone for 30 minutes. Because of her reluctance to participate, I have chosen not to include data from our conversation in my analysis. Those who chose not to be interviewed explained that they wanted to put the past behind them. It is possible that I could have pressured them into talking with me, but I thought it important to respect their wishes.

Of the women I did interview, all who had children had reestablished relationships with them and made stable homes for themselves. The women may not be fully representative of the larger population of clemency recipients, which includes women living on the extreme margins of society. In addition, they may be more activist in their worldviews. There was wide variation in their participation in the battered women's movement, with some working for shelters, others speaking publicly about their experiences, and some working to help their daughters escape violent relationships. Every clemency recipient who chose to be interviewed expressed hope that speaking out might somehow prevent at least one woman from living through what she had experienced.

Of the women in my sample who desired employment, each had found a job. None was able to return to her place of employment prior to her prison sentence. Most had to abandon their original occupations, due to legal restrictions or the difficulties felons face in employment. One woman had worked as a preschool instructor. According to law, as a convicted felon she was no longer eligible to work in child care. Some of the women lived on Aid to Families with Dependent Children (AFDC). Others received Supplemental Security Income (SSI), for which they were eligible due to a variety of disabilities caused by emotional and physical abuse or advanced age. At the time I conducted the interviews, between 1992 and 1994, one woman had remarried and moved into a new house in a well-to-do subdivision in a suburb of a major urban area. Another lived in public housing, in close proximity to her emotionally abusive family of origin and to an abusive man with whom she had become involved. Perhaps the most fragile of the women in my sample, this woman struggled with alcohol and drug addiction and despaired over whether she would ever "get [her] life back." For most women, putting their lives back together after being released was a struggle. Most were sad about their losses but at the same time proud of their clemencies and of what they had accomplished since being released from prison.

Of the 11 women whose lives are profiled in this chapter, two killed stepfathers who had sexually abused them for years. Two other women hired men to kill their husbands to protect their children from ongoing physical, and in one case sexual, abuse. At least two of the homicides were unintentional. One woman's husband was killed as they wrestled over the gun with which she intended to commit suicide; another's boyfriend ran into the knife she was holding to prevent him from attacking her. Only one of the women's batterers was killed in a traditional, confrontational situation, in which he had started the altercation and was beating her at the time he was killed and in which she was the person who killed him. One woman's son shot and killed her husband while he was beating and choking her, and another shot and wounded her boyfriend when he threatened her. Six of the women killed men who had threatened to kill them when an assault was not taking place. One of those women killed her husband while he slept, and another killed her sleeping stepfather when she learned he had molested her younger sister. Another woman killed her stepfather while he was gardening, after learning that he had sexually molested a niece after years of abusing her. Another killed her husband after he had beaten her. She went up to the bathroom to clean herself and found his gun. She did not remember shooting him.

The women in this chapter have had their lives opened to public scrutiny in ways most people would find unimaginable. Many of them have continued to speak out about their experiences and the need for better laws and resources for victims of family violence. Despite the openness with which many of them live, I assured all of them of confidentiality. Interview data include information and details not contained in court records or newspaper accounts of the women's lives. If clemency recipients wish to be publicly known, that is their prerogative. To ensure that they have the option of maintaining a comfortable level of privacy, I have concealed their identities. This may appear contrary to the feminist idea that the personal is political; however, the relationship between researcher and subjects is one in which power is vested in the former. By protecting their identities as much as possible, I have attempted to give them the power to decide how open or closed they wish their lives to be. In social science research, it is common to alter minor facts about respondents to protect their confidentiality. I have chosen not to do so because I believe it is important for readers to have all relevant factual evidence.

Lives of Violence

The violence, abuse, sexual assault, and torture these women endured is almost beyond imagination. Three women jumped from second-story windows and another leapt from a moving vehicle to escape brutal beatings. One woman had drain cleaner poured down her throat when her husband suspected her of having an affair. Apparently, doubt that she could have lived through such an ordeal showed on my face while I was interviewing her. She opened her mouth to show me. Her tongue and the inside of her mouth were deeply pitted and scarred where the drain cleaner had eaten away her flesh. Before her husband would allow her to go to the hospital, he made her promise she would tell emergency room personnel she had attempted suicide. She described the incident, saying,

He had took the kids over his mother's house. He said, "So when I come back . . . this may be the last time you see your kids." . . . And so when he came back . . . he said, "Now you're gonna tell me who you had in this house." And I said, "No one." . . . And he said, "You're either gonna tell me who . . . you had sex with, or I'm gonna kill you." . . . And so he tied me up . . . then he put his knees in my chest and he just literally started beatin' me, hittin' me all in the face. . . . And he would beat me, cuss me, in the face, and my face, my nose was bleedin', my face was bleedin'. And so he kept on sayin', "Now tell me who."

To stop the beating, this woman lied and said she had been with someone. Her husband's assault became even more vicious. She continued,

And that's when he drug me out the bed, in the bathroom, and he started chokin' me. And then he had my head and he pulled my head back, and he said, "Bitch, you gonna die tonight." He said, "I hate you." And there was a container of Drano that he poured down my throat. And immediately I started throwin' up. He threw me on the floor. [She begins to cry.] He said, "You gonna die, bitch. You're gonna pay." And, uh [long pause while she cries], and I began to, uh [pause], throw up blood clots and I begged him to please take me to the hospital. He said, "No. You gonna die. You'll never see your kids again."[1]

Women were often entrapped in violent relationships by threats that their children would be kidnapped. Their misery was often compounded by emotional, physical, and sexual abuse of their children. This same woman described an incident in which she was fleeing her house with her son, who was also being beaten. She turned back abruptly. She explained why, saying,

He grabbed my daughter. She was about 10 years old. And he held her over the banister, head first, feet up, and he, you know, was threatening if I didn't come back, that he was gonna drop her. And so she was screaming. So me and my son went back in the house. And then he jumped on me again . . . beat me, you know, fists, feet, whatever. And he would kick me in my back and my stomach and he would push me down the steps. . . . And he always told me everything was my fault, you know, I brought it on myself.

Another woman, who had been beaten by her husband for over 20 years, watched in horror as he beat their eight-year-old son with a chain. When she and a teenaged son tried to protect the child, they were beaten. An older son, who later confronted his father about the abuse, was threatened with a knife and beaten with a black jack.

These women had begged for help from the police, who repeatedly told them there was nothing they could do. They had sought advice from clergy, who told them to pray for their husbands and to try to react to beatings with love. And they had confided in their families. When one woman told her father about her husband's abuse, he came to her home to confront her husband. After her father left, her husband told her that he would kill her father if he ever set foot in their house again. Like many women, she reacted by isolating herself in order to protect family members from a man she knew to be capable of horrendous acts of violence.

Women who had been sexually abused by stepfathers for their entire lives listened in horror as younger family members revealed that the men had turned their abuse on them. After a lifetime of sexual abuse, these women killed their stepfathers to protect younger women from the years of sexual assault they had endured. Mothers, who had lived through decades of physical and sexual assault, listened with shock and horror as their daughters told them about incest that had been happening to them for years. One woman explained that her daughter had told her about the child's father's sexual abuse, which had been occurring for six years. She said, "That's when my deception began." Within a year, she had contracted with someone to kill her husband, who is now dead as a result. Another young woman had decided to run away from home to escape her stepfather's sexual abuse, which had begun when she was six. When her sister revealed that he had begun abusing her, the girls waited until he went to bed. They tied his bedroom doorknob to the stairway railing, doused the house with gasoline, and lit a match. The older sister was tried as an adult and sent to the Ohio Reformatory for Women.

Decisions to kill abusive partners and stepfathers were not made lightly. In three instances women believed their lives were in imminent danger at the time the assault or homicide occurred. One woman's boyfriend had taken her car, threatened to kill her boss, demanded that she stop seeing her children, and beaten her brutally for over a year. She had told him she would not cosign for a loan he wanted. When he threatened that she had better sign the papers "or else," she told him that their relationship was over and asked him to leave. He was enraged. She explained what happened, saying,

He says, "You're signin' the papers. You're never gonna leave me." And I says, "You're not comin' near me." That's all I can remember. It's like slow motion. I don't know how to explain it. . . . It's like, you know, he's coming, I ran, I got the gun, pointed it at him. My hands were shakin'. I had both hands on the gun. I remember that. I said, "Take another step and I'm gonna shoot you. Please don't make me do this." I asked him, I said, "Please go." And he took one step, and boom! He fell to the ground. I remember that. I saw blood. I don't know where I shot him. I closed my eyes (interview, 31 October 1992).

Another woman's son shot his father when he found him beating and choking his mother. To protect her son, she lied to police and her attorney, saying that she had killed her husband. As her trial approached, her son confessed. They were both charged with conspiracy to commit murder. Both were convicted. The son remains in prison. The mother was so racked with remorse and guilt that it was difficult for her to rebuild her life.

Some social scientists have focused upon the learned helplessness of battered women. One of the objections to battered woman syndrome has been its focus on women's failure to escape rather than on the numerous strategies they use to survive abusive and violent relationships (Callahan 1994; Dutton 1993; Hoff 1990). Like hostages, victims of terror, and prisoners of war, victims of ongoing abuse often experience a form of post-traumatic stress disorder that results from the unequal power dynamics in the relationship as well as from the batterer's abuse of power. Women's reactions are specific to the culture in which they live. They are the product of the social supports and options available to them, as well as of factors specific to their own biographies, including gender socialization, religious beliefs and convictions, and history of abuse in the family of origin.

The trend in the social-scientific literature has shifted away from an examination of women as helpless victims and toward one that incorporates their agency as survivors. Women react to violence in ways that will ensure their own and their loved ones' short-term survival while they devise ways to survive over the long run. Sometimes the appeasement gestures and other tactics they rely upon to ensure immediate survival are interpreted as evidence of learned helplessness. The only thing helpless about these women is the society that fails to fully protect them from certain danger and probable death and the legal system's tendency to judge them according to androcentric standards.

Although these women killed or tried to kill someone who had abused them, the decision to defend their lives was made after numerous other efforts to fight back, escape, or appease the abuser had failed. At their trials, they were prohibited from introducing evidence of the abusive relationship, the abuser's history of mental illness or substance abuse, or evidence that would have corroborated their arguments of self-defense. Some of them were not permitted to argue self-defense at trial, which made explaining to the jury why they killed or tried to kill the abuser a particularly onerous task.

Protecting Others   One of the integral components of femininity and motherhood in Western society is a woman's concern for the well-being of others (Gilligan 1982). By law, parents are required to protect their children from abuse. Failure to do so may result in criminal charges or in the removal of the child from the parent's custody. By custom, women have taken on greater responsibility for maintaining familial relationships and tend to feel more responsible for family problems or the failure of a marriage. In my sample, five of the six women whose children were involved in their relationships with abusive men said they stayed with or went back to their partners because their children convinced them to do so, because the men threatened that the women would never see their children again if they left, because they lacked resources to provide for their children, or because they felt sorry for their husbands and believed in the sanctity of marriage. In addition, as previously discussed, one woman stayed with her abusive husband and isolated herself from her family of origin when the abuser threatened to kill her father. In describing their husbands and abusive stepfathers, women often focused on the abuse the men suffered as children, their problems with mental illness, the stresses they experienced at work, and their inability to care for themselves. Even when their children were abused by their husbands, these women frequently gave in to the children's pleas to reunite the family. Often the children's requests came at the same time that the husbands were apologetic.

Common to most of the women in my sample was a self-sacrificing means of survival in which the needs and safety of others were placed above their own well-being. Decisions were often made from a position of economic, political, social, and physical vulnerability. Options were few. Ultimately, their desire to protect others put them in a situation in which they believed they had to kill their abusers, be killed themselves, or endanger family members and have their children continue to suffer. Had these women been given an opportunity to prioritize their own needs on a level with those with whose care they were charged, and had they been given adequate social supports to insist that their own needs be met, they would have been better able to avoid a situation in which a choice between their own safety, the well-being of others, and the life of the abuser would have had to be made. In prison, they were given the chance to do that, often for the first time in their lives.

The Prison Experience

Prisons are institutions. Inmates are virtually cut off from the rest of society and surrender personal control over their lives to public officials whose function it is to punish and/or rehabilitate a nonvoluntary population of inhabitants (Goffman 1961). Prison officials and employees must control and regulate the lives of inmates, provide for their basic needs, maintain order and discipline, and prevent individual escape or mass insurgency. Within such a setting, inmates are deprived of basic liberties, including autonomy and freedom of association, as well as basic needs, including the security of being free from physical, sexual, or psychological harm. Aside from the use of physical force, inmates are controlled through a system in which they may earn rewards but must also avoid punishment (Sykes 1958). Some inmates approach such a situation as a war of all against all, in which they work to improve their own well-being without consideration of the needs of others. Other inmates look for ways to establish "ties of mutual aid, loyalty, affection, and respect" (Sykes 1958, 82).

Liberal social movements of the 1960s advocated establishing more rehabilitative prison policies. As a result, support, educational, and recovery programs expanded in U.S. prisons. After the heyday of the 1960s movements, however, and with the recession of 1974–1975, federal grants for innovative programs dried up, and prisons became oriented more toward punishment and less toward rehabilitation (Colvin 1992). When women who would later work for clemency entered prison, they tended to do so in the late 1970s and the 1980s, a period of anticrime sentiment and prison expansion. Prison-based or government-sponsored opportunities for recovery were increasingly rare. Despite officials' efforts to thwart the development of collective identity, particularly in the wake of the Black Power and Chicano bases of inmate militancy during the 1960s (Colvin 1992), inmates sought out and created ways of establishing relationships based upon a commonality of interest, experience, and identity.

Most of the women who would later fight for clemency arrived at prison disoriented as a result of cumulative traumatic experiences. With few opportunities to talk openly about their crimes and the history of abuse that led up to them, most women were still in shock when they arrived at prison. There, any self-esteem or self-respect that the abuser might have left intact was assaulted.

One woman, who had lived with physical and sexual assault for years and whose husband had beaten and threatened to kill her children, eventually escaped that relationship. She then became involved with another abusive man. Upon returning home from having surgery (due to injuries inflicted by her husband), her boyfriend attacked her. When her daughter intervened, she was assaulted. The woman demanded that her boyfriend move out of her home. He attacked her, repeating the words, "This time I'm gonna fuck you up." When he knocked her onto a bed, continuously beating and yelling at her, she managed to get to a gun he kept hidden under the mattress. She shot him dead. Despite all of the emotional, physical, and sexual abuse this woman had endured, she found the strip search required of all inmates entering prison to be demoralizing and degrading. Somehow, even after the efforts of her husband and her boyfriend to take away all her self-worth and sense of humanity, some shred of dignity remained. The prison managed to find it. She said, "When it was my time to go, leave the county jail, we had to dress alike and it made me think I was going to the electric chair—that I was going to die.... When I got there, it's a room that after they take the shackles off you, call your name, that you have to take off all your clothes in front of a bunch of women. That was the downgradingest, hurtingest. I lost something there.... You drop your clothes and squat in front of them" (interview, 20 August 1993).

Among the women in my sample, perceptions, survival strategies, and worldviews differed by age. Older women felt afraid, humiliated, and degraded. To cope with prison, they sought friendships with other inmates they perceived to be like themselves. Among women over 50, there was a tendency to avoid participation in formal support networks, except as they were sponsored by religious groups. Two women said they avoided inmate organizations because of the lesbianism they saw there. One elderly woman said, "The only group that I joined in with was the church groups. But anything else, I did not partake in it because I did not believe in all that bull dykin' and stuff that was goin' on with them girls" (interview, 1 November 1992). In prison, women had more time to devote to friendships, but they had to be careful about whom they trusted. One of the women explained, "You're closer with the prison family because you're going through the same things together and you find a person you can talk to. . . . There are some very tough people in prison. . . . You meet people . . . and you get this closeness and you know that if you're depressed, somebody's there for you, and they're going to understand because they're there" (interview, 1 November 1992).

Although they supported each other in their quest for clemency, older women tended to see their release from prison as a personal issue and to devise more individualistic strategies to avoid or survive abuses of power. One woman, in her 70s when I talked with her, explained her strategy of avoiding problems. She said, "I just kept to myself most of the time, and I just looked at them like I was crazy, because all they wanted to do, they was screwing the girls up there, and I wasn't about to let that happen to me. There was a bunch of the guards that got fired because they was taking advantage of the girls" (interview, 1 November 1992).

This individualistic survival strategy is one product of a worldview that fails to make the connection between personal problems and political power structures. This perspective on the world reflects some women's lack of participation in prison support groups and their concomitant failure to internalize the movement's collective action frame. Although these women successfully avoided violence in prison and afterward, after their release they were more dependent upon others to provide their housing, food, and medical care and to make decisions for them. Those who were physically able to do so completed their 200 hours of service in a battered women's organization but were less involved in the movement than were women who had attended support and education groups in prison. Nonetheless, these apolitical women did come away from prison determined never to become involved in an abusive relationship again, and they watched over daughters and granddaughters, encouraging them to leave anyone who did not treat them well.

Women who entered prison as teenagers tended to feel hurt and anger, emotions that were undoubtedly one result of a life of abuse. They were not predatory in their behavior. To them, prison was a war of all against all in which they were the prey. Initially, their survival strategy was individualistically combative. Eventually, they began to trust other women and to join support groups, in which their strategies and worldviews were transformed. One young woman, who had been sexually and physically abused by her stepfather from the age of six, went to prison determined to survive. She described how she coped with prison life, saying, "I was the youngest girl in the penitentiary for a long time, and everybody thought they could beat me up, get over. And I ended up tearing a lot of people up. I got into a lot of fights. A lot, until they learned to give me my respect. . . . I didn't come here to be bothered by anybody, and once they realized I wasn't to be messed with, because when it comes to my life or yours, I'm not gettin' hurt. I've been hurt enough" (interview, 18 July 1994). Another woman, a teenager when she entered prison, explained that she protected herself by displaying a bad attitude and a willingness to fight. She said, "I had women that bothered me . . . but I kept this dog on. . . . I had this one woman come to me [after I got involved in a support group] and [she] said that she thought I was so hateful she would never speak to me" (interview, 8 August 1993).

For women who had been abused throughout their lives, violence was the only means of survival they knew. But fighting, disobeying orders, or other violations led to confinement in "the hole," a place of solitary confinement where inmates were given only a gown to wear. Because of their defensiveness and highly combative reactions to others, these women repeatedly encountered other inmates who wanted them to be punished and prison authorities willing to enforce the rules. Joining groups was virtually beyond their comprehension or emotional capability. Learning to trust other women enough to listen to their stories and share their own experiences was extremely difficult for younger women. The identity transformation necessary for empowerment was the most difficult among this group of women.

Women who were in their late 20s through their mid- to late 40s when they entered prison coped with prison life by forming informal friendship networks, similar to those older women engaged in, and by founding formal support groups. Although age may not inherently cause some women to cope by fighting and others to cope by withdrawing, it appears that in my sample, older women were more resolved to doing their time and younger women were more determined not to let anyone "get over" on them. Women in the age range between older and younger inmates tended to become movement leaders, although in such states as Ohio and California, older women—perhaps because their cases had the potential to build public support for the clemencies—were often more publicized spokespersons.

Recovery

For most women, life in prison was a balance between the total control of the institution and the opportunity to take care of themselves, often for the first time in their lives. Where formal support and recovery groups were lacking, women made friends and protected, supported, and provided for each other. Women talked among themselves about their problems. Primary among their concerns were children they had left behind. They worried about whether they would be able to maintain legal rights to their children, and about how their children were coping with the loss of both parents, whether they were being abused where they lived, whether they would be able to visit, how they seemed when they visited, and most anxiety producing of all, whether their children would forgive them for killing their father. One woman's son, who had always been a good student and, in her opinion, a model child, became extremely depressed when his mother was sent to prison for killing her live-in boyfriend. She described his visits, saying, "During that time my son was there . . . he would have his head hanging down. And he was always nervous. He was a behavior problem too, and he would not respond to nobody. . . . He told me he didn't want to live because I was gone and I was all he had and when he come to see me, it was so bad, because my son wouldn't look at me. He'd just rock and rock and rock and cry. Rock and cry all the time" (interview, 20 August 1993) Like other women, she worried about her son constantly. But she had to learn to take care of herself, knowing there was little she could do to help him.

In this environment, women learned to focus on themselves, though concern for loved ones was always there. One woman, who was sentenced to 25 years-to-life for killing her husband, said, "I was in the institution. I took that as, OK, I'm gonna be here, so there's nothing that I could, you know, I need to keep myself busy, and there was a lot of education" (interview, 17 August 1992). She worked at a job she found satisfying, and at the end of a hard day's work, she explained, "[y]ou sit there, and you make all kind of plans, how your future's gonna be when you get out. And everything's so . . . peaceful. You're so relaxed. You have taken care of your body, you have just read until you can't read. You have written letters. You have explored everyplace. You have done everything in there that you could. . . . You need to feed this [points to her head] to keep it healthy, and then when you get out, OK, we're gonna unfold all these plans that we had."

In the places of solitude they created, they focused on taking care of themselves. But they still had to survive within the system. An older woman, in prison for killing her husband, described the near absolute control prison employees could exercise, saying, "It's easy for you to get into trouble because if you don't know the rules, then you'll get in trouble. . . . You got to eat when they say eat; you got to go to bed when they say go to bed. If you get off your bed and it's count time, you'll get in trouble. You'll go to the hole, because that's considered escape, because they can't see you" (interview, 20 August 1993). For some women, adapting to the absolute control reminded them of their relationships with their abusers; for others, coping with prison authority was easier than living with an abusive family. One woman, who had been sexually abused by her stepfather and emotionally and physically abused by both parents, said, "I never got one disciplinary ticket or anything like that. You know why? Because very early in prison . . . I said to myself, 'This is a piece of cake. I could do this!' I said, 'Because it's nothing but a mind game, and these people, compared to my parents, these people aren't even rank amateurs.' So I knew I could do this time . . . because all my life I'd done nothing but take orders" (interview, 9 July 1994)

Empowerment

Although this woman found that "doing her time" was easy compared to living with her abusive parents, she and all the women I interviewed talked about the abuse of power by corrections officers (COs), which included arbitrary and unfair punishment, beatings, sexual harassment, and sexual assault as well as violence between inmates and toward COs. As one woman described it, "The atmosphere was like, it was just like hell. And it was how the COs treat you. I seen girls get beat by COs, I seen vice versa. COs jump some girls, girls jump some COs. Sexual harassment there. I mean, it's like a hell hole . . . girls up there were fightin' and doin' all kinds of things. . . . It was really terrible. It was a hell pit" (interview, 20 August 1993).

Having arrived in prison beaten and convicted, all of them facing terms ranging from 15 years to life, these women had to find ways to survive. Talking about their crimes and their problems was discouraged by the prison administration, but it happened anyway. One woman explained, "I had a lot of friends there, and if I ever needed to talk to anybody or they needed to talk to anybody, we had each other. I had a lot of good friends. . . . A lot of them were—are—the best friends I've ever had in my whole life" (interview, 10 September 1993). Although friends were important, they typically failed to provide a political analysis of an individual woman's experiences or situation.

Prison support and educational groups were the organizational links through which the movement's collective action frame was transmitted from career activists to movement beneficiaries. As incarcerated battered women reclaimed and redefined their experiences and identity, they began to think of themselves as survivors. In their minds, the major difference between a victim and a survivor is that the former runs the risk of future abuse, whereas the latter will not stand for it. Women who were involved only in friendship networks and who avoided association with women in support and empowerment groups tended to devise individual solutions to potential threats of abuse. Some fought; others tried to "look crazy." Those who were members of support groups recognized that the abuse of power had political roots, and their resistance went to the source of the problem.

Resisting Oppression

Some prison employees were interested in finding ways to help women recover. Many worked to empower inmates so they could end the victimization that had led so many of them to prison. Despite the benevolence of many employees, however, some abused their authority and power. The most powerful example of inmates' acts of resistance was told to me by a woman who had tried to escape her abusive boyfriend several times before she shot him as he threatened to kill her. She told me about the sexual assault of one of her roommates:

I had a roommate that was very heavy. A little, short shit, but she had breasts out to here [holds her arms out straight]. . . . She was real sweet. . . . And this one guard, he was after her. . . . And many a times, he'd make nasty insinuations about her breasts and what he would like to do to them and how he would like to do it and what he'd do to her. I mean, gross things, OK? . . . And the girl across the hall, she was our friend. . . . And she said, "Oh, there's something wrong here." . . . I said, "I know, but we're in the penitentiary," and, you know, you're a little confined. . . . Who do you go talk to? Well, you don't go talk to anyone. Who do you trust? You trust none of them. . . . This man . . . threatened us. Cocaine, he'd put in our bag if we said anything about what he said to her. . . . Well, you know, you get scared. . . . Well it was one evening at dinnertime, and the only person in the building was him, downstairs, and us. . . . And next thing I know, we hear screaming, you know, and the screaming was frantic. . . . We ran. . . . He's comin' down the third flight of stairs, you know? And he saw us, right? We run up the steps. She's all ripped up. You know, she's got semen all over her face. Her body here [around her breasts] is all red. . . . And now we're in a situation. What do we do? Who do we tell? Who do we trust? Where are we gonna go? . . . We're in the penitentiary. She's cryin'. She's frantic. I had to rock her, hold her. . . . We decided we would go to [a female guard]. . . . Scared to death, not knowin' what's gonna happen. . . . You know, we just had to take the chance. Are we gonna have to take abuse forever? Are we going to go through anymore shit, or what? And I told them, I said, "Well I'm not for no more abuse. You know, I'm not going to let it happen to me no more. I'm willing to do whatever I have to, for whatever it be. It may not be easy. It may not be the best. But that's my choice." And the other two decided we'd go together. We did (interview, 31 October 1992).

These three women, one of whom had formally been involved in a support group for battered women, filed a complaint with prison officials, who asked if they would be willing to talk to the prosecuting attorney. The three of them discussed it and decided they would go as far as needed to end the abuse. They testified before the grand jury and watched as the CO was arrested and escorted out of the prison yard in handcuffs. As a result of their testimony, they endured harassment from women who had traded sex for favors and from prison officials who did not approve of what they had done. Such determination in the face of near-total domination is testament to the degree to which support groups have the potential to empower women, who can then demand social change in their daily lives.

The same woman told me that ultimately the guard was tried and convicted and that other women began to resist the abuse of power by COs. I asked her where she found the strength to go through the entire process. She said,

I don't know. It's maybe just the healing and not wanting no more of any kind of abuse going to anybody. She was such a gentle girl, woman, you know? . . . And yeah, she made a mistake, but that didn't mean she had to go through that. And she was just hurt and afraid and scared. And together we united. And we could never clean up the penitentiary or never change a lot of people's minds. But you get rid of one nasty apple. . . . It was a funny thing after that happened. A lot of the nastiness and that vulgarness . . . was seeming to cease a little bit and to ease up a little bit, because they began to get nervous. And more women stood up, and two other officers were escorted off because the women found enough courage to stand up. So you know, even though you have to go through some hurt and abuse, some good came out of it because . . . they found the strength to say, "Hey, if they can do it, why can't we?" And they did.

Career activists can institutionalize rules and laws that make abuse illegal. But they live in a different world than inmates and battered women. With the partnership between feminists in positions of authority and movement beneficiaries, who are determined to resist abuse and oppression in their everyday lives, the women's, battered women's, and clemency movements have a much greater chance of succeeding. The empowerment of women is an essential strategy in the movement's dissemination and the achievement of its goals.

Identity-Oriented Movements and Social Change

Identity-oriented movements must work toward social change at many levels. In the case of the battered women's and clemency movements, activists must confront cultural beliefs that condone violence toward women and classify wife abuse a "private" issue while considering the homicide of an abusive spouse a "public" offense against the state. They must demand structural changes in all major social institutions, and activists must be willing to work for social change in their careers and personal lives, as well as in their roles as protesters. But although social change is important, the transformation of identity and the development of the belief that individual women should take "no more abuse" is a crucial component of the battered women's movement's goal of eliminating violence toward women. As women demand, through accessible social and legal systems, that the abuse stop and as their allegations are given credibility, those who perpetrate violence and even those who ignore it will begin to "get nervous." It is here that change is most likely to have an impact.

Laws against wife abuse, child abuse, and other forms of family violence are necessary, as are legal protections for those attempting to end abusive relationships. But until the resistance to family violence goes into the trenches, where battered women and their children live, the movement will only be able to continue to help women escape violent relationships, rather than end the violence altogether. Every time a woman is empowered to resist the abuse of power, whether on the job, in an intimate relationship, on the streets, or in prison, every time a woman will not be silenced into submission, the movement to end violence against women gets stronger. Every act of resistance witnessed by another woman raises in her consciousness the idea that catcalls, wolf whistles, sexual propositions, insults, slaps, demands, punches, kicks, rape, and other forms of abuse are not normal, are not deserved, and will not be tolerated. Those women who witness everyday resistance are more likely to say, "Hey, if she can do it, so can I."

The battered women's movement recognized that it needed activists in the government, as well as outside the system, to exert pressure for change (Schechter 1982). From its inception, the movement recognized the importance of empowerment so that "victims" could become "survivors" who would resist abuse. Without the resolve and resistance of victims, the success of activists, whether inside the government or outside the system, will have a limited effect. It is through the acts of everyday resistance of survivors who have decided to take "no more abuse" that the movement will ultimately succeed. It is at that level that cultural traditions and beliefs that condone violence toward women will be challenged and ultimately eliminated.

Collective Identity, Beloved Community, and the Challenge of Clemency

Between February 1990, when Governor Celeste's intention to review the cases of battered women who had defended their lives was revealed to inmates, and the following December, when the decisions were announced, solidarity among clemency applicants grew. Women encouraged their friends to apply, and when new women came to the prison, inmates inquired about their crimes and encouraged anyone who fit the criteria to submit a petition. One woman, who arrived in prison early in 1990, said, "A couple of ladies there that had applied for it, they came up to me and they asked me what I was there for. And I didn't want to tell them. But, of course . . . there's like a grapevine. . . . [I]t's real there, so some of them already knew. So I told them. And so they told me about the clemency and they told me about the lady that was in charge of it, that I should talk to her" (interview, 31 October

1992). When encouragement from other inmates was not enough to convince some of the women to apply, activist prison employees talked to them. One of the women who had been in prison since she was a teenager said, "She [a prison employee] thought of me doing this. I didn't even think of filing for commutation. She had me come into her office. She knew my whole case history. . . . We sat down together, and what I wrote, she helped me type it up. . . . [I applied only] because everybody else was so supportive. . . . If it wouldn't have been for everybody else, I might still be there" (interview, 18 July 1994).

As they waited for the decisions to be announced, a sense of community grew among clemency applicants. There were minor jealousies among the women, with less vocal inmates suggesting that some of the leaders were "in it for the glory," but overall the women shared information rather than hoarding it. Rather than discouraging each other from applying, perhaps in the fear that more applicants would decrease the odds of their own release, they encouraged other women to submit petitions, write letters, and find corroborating evidence, and they reassured those who had doubts. In light of the women's strong feeling of solidarity and community, it was almost inevitable that the clemency announcements would cause a fissure among applicants. The governor's decision effectively created three groups: those who received clemency, those who were denied it, and those whose cases were returned for further documentation. The divisions among women that were most apparent were among those who were granted clemency and those who were not.

By the time the clemencies were announced, rumors had been circulating around the prison for weeks. That day, women were escorted to different rooms, depending upon how their cases were decided. As they walked to designated areas, they were separated from their friends and sent to hear their fates. The tension was unbearable. What follows is several women's descriptions of what happened.

There had been talk that the governor was making a decision . . . but I would just not let myself think about it. . . . I left the school, [and] walking back to my living unit, there was all these women going toward the gym. . . . I was just told I had a pass to go to . . . some room in the main building. And I was thinking to myself, saying, "Why am I going there and everybody else is going to the gym?" And I said, "Well, I haven't got it" (interview, 31 October 1992).

We were all walkin' down the hallway and they started pullin' me toward another room, and I guess I had some bad vibes or somethin', 'cause I started hollerin' and screamin' about, "Where are you takin' my friends?" (interview, 17 August 1992).

We got a pass to meet in a room off the warden's office. They didn't tell us nothin'.... They put the ones that didn't get it in the gym, and they had psychologists and everybody there to help them. And the ones of us that got it, they put us in this little room and locked us in there (interview, 18 July 1994).

I seen the doctors and the preacher go over to the gym and I said, "Oh no, I don't want to go over that way. That's where the answer is no." ... My stomach was like in knots and my heart was goin' bam, bam, bam and I just started shakin' (interview, 20 August 1993).

And we were in that room from like three o'clock until quarter after four, just sittin', not knowin' what was goin' on. They didn't tell us anything (interview, 31 October 1992).

All of a sudden we saw women being escorted back, and they were screamin', hollerin', cryin' and stuff (interview, 17 August 1992).

Oh! It was, I mean, you could hear the pain ... and the pain rolled through, and just in the very next room.... The tears were pourin' outside the door, just, I mean you could hear 'em. It was horrifying (interview, 31 October 1992).

There was some women [in the clemency room], they was prayin' in the back and some was cryin', and I said, "This is like death warmed over in this room. I don't know what's goin' down." ... Then they came into the room ... they told us ... we were the elite bunch from the clemency, and we were lucky, and we were fortunate (interview, 17 August 1992).

One girl almost fainted beside me, and I couldn't believe it. I been tricked and played so long. I was just sittin' there, tears runnin' down my face. I couldn't say nothin' (interview, 18 July 1994).

The joy of just a handful of women that were getting their freedom, unite and explode! And to have to bring that right down, real rapid, 'cause we're going out into the population. We all brought it down (interview, 31 October 1992).

The women who received clemency were counseled to keep their happiness to themselves, to be sensitive to those whose petitions had been denied, and to "show compassion for the other person." They were sent back to live among the women with whom they had shared their hopes and dreams and with whom they had built a community. Some women received support from their friends. One woman said,

"When I got back to the cottage, all the girls, they picked me up and they welcomed me, you know. They said, 'We told you you was goin' home!' " (interview, 20 August 1993). Strong support came from women who had not applied for clemency. Among those who had been denied, such enthusiasm was impossible. Another woman said, "We went back to our living unit. There was people who was sick, who had nervous breakdowns. . . . You were happy for yourself, but you felt so bad" (interview, 17 August 1992). Clemency recipients were joyous for themselves but felt guilty and sad for those whose petitions were denied. For most, the rift between those whose sentences were commuted and those whose applications were denied was too great to overcome. For a few, reconciliations were possible, though difficult. One clemency recipient said, "I did [feel guilty] at first, especially when my best friend didn't get it. It was hard for us to talk. Then she came to me and said, 'Look, it's not you. But I thought I deserved it, too.' And I did too. I told her and we broke down cryin' and stuff, because she did deserve it. I couldn't even look at her" (interview, 18 July 1994). When support group members came together after the clemencies were announced, the tension among the women was insurmountable. The solidarity that had depended on a common goal and a collective identity was broken, and the beloved community was split in two. One woman described what happened:

Out in the honor camp we had a support group, and it was bitter. It was horrible, because there was only I think five of us or six that received the clemency. And maybe 25 in the honor camp that had filed that did not get it, and a lot of them were in that group. And when we first had the group, we were all in, great, no problem. And when the clemency thing came through, hostility feeling, uh, hatred-type "I hate you because you got your freedom, I didn't get mine" feeling came across. And we took a vote whether we should separate the meeting for the ones who didn't get it to the ones who did. The majority voted to separate, because they couldn't deal with the ones that did. And we did. . . . That was extremely painful to live through, because I loved these women, do you understand? I cared and I shared time and some I talked with and we got closer and became friends. . . . And I shared their hurts and they shared mine. And here I'm getting my freedom and you're not (interview, 31 October 1992).

The collective action frame failed to account for why some women would be battered, incarcerated, and released, and others would remain in prison. With their ranks diminished in size and their release from prison pending, clemency recipients had little time to mourn the loss of community. They had to prepare for the road ahead.

Life after Prison: The Challenge to Feminist Theory

According to feminist theory, empowerment enables a survivor to re-sist oppression and to advance feminist goals. This theory appears to gain some credence among clemency recipients who participated in support and recovery groups. But it has a tendency to overestimate the impact of empowerment and to underestimate the oppressive and abusive conditions with which some women live. It also fails to ac-knowledge that empowerment comes as a result of an ongoing process of recovery, in which the survivor gains new strength as she interacts with her environment and, with the support of others, resists abuse and oppression. Battered women, like all survivors of violence, can benefit from participation in a community of survivors, first as novices and ultimately as mentors to others.

Despite the hopes, dreams, and plans they had, life on the outside was overwhelming for many clemency recipients. The woman who talked about being able to take care of her body, mind, and spirit when she was in prison talked about her life after she was released:

Life is so fast movin', and your plans get throwed away, because you're back into society and society doesn't function normal. And they're fast movers, so now you gotta figure out, how do you fit in? Cause you're different, you know, you're not the same, and everybody looks at you. [They say,] "Oh, I don't know what's wrong with you, you know, you wasn't like that before." And "Where'd you get all this righteousness from?" . . . And you try to be OK and not let stress enter you, but a lot of time stress does, and it gets the best of us (interview, 17 August 1992).

Few appropriate supports were available for women who had killed an abuser, been sent to prison, and then been set free. Some women went to halfway houses, where they were assisted in finding employ-ment. Some of them found apartments and adjusted; others became homeless. Many women depended upon the kindness of relatives, some of whom were already in marginal situations. Six women applied for and received Supplemental Security Income (SSI) for disabilities caused by battering and abuse. Some worked part time, often as aides to elderly women. One woman got pregnant while she was homeless.

When the women got out of prison, their most immediate needs were a suitable place to live and a source of income. One woman de-scribed the mixed emotions that came with her release:

You know, when you come out of a place and you've been incarcerated for a length of time, and I'm not talkin' about just a week or month or two months or six months. Time. You have to do a lot of adjustment. I mean, severe adjustments. You're a little hyper. You're nervous. You're scared. Now you gotta go out in this world and get a job. How do you do that? Where do you go? . . . You have to depend on you now to eat, to sleep, put a roof over your head. . . . You need a little support group of some type. It's a scary thing comin' back out. Some people can't deal with it (interview, 31 October 1992).

Older women relied on family members for monetary, physical, and emotional support. Once they had completed their community service, they lost contact with the movement and focused on improving their personal situations. Those who had been involved in support and recovery groups were more activist in their world views and activities.

The support, opportunities for recovery, and empowerment they received in prison would serve most of the more activist clemency recipients well. Those women whose abuse had begun during adulthood gained insight into the violent relationship and the social conditions that allowed it to continue and learned strategies to ensure they did not become entrapped again. Women who had been abused since childhood, particularly in cases in which the abuse was sexual, had more difficulties.

Gilmartin (1994) refers to the confusion and emotional trauma victims of incest or child sexual abuse experience as "soul murder" or the "shattered soul." Neither is a clinical diagnosis. They refer to the emotional numbness, isolation of feeling, confusion, denial, identification with the perpetrator, and diminished sense of self and identity that result from severe sexual abuse. Two of the women who had experienced incest had devised survival strategies that, despite a number of problems, helped them function in society. The third woman lived in a state of confusion, anger, denial, and anxiety. She continued to be emotionally abused by her family of origin and became involved with a physically and sexually abusive married man. To cope with and repress her anger, she drank. Whether abused as children or adults or both, all of these women would have benefited from additional support.

Pragmatic Concerns   Finding jobs with a felony record was difficult for those seeking employment. Two strategies seemed to work well. Some women lied about their felony record. This is a strategy that may work better for women than for men, because people expect women to have prolonged absences from the workforce. One woman explained how she got a job right out of prison, even when the application asked if she had ever been convicted of a felony. She said, "I lied. I did, and it worked. But I think they knew" (interview, 16 August 1993). Most women told the truth. Some lost jobs for which they were qualified. One woman explained, "I have . . . applied for jobs that I know I was qualified for, and I never lie on applications. . . . I know that if I put a lie down there, like some of the women do, and say I have never had a felony conviction and they found out that I did, and they could fire me on the spot. So I always told the truth. The minute they look at that, they don't hire you. They don't tell you that's the reason, but that's the reason" (interview, 9 July 1994). Some women became proactive in their search for employment. One woman who used this strategy explained,

I got the first job I applied for. So I was very blessed. I had a very nice person interview me. Asked me had I ever been incarcerated for a felony of any type, and I said yes. I didn't lie about it. I explained to her why . . . and told her I received my clemency from the governor . . . and I was released under the battered woman syndrome. And tried to enlighten her eyes so that she'd understand a little more about that. . . . She was very compassionate, but I could've got one that wasn't. But she said, "There's no reason why that should stop you from havin' a job." So she gave me my job right away (interview, 31 October 1992).

Although rare, this was a strategy that paid off with an entry-level position. From there, this woman became certified as a nurse's aide and advanced in her new career to a satisfying job.

Finding homes was another concern. Most women went home to their families. Two women, each of whom had killed incestuous stepfathers, had no family to which they could return. They moved into halfway houses, where they were assisted with finding jobs and housing. One was able to make a relatively smooth transition from the halfway house to independent living. The other woman, and another who had lived with sexual abuse since a young age, had greater problems adjusting to life outside prison.

One young woman explained that she had grown up in prison. When she was released, her stepfather was dead, her mother had abandoned the family, and her younger sister refused to have contact with her. For her, the halfway house experience was helpful, but it was not enough. She explained,

The only place I could go, because I didn't have no family, was a halfway house. They give you 60 days to try to get a job and save up enough so you can get your own place. Plus, if you need counseling or whatever, you know, they help you get up on your feet. Which, I ended up stayin' an extra 30 days, because I hadn't found a place to stay, and I didn't know how to manage money, and I was still livin' like I was 16. That was the problem about me growin' up in jail. . . . So I worked for Taco Bell while I was there. And finally, a guy I met let me move in with him. Come to find out, he was on crack and everything else. And I ended up on it (interview, 18 July 1994).

Before long, this young woman was selling drugs. She rented a house and bought a car, but with her drug habit outrunning her ability to earn money she fell behind on the rent and was evicted and became homeless. She slept in her car, later selling it and moving in with a couple who also used and sold drugs. By the time she had been out of prison seven months, she was homeless, addicted to drugs, and pregnant. Her pregnancy made her realize that if she did not get help, her child would run the risk of repeating the intergenerational cycle of violence. It was concern for her child that made her reach out for help, and it was her pregnancy that made her eligible for the support she needed all along. She said,

When I first found out I was [pregnant] with her, I was really scared about that. . . . Everything's supposed to be hereditary and all that, but I think you can break the cycle. I'm determined to do that. . . . I called the Y[WCA] . . . and they're like my family to this day. I called her, I told her I was two months pregnant. I explained my situation, the drugs and everything. She said, "Come." Right then and there. And they let me in, and they took good care of me. . . . They give you counseling, they clean you up. . . . They help you find someplace. . . . They give you all the resources, and it's up to you to do it. . . . They're just so giving. And they just made me see a whole 'nother side of life that I knew I could have, and I wanted it. But I was just messed up so bad.

Through the YWCA, this young woman got involved in a number of support groups, including Alcoholics Anonymous, Narcotics Anonymous, and Born Free—a program for drug addicted pregnant women. She got counseling and found people who cared about her. She said, "They're like a big family down there. They are really nice." With the support of her new family of choice, she found an apartment and enrolled in a community college. But life was not without its struggles. After the birth of her first child, she became involved with a man who abused her. She resisted his violence and intimidation and told him she would not tolerate his abuse. She explained, "He's never hit me, but he's pushed me around and he like, pulled my hair once. And I told him, 'I will not let this happen again.' I said, 'You know what I've been through. Now, I'm not going back to the penitentiary. I'm not losing my family. My kids is everything I own and it's not worth it.' So I did what I had to, I called the police and I had him arrested and I prosecuted him. I got the charges and I went to court and I testified against him." When I talked with this woman, she had given birth to her boyfriend's child. His violence had stopped, and both of them were working recovery programs. She was hopeful that by getting her college degree she would be able to get off welfare and that life would hold better things for her children than it had for her.

In Ohio, members of the Friendship LIFE Group attempted to provide support to clemency recipients. But because they were so widely dispersed, it was difficult to establish meaningful contact with most women. The lack of ongoing empowerment programs for women released from prison is, perhaps, the greatest oversight of the Ohio movement. It is one that was addressed by movements in Florida, Massachusetts, and Maryland, and in an informal manner, in Kentucky. Nonetheless, the women I interviewed repeatedly astonished me with their ability to resist oppression.

The requirement that these women serve 200 hours in a program for battered women was intended to provide them with a forum in which they would be understood. Some found the understanding and sense of belonging they needed. Others found the experience alienating, perhaps because they were assigned jobs at which their contact with shelter residents was minimized. I have no data from shelter directors or employees to support the claims of some women that they were looked upon as examples of the way battered women should avoid solving their problems. Like women who found support in the shelters where they did their 200 hours, the women who were shunned would have benefited had they been formally introduced to programs that provided them with support, encouragement, and empowerment.

Everyday Resistance

Only two women in my sample became directly involved in relationships in which men abused them. One of these was the woman who prosecuted her boyfriend for pushing her and pulling her hair. The rest of the women avoided violent and abusive men and sometimes relationships altogether. One middle-aged woman said, "Right now, I'm still very, very untrusting of men . . . of relationships. I haven't thought about a relationship, and I'm mostly just a loner" (interview, 31 October 1992). The recovery process differed among women, with some coming out of prison ready to speak out against violence and others wanting to spend time alone. Even the well-intentioned efforts of family members caused more stress than comfort for some women, who needed time and understanding to adjust to their freedom.

Some clemency recipients had to cope with the anger of family members of the men they killed. One woman asked to be sent from prison to an area of the state in which she had never lived so she could avoid her abuser's family. Talking about his family, she said, "I've had them say that if I ever come that way, they'll blow me away." Another woman, whose abusive boyfriend did not die, worried that she might see him on the street, particularly because her job required her to travel around the city. She said, "I'm very cautious when I start to proceed into areas where I think he could be driving or working. I'm always looking. My eyes never stop roaming, you know?" (interview, 31 October 1992). This woman explained that because of the requirements of the victim notification system in Ohio, the man she shot was notified when she was released from prison. Because there was no police record of his violence toward her, she was not entitled to any notification of his whereabouts.

Empowering Others   Although they resisted or avoided violent men in their own lives, a pressing issue for women who had teenaged or adult daughters was the violence with which their children lived. Having lived with violence, killed their abusers, and spent time in prison for their crimes, they were adamant that their daughters would escape. One mother's efforts paid off when she convinced her daughter to leave an abusive relationship. She said, "He would beat her up, and he hit her in the head with some type of object. He tore up her car, and this was all while I was in lock up, and plus before I went to lock up he was doing that. . . . [When I got out,] I talked to her and I told her, 'You don't wanna repeat, you know, you see what I went through.' And I said, 'You don't have to go through that.' And I talked to her, and so she's out of the relationship" (interview, 20 August 1993).

Other mothers' efforts to talk to their daughters were not as successful. One woman explained her efforts to convince her daughter to leave an abusive husband:

[My daughter] got into the situation while I was [in prison]. . . . And so when I came home, the boy thought that he could still, you know, give some abuse.

And she was pregnant at the time, and she called and she was crying. . . . I
called the police before I left home. . . . I said, "I get my chance to act out the
real way to do this stuff," and so when I got to her house, the police came and
they arrested him. She did not know what was going on. She did not know anything about the . . . cycle of violence or nothin'. But I knew, so I said, "Well, I'm
gonna take her right to the hospital, 'cause she's pregnant, 'cause she's real upset." . . . The police came to the hospital, did the police report. . . . So he said,
"Now listen, you don't need to take this" (interview, 17 August 1992)

The next day, this woman took her daughter to the prosecutor's office,
but by then the younger woman was having second thoughts. The
mother recognized she was too heavy handed in her attempts to help
her daughter, so she took her to the Witness Victim program, where
counselors talked with the younger woman. After the meeting, she
called a woman from the Friendship LIFE Group. They talked about
the mother's need to allow her daughter to make her own decisions.
The next day, the Friendship LIFE volunteer met the mother and
daughter at court. The woman explained her frustration with her
daughter, and her sense of satisfaction that a criminal record had
been established for her son-in-law. She said,

When we went to court the next day, I went down, but [my Friendship LIFE
friend] went in the courtroom with [my daughter] and sat with her. . . . So she
interacted with [her]. And at the end of the day, [my daughter] was very an-
gry with me. . . . But [my son-in-law] did end up getting on the record, and
that's what I wanted. And he ended up with probation that time, because it
was like the first incident.

When her son-in-law assaulted her daughter a second time, her
daughter pressed charges, and the man was sentenced to 10 days in
jail. She was dismayed when the third incident resulted in probation,
because "[h]is previous record didn't surface." But she was vigilant in
resisting his abuse and continued to look for ways to educate and empower her daughter.

Clemency recipients expressed frustration over their female relatives' entrapment in violent relationships. Nonetheless, their everyday
resistance to violence in their own lives and those of their families was
steadfast. They hoped to break the cycle of violence and teach their
daughters that they deserved lives free of male domination.

Shelters, police, victim assistance programs, and reformed laws are
parts of only one side of the movement to end violence against women.

For the movement to succeed, victims need to be empowered to resist violence in their own lives and to reach out and help other women. The potential power of this ripple effect is expressed by the following woman, who became a public speaker after being released from prison. Two of her sisters, having witnessed the way this woman turned her life around, told her about the impact her life had on their own. She explained, "Some of my sisters was goin' through [violent relationships]. They left their husbands, they're in college. Two of 'em is in college and graduating. . . . You know, they told me that 'You made me strong. . . . I look at your life and see all the hell you went through, and that changed my whole mind. It made me want to go do somethin' for myself. You know, you inspire me to' " (interview, 20 August 1993).

Shelter Activism and Speaking Out

The desire of clemency recipients to become involved in the movement ran a full range, from wanting to avoid it and a willingness to do it to the wish to be involved in the day-to-day operations of the shelter. Shelters provided a variety of opportunities for women to fulfill the 200-hour requirement, allowing as much or as little client contact as they desired and permitting them to take on an activist agenda. It appears that shelters did not encourage activism unless women expressed an interest in it. But they nurtured and encouraged women who wanted to speak out and provided them with opportunities that suited their needs.

For a minority of women in my sample—those who were movement leaders in prison—working for and receiving clemency was a critical turning point, in which their lives and worldviews were politicized. This transformation of identity, from victim to survivor to activist, is related to the degree of commitment these leaders made to the movement while they were incarcerated (see McAdam 1988). Before going to prison, survival was their primary focus. In prison, their focus shifted to recovery and then to activism. Clemency was the goal. After prison, they became resolute in speaking out against violence against women. Similar to the Framingham Eight in Massachusetts, who incorporated as a way of organizing their public speaking, several Ohio women sought opportunities to share their experiences with others as a way of educating the public and building support against wife abuse.

For most of these women, movement activism, primarily through public speaking and shelter work, was an important component of their ongoing empowerment and recovery process. For example, one woman got a job as a shelter advocate when she learned she would be unable to return to her previous occupation. She had teenaged children at home and a married daughter who was in an abusive relationship. She found the shelter to be a place of solace, understanding, and acceptance and a place where she could do the most good in society. She said,

When I get [to the shelter], I calm myself, because I'm getting ready to do something that is good and that I believe in . . . and I'm going to give them the best that I can. [My original occupation] was all I ever wanted to be. . . . I never thought about doing anything else. And so now with being a victim of DV and then working in a shelter . . . to me it's relaxing. . . . And I don't have any problem with saying I think I need it, you know, for my own self-worth, because it keeps me abreast of being OK, because of what happened to me and to look at other women and still know and recognize that it's happening, you know, full blast (interview, 17 August 1992).

Shelter work, like support group work, was an interactive process of helping others see their situations in a more realistic light and then realizing one's own life was not so different. One woman talked about the benefits she received from her community service. She said, "I got a lot out of the service with [the shelter]. Like I said, I feel good about myself now knowin' . . . [states her name] is takin' control of her own life. I don't ever have to worry about nobody else that has power and that control over me, whereas I cannot even dress myself or fix myself up to look like I'm someone or somebody. . . . If you're in a relationship that is not good for you, then get out of it. . . . I'm in control. [States her name.] Nobody else is" (interview, 20 August 1993). Whether they spoke publicly about their experiences, worked as shelter advocates, spent volunteer time talking with shelter residents, sat in on support groups, or helped daughters and sisters escape violent relationships, the majority of clemency recipients have worked to change the world around them. Just as the Celeste clemencies have rippled through other states, in which activists realized that such a goal might be attainable, they have rippled through the lives of the women who were released from prison with the resolve to tolerate "no more abuse."

Conclusion

To have a permanent impact on society, identity-based social movements must alter established social arrangements at every level of society. The battered women's and clemency movements have done this by challenging assumptions about women and empowering women to resist oppression in their daily lives. They have worked to alter gendered belief systems, particularly surrounding the idea that women are naturally subservient to men. They have challenged the codification of gendered belief systems in the law, including the right of a man to beat his wife and the ways in which self-defense laws are biased against women. They have worked to establish laws to protect women from violence and shelters in which they may hide when the law fails. Although all of these changes, and more, are necessary to end violence against women, the greatest insurance against abuse is the ability of women to stand up against men who would beat and abuse them and to take legal steps to protect themselves and prosecute men who abuse them. Particularly in the battered women's movement, in which clients have a tendency to hope and believe that abusive men will change, a transformation of identity—from victim to survivor to activist—is one of the movement's greatest achievements. Movements that work for identity transformation can find no greater success than to have their goals expressed in the everyday lives and acts of resistance of their beneficiary groups. To achieve such success, however, requires structural change and a radical alteration of the belief systems that underlie the status quo, and a partnership among activists at all levels, including those in government and in national movement organizations, grassroots activists, and movement beneficiaries. And it requires that the movement provide ongoing support and empowerment for those upon whom the ultimate success of the movement depends.

Battered Women's Clemency Movement Time Line

1972   Chiswick Aid, the first feminist shelter for battered women, opens in Chiswick, England.

1974   Women' Advocates opens the first U.S. feminist shelter in St. Paul, Minnesota.

         Joan Little stabs a jailer who is raping her. She is acquitted.

         Inez Garcia shoots and kills a man who had raped her and threatened to do so again. She is convicted.

1976   Women Together, Inc., opens a feminist shelter in Cleveland, Ohio.

         Beverly Ibn-Tamas shoots and kills her abusive husband, Dr. Yusef Inb-Tamas. Expert testimony on "battered women" is excluded. She is convicted.

1977   Inez Garcia (1974) is acquitted.

         Yvonne Wanrow's conviction is overturned on appeal.

         Beverly Ibn-Tamas (1976) is retried for killing her husband. She is convicted.

         International Women's Year Convention is held in Houston.

1978   National Coalition against Domestic Violence and Women's Self-Defense Law Project are founded.

         Kathey Thomas shoots and kills her abusive common-law huband.

1980   Donald Baker tries to kill his wife. He pleads not guilty by reason of insanity. The prosecution enters expert testimony on "battered wife syndrome" to show that his abuse of his wife was not related to insanity. He is convicted.

1981   Citing Ibn-Tamas's case, expert testimony on battered woman syndrome is admitted on appeal in the case of a battered woman who killed her abusive live-in boyfriend (*Smith v. State*) in Georgia.

The Ohio Supreme Court rules that expert testimony on battered woman sydrome is inadmissable in *State v. Thomas*.

1984   Looking Inward for Excellence (LIFE) Group is founded by Rebecca Cardine at the Ohio Reformatory for Women at Marysville as a support group for women serving life sentences.

1987   National Clearinghouse for the Defense of Battered Women is founded.

Missouri enacts legislation recognizing battered woman syndrome.

Ohio governor's Interagency Council on Women's Issues is founded by Executive Order.

1988   California inmates found Women against Abuse.

Direct service providers in Ohio split from Action Ohio and form the Ohio Domestic Violence Network (ODVN), whose purpose is to effect social change on behalf of battered women.

1989   Massachusetts female inmates, with assistance from Stacey Kabat, found Battered Women Fighting Back! (BWFB!)

Maryland Clemency movement is organized via information of the Public Justice Center's Domestic Violence Taskforce.

Maryland's Taskforce produces *A Plea for Justice*.

Louisiana passes legislation stating that in cases where there is a history of violence between an intimate couple, it is not necessary to first show a hostile act on the part of the victim and that expert testimony about the impact of the victim's assaultive behavior on the state of mind of the defendant shall be admissible.

1989–90   Maryland Taskforce interviews women for potential clemency petitions.

1990   Recovery groups for incarcerated battered women are established at the Ohio Reformatory for Women.

Maryland Taskforce premiers *A Plea for Justice.*

Maryland governor William Donald Schaefer sees *A Plea for Justice* and later meets with incarcerated battered women.

Florida activists found the Women in Prison Committee as a project of the Florida Coalition against Domestic Violence.

March: The Ohio Supreme Court recognizes battered woman syndrome in *State v. Koss.*

August: Ohio governor Richard Celeste signs into law House Bill 484, recognizing battered woman syndrome.

December: Ohio governor Celeste grants clemency to 26 women after reviewing 115 application.

Maryland governor Schaefer contacts House of Ruth, which was working with the Maryland Taskforce, for help in identifying women for clemency consideration.

1991   Philadelphia
National Clearinghouse for the Defense of Battered Women adds clemency to its focus on battered women.

Maryland
U.S. Representative Constance Morella (R-Md) introduces a nonbinding resolution expressing a sense of Congress that expert testimony concerning the nature and effect of domestic violence should be admissible when offered in a state court by a defendant. It is signed by President George Bush.

23 January: Maryland Taskforce submits a confidential report recommending clemency for 12 women.

19 February: Maryland governor Schaefer grants eight clemencies.

April: Maryland passes a "Battered Spouse Syndrome Bill."

July: Maryland governor Schaefer grants early parole to two more clemency applicants and denies the remaining two.

Massachusetts

Massachusetts Task Force on Battered Women and Self-Defense is founded by human rights and feminist activists, led by Stacey Kabat.

September: Massachusetts revises clemency rules for incarcerated battered women.

California

March: California inmate group Women Against Abuse writes a letter to Governor Pete Wilson asking him to review the cases of battered women serving time for killing their abusers and to consider commuting their sentences.

August: California Coalition for Battered Women in Prison is founded as a consortium of progressive legal and community groups and private and public interest attorneys.

Eight members of a Claifornia inmate group, Women against Abuse, testify before 10 legislators at the California Institution for Women at Frontera.

October: California passes legislation granting right to expert testimony on the physical, emotional, and mental effects of battering.

Florida

Florida governor Lawton Chiles revises clemency application rules and forms a domestic panel of three experts to review the petitions of battered women.

Jan. 1992 to   15 Florida inmates apply for clemency.
Sept. 1993

1992   Kentucky passes legislation redefining the meaning of imminence in the context of domestic violence and permitting victims of domestic violence to have their cases reviewed in the courts where they were tried.

14 February: In Massachusetts, eight women apply for clemency.

March: In California, 34 women apply for clemency.

July: California passes legislation requiring parole board members to recieve domestic violence training.

1993   Illinois Clemency Project for Battered Women is founded.

Massachusetts governor William Weld grants four clemencies:
>   April: one sentence communted
>   July: one sentence reduced to "time served"
>   November: one sentence commuted, one granted early parole.

May: California governor Pete Wilson reduces two sentences, denies 14 other clemency petitions.

Florida governor Chiles grants two clemencies: one in May, one in July.

November: Floria governor Chiles sends a clemency recipient to work release.

1994   14 January: Massachusetts governor Weld signs legislation permitting evidence of past abuse and expert testimony on the dynamics of abusive relationships and effects of battering on perception of imminence.

March: Massachusetts governor Weld grants two more clemencies and denies two.

Illinois Clemency Project files 12 clemency petitions.

May: Illinois governor Jim Edgar grants 4 of 12 clemency petitions.

1995   Illinois Clemency project submits 18 petitions; Governor Edgar reduces one sentence, denies 17 petitions.

California passes legislation recognizing battered woman syndrome

December: Kentucky governor Brereton Jones grants nine clemencies and one pardon.

1996   January: Florida Battered Women's Clemency Project hires two full-time staff attorneys

Florida Battered Women's Clemency Project files 10 petitions and receives two waivers; Governor Chiles has not acted on any of them as of January 1997.

Illinois Clemency Project submits eight petitions; Governor Edgar has not acted on any of them as of December 1996.

California governor Wilson fails to review the clemency petitions before him.

California Coalition against Domestic Violence becomes defunct.

Glossary of Social Movement Organizations

National Organizations

National Coalition against Domestic Violence (NCADV)—Founded in 1978 in Washington, D.C., as a membership organization for local programs and state coalitions to provide a national voice for local programs, define the movement's philosophy, and give voice to underrepresented women.

Women's Self-Defense Law Project—Founded in 1978 to help lawyers in the United States more effectively represent female victims of violence who defend themselves from attackers.

National Clearinghouse for the Defense of Battered Women—Founded in 1987 as the first national organization focusing exclusively on legal defense strategies for battered women charged with criminal activity.

California Organizations

Women against Abuse—A support group for incarcerated battered women founded in 1988 by inmates. This group has been the organizational center of incarcerated battered women's activism for clemency in California.

California Coalition for Battered Women in Prison—A consortium of progressive legal and community groups and private and public-interest attorneys whose goals included identifying battered women in prison for killing or assaulting batterers and assisting them with the clemency application process.

Florida Organizations

Women in Prison Committee (WIP)—Founded in 1990 as a project of the Florida Coalition against Domestic Violence.

Florida Battered Women's Clemency Project—Founded in 1994 by the Florida Bar Association to assist incarcerated battered women in applying for clemency.

Illinois Organizations

Illinois Clemency Project—Founded in 1993 as a coalition among Chicago-area feminist law professors, law students, and battered women's advocates.

Kentucky Organizations

Battered Offenders Self-Help (BOSH)—Founded by a prison employee as a support group for women who kill or assault their abusers.

Kentucky Commission on Women—Established by executive order in 1964 and as a state agency in 1970. The commission's mission is to enhance economic opportunities for women, promote women's legal rights, and increase women's voice in state politics.

Kentucky Domestic Violence Association—A statewide social movement organization made up of the 17 domestic violence shelters in Kentucky. Its purpose is to provide advocacy for domestic violence victims and technical assistance for shelters. KDVA helped to coordinate the clemencies achieved during the Jones administration.

Maryland Organizations

Maryland Domestic Violence Taskforce—Founded in 1989 by a coalition of private and public-interest attorneys from private law firms, the Office of the Public Defender, and students and professors from the University of Maryland Law School.

House of Ruth—The Baltimore battered women's shelter, which played an important role in assisting the Domestic Violence Taskforce in researching and identifying women to apply for clemency.

Massachusetts Organizations

Battered Women Fighting Back! (BWFB!)—A support group founded in 1989 by prison inmates to free women in prison for defending their lives and to seek justice for battered women.

Task Force on Battered Women and Self-Defense—Founded in 1991 by human-rights and feminist activists, with goals including clemency for women in prison for defending their lives, legislation to permit battered women to fully defend themselves at trial, and better legal protection for battered women.

Ohio Organizations

WomenSpace—Founded in 1975 as a feminist organization of programs in Cleveland. Its purpose is to coordinate activities among social movement groups and facilitate the development of feminist organizations.

Women Together, Inc.—An ad hoc group of feminists from organizations throughout the greater Cleveland area that founded the first shelter in Ohio.

Looking Inward for Excellence (LIFE) *Group*—Founded in 1984 by a prison employee at the Ohio Reformatory for Women at Marysville as a support group for women serving life sentences.

Friendship LIFE Group—Founded in 1986, this group of volunteers coordinated programs for, visited with, and provided support to members of the LIFE Group.

Governor's Interagency Council on Women's Issues—Formed by executive order in 1987 to monitor legislative and agency efforts on behalf of women, assess women's needs, and coordinate discussion between the governor and women's organizations.

Ohio Domestic Violence Network (ODVN)—Founded in 1988 by agency directors who split from Action Ohio as a network of direct-service providers. ODVN focuses exclusively on effecting social change on behalf of battered women.

Notes

1. Introduction

1. In a subsequent review, one additional woman also received clemency.

2. A. Johnson, "Twenty-five Women Granted States' Clemency," *Columbus, Ohio, Dispatch* (Saturday, 22 December 1990): 1–2.

3. J. Blum, "Celeste's Clemency for 25," *Columbus Monthly* (March 1991): 55–58; I. Wilkerson, "Clemency Granted to 25 Women Convicted for Assault or Murder: Ohio Governor Says They Were Battered by Men," *New York Times* (Saturday, 22 December 1990): 1A, 10A.

2. The Historical, Social, and Legal Context of the Clemency Movement

1. See Burgess and Draper (1989).

2. A prominent exception to this trend is the effort by the American Psychiatric Association to include diagnostic categories in the *DSM-III-R,* including a "masochistic personality disorder" and later a "self-defeating personality disorder," both of which contain criteria that could easily have been confused with battered woman syndrome. Feminists from numerous fields have opposed such an inclusion (Walker 1987). Whereas battered woman syndrome suggests that the psychological characteristics of battered women result from abuse, the masochistic and self-defeating personality disorder diagnoses suggest that tolerance of abuse rests in an abnormality in the personality structure of the victim.

3. See Browne (1987), Fiora-Gormally (1978), and Walker (1987) for excellent discussions of the cultural, structural, and legal contexts of battering relationships and their impact on battered women.

4. American Psychiatric Association, *Diagnostic and Statistical Manual of Mental Disorders,* 4th ed. (Washington, D.C.: 1994), 428–29.

5. Graham, Rawlings, and Rigsby (1994) have shown that PTSD may develop over a period as short as three hours.

6. Maguigan (1991) argues that the majority of homicides battered women commit are carried out in confrontational situations; however, her sampling procedure relied on appellate cases, which eliminated cases that were settled before trial. There is no way of determining whether most cases settled before trial were confrontational or nonconfrontational.

7. Confidential interview conducted by Patricia Gagné on 31 October 1992.

3. Political Trials and Legal Reform

1. I am not suggesting that research on socialization or women's status in society is less scientific than that conducted on psychological reactions to abuse. I am arguing that the courts were biased against research and expert witnesses who could not establish that their expertise was based upon standardized methodologies recognized within a scientific community, such as the American Psychiatric Association or the American Psychological Association.

2. *Federal Rules of Evidence* (St. Paul, MN: West Publishing, Co., 1987), 132–133. *Dyas v. United States,* App. D.C. 376 A.2d 827 (1977), certiorari denied 434 U.S. 973. *Ibn-Tamas v. United States,* App. D.C. 455 A.2d 893 (1983).

3. See, for example, *Pugh v. State,* 401 Ga. S.E.2d 270, 271 n.1 (1991).

4. See, for example, *State v. Martin,* 666 Mo. S.W.2d 895, 899 (1984).

5. See, for example, *Pruitt v. State,* 296 Ga. S.E.2d 795 (1982). Expert testimony excluded as irrelevant when defendant failed to demonstrate on the record that she was a battered woman.

6. Confidential interview conducted by Patricia Gagné on 6 August 1992.

7. *Ibn-Tamas v. United States,* 407 A.2d 626 (1979).

8. *State v. Baker,* N.H. 424 A.2d 171 (1981).

9. *Smith v. State,* 247 Ga. 612, 277 S.E.2d 678 (1981), and *State v. Anaya,* Me. 438 A.2d 892 (1981).

10. See, for example *State v. Thomas,* 66 Ohio St.2d (1981), and *Hawthorne v. State,* 408 Fla. So.2d Dist. Ct. App. 801 (1982).

11. See Schecter (1982) for a discussion of the Carter administration's leadership on family and domestic violence issues.

12. "Program Description," undated, National Clearinghouse for the Defense of Battered Women, Philadelphia.

13. "Organizational Description," undated, National Clearinghouse for the Defense of Battered Women, Philadelphia.

14. Confidential interview conducted by Patricia Gagné on 5 October 1992.

15. *Double-Time: Newsletter of the National Clearinghouse for the Defense of Battered Women* 2.3 (December 1993): 20.

16. Ibid., 11.

17. Ibid., 2.

18. See note 12.

19. Ibid.

20. Ibid.

21. Sue Osthoff, "Become a Supporting Member of the National Clearinghouse for the Defense of Battered Women," letter, October 1992, Philadelphia.

22. *People v. Garcia,* Monterey County, Cal., Sup. Ct. 4259 (1977).

23. *State v. Wanrow,* 88 Wash. 2d 221, 559 P.2d 548 (1977).

24. Ibid., 551.

25. Ibid., 550.

26. Ibid., 550.

27. *Ibn-Tamas v. United States,* 1979.

28. Ibid., 640.

29. *Ibn-Tamas v. United States,* 455 A.2d 893 D.C. App. 894 (1983).

30. Cases that have cited *Ibn-Tamas* on appeal include the following: *Hawthorne v. State,* 408 So.2d Fla. Dist. Ct. App. 801 (1982); *Smith v. State,* 247 Ga. 612, 277 S.E.2d 678 (1981); *People v. Minnis,* 118 Ill. App. 3d 345, 455 N.E.2d 209 (1983); *State v. Hodges,* 239 Kan. 63, 716 P.2d 563 (1986); *State v. Anaya,* 438 Me. A.2d 892 (1981); *State v. Hennum,* 441 Minn. N.W.2d 793 (1989); *State v. Williams,* 787 S.W.2d Mo. Ct. App. 308 (1990); *State v. Kelly,* 97 N.J. 178, 478 A.2d 364 (1984); *People v. Torres,* 128 Misc. 2d 129, 488 N.Y. Supp. S.2d Sup. Ct. 358 (1985); and *State v. Allery,* 101 Wash. 2d 591, 682 P.2d 312 (1984).

31. *Ibn-Tamas v. United States,* 1983, 895.

32. *State v. Baker,* N.H. 424 A.2d 171 (1980).

33. Ibid., 172.

34. Ibid., 173.

35. *Smith v. State,* 682.

36. See *Smith v. State* and *State v. Anaya.*

37. *Smith v. State,* 682.

38. Ibid.

39. Ibid., 679.

40. Ibid.

41. Ibid. This reasoning addresses the "beyond the ken of the average juror" criteria of the rules of evidence.

42. Ibid., 680.

43. *Hawthorne v. State,* 408 So.2d Fla. Dist. Ct. App. 801 (1982); *State v. Allery,* 682 Wash. P.2d 312 (1984); *State v. Kelly,* 478 N.J. A.2d 364 (1984).

44. *State v. Anaya,* 438 Me. A.2d 892 (1981).

45. Ibid., 893.

46. Ibid., 892, 893.

47. Ibid., 893.

48. Ibid., 894.

49. For examples, see *State v. Kelly* and *People v. Torres* 488 N.Y. S.2d Sup. Ct. 358, 359 (1985).

50. *State v. Hudley,* 693 Kan. P.2d 475, 479 (1985).

51. See Ohio H.B. 484 (enacted 1990) and *State v. Koss,* 551 Ohio N.E. 2d 970 (1990), which overturned *State v. Thomas,* 66 Ohio St. 2d 518 (1980); Louisiana Evidence Code, Article 404 (enacted 1989), which overturned *State v. Necaise,* 466 La. So.2d 660 (1985).

52. *People v. Minnis,* 455 Ill. N.E.2d App. 4 Dist. 209 (1983).

53. Ibid., 215.

54. Ibid., 217.

55. *State v. Leidholm,* 334 N.D. N.W.2d 811 (1983), 816.

56. Ibid., 813.

57. *State v. Hudley.*

58. Ibid., 475, 476.

59. Ibid., 476.

60. Ibid.

61. Ibid., 477.

62. Ibid., 478.

63. Ibid., 479.

64. *State v. Norman,* 89 N.C. App. 384 (1988).
65. Ibid., 587.
66. Ibid.
67. Ibid., 588.
68. *State v. Norman,* 378 N.C. S.E.2d (1989), 10.
69. *State v. Norman,* 89 N.C. App. 384 (1988), 589.
70. *State v. Norman* (1989), 8.
71. Ibid., 15.
72. *State v. Norman* (1989), 15.
73. *State v. Stewart,* 763 Kan. P.2d 572 (1988).
74. Ibid., 579.
75. Ibid., 574.
76. Ibid.
77. Ibid., 573.
78. *State v. Mott,* Ariz. CR-95–0247-PR (1997).

4. The Ohio Battered Women's Movement and the Celeste Clemencies

1. Prior to the case of *State v. Thomas* (66 Ohio St.2d 518 [1981]), in Ohio the admission of expert testimony about battered woman syndrome was left to the discretion of individual judges.
2. Ibid.
3. *State v. Koss* (49 Ohio St.3d 213 [1990]).
4. Mo. Ann. Stat. (Crimes and Punishment) sec. 563.0332 (Vernon 1991; enacted 1987).
5. La. Code Evid. Ann. art. 404(A)(2) (West 1989; enacted 1989).
6. Ariz. Rev. Stat. Ann. sec. 13–415 (approved 1992).
7. Cal. Evid. Code sec. 1107 (West 1993; effective 1991).
8. Ga. Code Ann. sec. 16–3-21(d) (Michie 1994; approved 1993).
9. Ky. Rev. Stat. Ann. sec. 503.010(3) (Michie 1994; effective 1992).
10. Md. Cts. and Jud. Proc. Code Ann. sec. 10–916; (enacted 1991).
11. Mass. Gen. Laws Ann. ch. 233, sec. 23E (West 1994; effective 1994).
12. Nev. Rev. Stat. sec. 48.061 (effective 1993).
13. Okla. Stat. Ann. tit. 22, sec. 40.7 (effective 1992).
14. S.C. Code Ann. sec. 17–23–170 (Law. Co-op. 1995; effective 1995).

15. Tex. Penal Code Ann. sec. 19.06 (West 1992; effective 1991) and Tex. Code Crim. Pro. Ann. art. 38.36 (Vernon 1995; effective 1994).

16. Utah Code Ann. sec. 76–2-402(5) (effective 1994).

17. Va. Code sec. 19.2–270.6 (effective 1993).

18. Wyo. Stat. (Crimes and Offenses) sec. 6–1-203 (1993; enacted 1993).

19. National Clearinghouse for the Defense of Battered Women, "Legislative Update," February 1997, Philadelphia.

20. H. Con. Res. 89, 102nd Cong., 1st sess.; Public Law 102–57 (enacted 1992).

21. G. Caplan, "Battered Wives, Battered Justice," *National Review* (24 February 1991): 39–43; D. Iseman, "Clemency: The Decision Heard 'Round the World,' " *Youngstown, Ohio, Vindicator* (Saturday, 6 January 1991): 2B; A. Rooney, "Celeste Declares Open Season on Ohio Men," *Columbus Dispatch* (Wednesday, 12 December 1990): 11A; R. Yocum, "Women's Clemency Angers Prosecutors," *Columbus Dispatch* (Sunday, 27 January 1991): 5F.

22. Although some scholars (e.g., Miller 1994) have called for gender-neutral changes in self-defense law, it appears that the general consensus within the movement has been to address the social and physical differences between women and men by focusing on and changing the inherent androcentric biases in the law.

23. Confidential interview conducted by Patricia Gagné on 28 September 1992.

24. "Announcements: Women Together Emergency Shelter House Opens," *WomenSpace Newsletter* (undated; ca. December 1976 or early 1977): 4–5; 3201 Euclid Avenue, Cleveland.

25. The majority of newsletters cited herein are undated. One of the founders explained that unfortunately the organization did not realize the potential historical value of its publications and was not very good at dating them. I have made an effort to determine approximate publication dates by referring to event dates listed in articles and announcements.

26. "Women Together Working for Crisis Housing," *WomenSpace Newsletter* (ca. 1976): 1.

27. "Announcements: Women Together Emergency Shelter House Opens," *WomenSpace Newsletter* (ca. 1977): 1.

28. Confidential interview conducted by Patricia Gagné on 9 July 1992.

29. Aides to the governor believed it was best to keep the clemency review out of the public eye as much as possible, thus precluding the involvement of grassroots support.

30. Confidential interview conducted by Patricia Gagné on 21 July 1992.

31. "Am. Sub. H.B. 484," undated, summary of the history of H.B. 484, Columbus.

32. Interview with former governor Richard F. Celeste conducted by Patricia Gagné on 13 August 1992 in Columbus.

33. Interview with former first lady Dagmar Celeste conducted by Patricia Gagné on 26 June 1991 in Columbus.

34. State of Ohio Executive Department Office of the Governor, "Executive Order 87–22: Creating the Governor's Interagency Council on Women's Issues" (10 June 1987), Ohio Historical Society, Box 2421, Columbus.

35. "Feminist Policy Criteria," undated, Ohio Historical Society, Box 2521, Columbus.

36. This bureau was headed by a cabinet member who was a Women Together founder.

37. "Attachment #1, Letter to Mr. George W. Wilson, Director, Ohio Department of Rehabilitation and Correction," 9 October 1989, included with "Memorandum to Dagmar," 28 December 1989, Ohio Historical Society, Series 4124, Box 4, Columbus.

38. Ibid.

39. "Interoffice Memorandum from Richard F. Celeste, Governor, to Linda Ammons and Paul Goggin," 8 January 1990, Ohio Historical Society, Series 4124, Box 4, Columbus.

40. Confidential interview conducted by Patricia Gagné on 17 August 1992.

41. "Memorandum: To Dagmar Celeste, First Lady, From Carl E. Anderson," 18 October 1989, Ohio Historical Society, Box 6, Columbus.

42. "Memorandum to Governor Richard F. Celeste Re: Battered Women's Press Conference Talking Points," 21 December 1990, Ohio Historical Society, Box 6, Columbus.

43. "Letter from the Office of the Governor to Elizabeth M. Schneider, Ph.D.," 5 January 1990, and "Letter from the Franklin County Public Defender to the Office of the Governor," 17 January 1989, Ohio Historical Society, Series 4143, Box 2454, Columbus; "Letters" and "Drafts of Legislation," Ohio Historical Society, Series 4143, Box 2454, Columbus.

44. "Memorandum to Ohio Department of Rehabilitation and Correction Central Office from the Ohio Reformatory for Women," 15 February 1990, Marysville, Ohio.

45. M. S. Black, "Battered Spousal/Woman Syndrome" (report prepared for the Ohio Department of Rehabilitation and Correction, 17 April 1990, Columbus).

46. Confidential interview conducted by Patricia Gagné on 14 August 1991.

47. "More Information Needed on Support Groups for Incarcerated Battered Women," *Double Time: Newsletter of the National Clearinghouse for the Defense of Battered Women* (October 1991), Philadelphia.

48. "The Road to Clemency for Battered Women: Learning to Utilize the Media," *Double Time: Newsletter of the National Clearinghouse for the Defense of Battered Women* (Spring/Summer 1993), Philadelphia.

49. "Manual on Clemency Now Available," *Double-Time: Newsletter of the National Clearinghouse for the Defense of Battered Women* (October 1991), Philadelphia. The manual, *Commutation for Women Who Defended Themselves against Abusive Partners: An Advocacy Manual and Guide to Legal Issues* (spring 1991), was written by three third-year law students, Lisa Sheehy, Melissa Reinberg, and Deborah Kirchwey, under the direction of feminist legal scholar Elizabeth Schneider in Boston.

50. "Clemency Organizing Projects," July 1996, National Clearinghouse for the Defense of Battered Women, Philadelphia.

5. Clemency after Celeste

1. Confidential interview conducted by Patricia Gagné on 18 March 1994.

2. "Governor Commutes Women's Terms," *Louisville, Kentucky, Courier-Journal* (Saturday, 29 May 1993): A4; Associated Press, "Governor Moves at Snail's Pace on Clemencies, Women's Group Says," Files/librarywire/96wireheadlines, 6 May 1996, Sacramento, Calif.

3. Confidential interview conducted by Patricia Gagné on 22 March 1994.

4. Ibid., 25 February 1994; "Battered Women Syndrome Defense Raised," *The Florida Bar News* (Monday, 1 March 1993), Tallahassee.

5. The cases in which expert testimony was disallowed, with the decision upheld on appeal, were *Kriscumas v. State,* Md. Ct. Spec.

App. 86–1072 (9 July 1987) and *Friend v. State,* Md. Ct. Spec. App. 88–483 (12 December 1988).

6. Judith A. Wolfer, "Maryland's Clemency Project: One Approach to Advocacy," *The Exchange: A Forum on Domestic Violence* 4.2 (1992): 1, National Abuse Prevention Center, Washington, D.C.

7. Ibid., 1, 8.

8. Ibid., 8.

9. Annotated Code of Maryland, Subtitle 5, Maryland Parole Commission, 4–501.

10. "Maryland's Clemency Project," 8.

11. Ibid.

12. Annotated Code of Maryland, Subtitle 9, Courts and Judicial Proceedings, 10–916.

13. "Maryland's Clemency Project," 9.

14. Ibid.

15. Battered women's testimony, hearings on H.B. 1252/53, 1992. Before the Subcommittee on Intellectual Property and Judicial Administration of the House Committee on the Judiciary, 102d Congress, 2d session (1992; statement of Governor William Donald Schaefer), as cited in Murphy 1993, 1285.

16. Interview, 18 March 1994; "Maryland's Clemency Project," 9.

17. "Maryland's Clemency Project," 9.

18. Ibid., 11; Public Justice Center, Domestic Violence Taskforce and the House of Ruth of Baltimore, "Twice Imprisoned: Confidential Report and Recommendation on Battered Women Incarcerated in Maryland," 23 January 1991, prepared for William Donald Schaefer, governor, Baltimore.

19. "Maryland's Clemency Project," 11.

20. Interview, 8 October 1996; Mary Becker, "Media Advisory News Conference, Tues., May 30, 10:00 A.M.@ The University of Chicago Law School: Illinois Clemency Project for Battered Women Petitions Gov. Edgar to Release 18 Convicted of Killing Partners," http://www-news.uchicago.edu/docs/5.25.95 _Battered_Women.html, 25 May 1995.

21. Confidential personal correspondence received by Patricia Gagné on 20 March 1997.

22. *People v. Aris,* 215 Cal. App. 3d 1178, 264 Cal. Rptr. 167 (1984).

23. Jane Gross, "Abused Women Who Kill Seek a Way Out of Cells," *New York Times* (Tuesday, 15 September 1992): A1, A12.

24. Ibid.

25. Confidential interview conducted by Patricia Gagné on 13 February 1997.

26. Gross, "Abused Women Who Kill," A1, A12.

27. Patt Morrison, "Legislators Listen to Women Who Killed," *Los Angeles Times* (Wednesday, 18 September 1991): A3, A17.

28. Confidential telephone conversation between Patricia Gagné and a California activist on 25 March 1997.

29. "34 California Killers Seek Clemency, Cite Battered-Woman Defense," *Columbus Dispatch* (Tuesday, 3 March 1992): 8A.

30. California Constitution, art. 5, §8.

31. Confidential interview conducted by Patricia Gagné on 14 February 1997.

32. Eli Rosenblatt, eli@holonet.net, "Self Defense Is Not a Crime," California Coalition for Battered Women in Prison, 2 April 1994, Berkeley, Calif., private e-mail message to Patricia Gagné from Lee P. Jones lpjone01@ulkyvm.louisville.edu, 3 April 1994.

33. Frank Phillips, "Weld Relaxes Prison Appeal by Battered Women," *Boston Globe* (Friday, 27 September 1991): 17.

34. Mass. Gen. Law, chap. 233, sec. 1, §23E.

35. *Commonwealth v. Rodriguez,* 633 Mass. N.E.2d 1039 (1994).

36. ABC News, "Framingham Eight: The Women Who Fought Back," Films for the Humanities, 1994, Princeton, N.J.

37. Confidential interview conducted by Patricia Gagné on 6 February 1997.

38. Stacey Kabat, "Battered Women Need Help, Not Jail," *Boston Sunday Herald* (23 June 1991): 23; the Massachusetts Clemency Project, "Battered Women Fighting Back!: A Massachusetts Advocacy and Defense Network for Battered Women," (Spring 1992): 1.

39. The Massachusetts Clemency Project, "Battered Women Fighting Back!."

40. Ibid.

41. National Clearinghouse for the Defense of Battered Women, "Clemency Organizing Projects," 20 May 1992, Philadelphia.

42. Kabat, "Battered Women Need Help," 23.

43. Ibid.

44. Governor William F. Weld, "Commutation Guidelines and Petition," memo "[t]o the Advisory Board of Pardons and Other Interested Parties," September 1991, Executive Department, State House, Boston, 2.

45. Kabat, "Battered Women Need Help," 23.

46. Toni Locy, "Weld Urged to Free 8 Women," *Boston Globe* (Saturday, 15 February 1992): 15.

47. Luz Delgado, "Woman Who Killed Abusive Lover Is Denied Commutation Hearing," *Boston Globe* (Tuesday, 21 July 1992): 3; ABC News, "The Framingham Eight."

48. Mass. Gen. Law, chap. 233, sec. 1, 23E.

49. Confidential interview conducted by Patricia Gagné on 29 January 1997.

50. *Rules of Executive Clemency of Florida,* undated (last amended revision, 18 December 1991), pamphlet.

51. "How WIP Works," Women in Prison Committee Project, undated, San Antonio, Fla.; Margo Harakas, "Can Panels Blaze Legal Trail for Battered Women?" *Ft. Lauderdale Sun-Sentinel* (Sunday, 13 December 1992): 1E, 6E.

52. "Waiver Procedures for Battered Woman Syndrome Cases," 1 January 1992, Modifying Rules of Executive Clemency of Florida.

53. *Hawthorne v. State,* 377 So.2d 780.

54. *Hawthorne v. State,* Fla. App. 408 So.2d 801 (1982).

55. *Rogers v. State,* 616 Fla. So.2d App. 1 Dist. 1098 (1993).

56. Jeff Schweers, "Battered Women Syndrome Defense Raised," *The Florida Bar News* (Monday, 1 March 1993): 14.

57. "Waiver Instructions for Battered Woman Syndrome Cases," Office of Executive Clemency January 1992, Tallahassee, Fla.

58. Schweers, "Battered Women Syndrome," 14.

59. Interviews, 25 February 1994 and 28 January 1997; Deborah Sharp, "Battered Women Who Killed Mates Fight for Freedom," *USA Today* (Monday, 7 December 1992): 12A.

60. Donna O'Neal, "Clemency May Be Last Hope for Battered Killers," *The Orlando Sentinel* (Thursday, 2 September 1993): B1, B5.

61. Orval Jackson, "Coalition Wants State to Free Woman Who Killed Husband," *Tampa Tribune* (Thursday, 28 November 1991): 6B.

62. Steve Orlando and Phil Willon, "Pinellas Woman Who Killed Husband Goes Free under New Policy," *The Tampa Tribune* (Thursday, 15 July 1993): B1, B4.

63. Ibid.

64. Rick Barry, "Killer's Sentence Commuted," *Tampa Tribune* (Tuesday, 9 November 1993): B1.

65. *Commonwealth v. Rose,* Ky. 725 S.W. 2d 588 (1987).

66. *Commonwealth v. Craig,* Ky. 783 S.W.2d 387 (1990), 387.

67. Kentucky Revised Statute 503.010, sec. 1(3).

68. Ibid., sec. 2(3).

69. Ibid., sec. 4(4).

70. Confidential interviews conducted by Patricia Gagné on 22 and 29 January 1997 and 24 February 1997.

71. "Clemency Organizing Projects," 7, National Clearinghouse for the Defense of Battered Women, July 1996, Philadelphia.

72. "Justice for Abused Women," *Louisville Courier-Journal* (Saturday, 17 June 1995): B5.

73. Fran Ellers, "Women's Networking Makes a Difference for Inmates," *Louisville Courier-Journal* (Tuesday, 12 December 1995): A1.

74. Sherry Currens, executive director, Kentucky Domestic Violence Association, "Clemency Plan," 22 June 1995.

75. Ellers, "Women's Networking."

76. Fran Ellers, "A Small Smile Can Be a Big Step for 10 Women Paroled From Prison," *Louisville Courier-Journal* (Friday, 5 January 1996): A1, A7.

77. Marguerite Neill Thomas, assistant public advocate, to Marsha Weinstein, executive director, Commission on Women, 21 November 1995.

78. Fran Ellers, "Jones Grants Women Clemency: Nine Inmates Say Abuse Led Them to Commit Crimes," *Louisville Courier-Journal* (Tuesday, 12 December 1995): 1A, 12A.

79. Ibid.

80. For examples, see "Justice for Abused Women," *Louisville Courier-Journal* (17 June 1995); "Retroactive Fairness: Battered Women Serving Time for Striking Back Need a Break from Lawmakers," *Lexington Herald-Leader* (Sunday, 18 June 1995; editorial); "Improve a Good Law: Sentences of Abused Women Can Be Reviewed More Easily," *Lexington Herald-Leader* (Saturday, 12 August 1995; editorial).

6. Identity, Strategy, and Feminist Tactics in the Clemency Movement

1. Willie Horton became a conservative symbol of the problems with liberal social policies and a liberal symbol of the racism inherent in conservative politics. His case was first raised by Senator Al Gore (D-Tennessee) in a presidential primary debate with Democratic Massachusetts governor Michael Dukakis. Horton was an African-

American convicted murderer who was on a weekend furlough in Massachusetts when he broke into the home of a white couple. He bound the man and raped the woman. Afterward, the couple identified him as the perpetrator. The Massachusetts legislature subsequently passed a law, overriding Dukakis's veto, rescinding the state's weekend furlough program for felons. In the 1988 presidential race between Dukakis and Vice President George Bush, conservative groups produced advertisements using Willie Horton to show the problems with liberal criminal justice policies. Liberals subsequently accused Bush of inflaming and capitalizing on white racist attitudes to win the election.

2. Confidential interview conducted by Patricia Gagné on 14 February 1997.

3. Ibid., 29 January 1997; Lindsay Campbell, "Kentucky Commission on Women 1994–1995," Frankfort, Ky., 13.

4. "Victims Deserve More Than Clemency," *The Frankfort, Kentucky, State Journal* (Wednesday, 13 December 1995): 4A.

5. Confidential interview conducted by Patricia Gagné on 6 February 1997.

6. Interview with former first lady Dagmar Celeste conducted by Patricia Gagné on 26 June 1991 in Columbus.

7. These reforms include a program of comparable worth for state employees, the establishment of a day care center in the state office tower, and recommendations to the governor on how to coordinate the services provided to victims of domestic violence and how to establish unified responses to batterers. The efforts of feminists in the Celeste administration are more fully explicated in Gagné 1993 and Taylor 1996.

8. See Kanter 1977 for analogous observations about the corporate world.

9. Confidential interview conducted by Patricia Gagné on 14 August 1991.

10. Interview with former Governor Richard F. Celeste conducted by Patricia Gagné on 13 August 1992 in Columbus.

7. The Dissemination of Identity-Based Movements

1. Confidential interview conducted by Patricia Gagné on 20 August 1993.

Bibliography

PRIMARY SOURCES

Newsletters

"Announcements: Women Together Emergency Shelter House Opens." Undated. *WomenSpace Newsletter,* 3201 Euclid Avenue, Cleveland, Ohio, 4–5. Copied.

"Battered Women Fighting Back!: A Massachusetts Advocacy and Defense Network for Battered Women." Spring 1992. The Massachusetts Clemency Project, 1. Copied.

"Clemency Organizing Projects." 20 May 1992. National Clearinghouse for the Defense of Battered Women, 125 South 9th Street #302, Philadelphia, PA 19107. Copied.

"Clemency Organizing Projects." July 1996. National Clearinghouse for the Defense of Battered Women, 125 South 9th Street #302, Philadelphia, PA 19107. Copied.

Commutation for Women Who Defended Themselves against Abusive Partners: An Advocacy Manual and Guide to Legal Issues. Spring 1991. Lisa Sheehy, Melissa Reinberg, and Deborah Kirchwey. Written under the direction of feminist legal scholar Elizabeth Schneider, Boston. Copied.

"Legislative Update." February 1997. National Clearinghouse for the Defense of Battered Women, 125 South 9th Street #302, Philadelphia, PA 19107. Copied.

"Manual on Clemency Now Available." October 1991. *Double-Time: Newsletter of the National Clearinghouse for the Defense of Battered Women,* 125 South 9th Street #302, Philadelphia, Pa., 19107. Copied. "Maryland's Clemency Project: One Approach to Advocacy," 4.2 (Winter 1992). Judith A. Wolfer. *The Exchange: A Forum on Domestic Violence.* National Woman Abuse Prevention Center, 1112 Sixteenth Street NW, Suite 920, Washington, DC 20036.

"More Information Needed on Support Groups for Incarcerated Battered Women." October 1991. *Double-Time: Newsletter of the National Clearing-house for the Defense of Battered Women,* 125 South 9th Street #302, Philadelphia, PA 19107. Copied.
"The Road to Clemency for Battered Women: Learning to Utilize the Media." Spring/Summer 1993. *Double-Time: Newsletter of the National Clearing-house for the Defense of Battered Women,* 125 South 9th Street #302, Philadelphia, PA 19107. Copied.
"Waiver Procedures for Battered Woman Syndrome Cases." 1 January 1992. Modification to *Rules of Executive Clemency of Florida.* Copied.
"Women Together Working for Crisis Housing." Undated; ca. 1976. *Women-Space Newsletter,* 3201 Euclid Avenue, Cleveland, Ohio, 1. Copied.

Private Collections

Private collection of a confidential activist. "Clemency Plan." Sherry Currens. Kentucky Domestic Violence Association, P.O. Box 356, Frankfort, KY 40602. 22 June 1995.
Private collection of a confidential activist. "Commutation Guidelines and Petition." William F. Weld, governor of Massachusetts. September 1991.
Private collection of a confidential activist. "Kentucky Commission on Women 1994–1995," 13. Lindsay Campbell. Frankfort, Kentucky. Undated.
Private collection of a confidential activist. Marsha Weinstein, executive director, Commission on Women, to Marguerite Neill Thomas. Letter. 21 November 1995.
Private collection of a confidential activist. "Twice Imprisoned: Confidential Report and Recommendation on Battered Women Incarcerated in Maryland." Public Justice Center, Inc., Domestic Violence Taskforce, and the House of Ruth of Baltimore, Inc. 23 January 1991.
Kentucky Domestic Violence Association, P.O. Box 356, Frankfort, KY 40602. "Clemency Plan." 22 June 1995.
Ohio Historical Society, Columbus, Ohio. Box 2421. "Executive Order 87–22: Creating the Governor's Interagency Council on Women's Issues." State of Ohio Executive Department Office of the Governor. 10 June 1987.
———. Box 4143, Series 2454. "Letter From the Franklin County Public Defender to the Office of the Governor." 17 January 1989.
———. Box 6. "Memorandum: To Dagmar Celeste, First Lady, from Carl E. Anderson." 18 October 1989.
———. Series 4124, Box 4. "Attachment #1, Letter to Mr. George W. Wilson, Director, Ohio Department of Rehabilitation and Correction." 9 October 1989; included with "Memorandum to Dagmar." 28 December 1989.
———. Box 4143, Series 2454. "Letter from the Office of the Governor to Elizabeth M. Schneider, Ph.D." 5 January 1990.

————. Series 4124, Box 4. "Interoffice Memorandum from Richard F. Celeste, Governor, to Linda Ammons and Paul Goggin." 8 January 1990.

————. Box 6. "Memorandum to Governor Richard F. Celeste Re: Battered Women's Press Conference Talking Points." 21 December 1990.

————. Box 2521. "Feminist Policy Criteria." Undated.

Ohio Reformatory for Women, Marysville, Ohio. "Memorandum to Ohio Department of Rehabilitation and Correction Central Office." 15 February 1990.

————. "Application Process for Application for Clemency." Memorandum from CRISP coordinator to president of the LIFE Group. 17 May 1990.

Public Document

Black, M.S. "Battered Spousal/Woman Syndrome." Report prepared for the Ohio Department of Rehabilitation and Correction. Columbus, Ohio, 17 April 1990.

Rules of Executive Clemency of Florida. State of Florida, undated. Pamphlet.

Video

Canny, Pauline, producer. *Framingham Eight: The Women Who Fought Back.* ABC News video collection. Princeton, N.J.: Films for the Humanities, Inc., 1994.

Internet

"Did you know that: Every fifteen seconds a woman in the U.S. is beaten. One California state prison study found that 93% of women who had killed their mates had been battered by them. There are hundreds of women in California state prisons for killing their abusers." Undated. http://www.igc.org/justice/prisons/women/ccbwp-brochure.html. California Coalition for Battered Women In Prison, 474 Valencia St. #230, San Francisco, CA 94103.

Becker, Mary. "Media Advisory: News Conference, Tues., May 30, 10:00 A.M. @ The University of Chicago Law School: Illinois Clemency Project for Battered Women Petitions Gov. Edgar to Release 18 Convicted of Killing Partners." 25 May 1995. http://www-news.uchicago.edu/docs/5.25.95-Battered_Women.html.

SECONDARY SOURCES

Books and Parts of Books

Acklesberg, Martha A. "Communities, Resistance, and Women's Activism: Some Implications for a Democratic Polity." In *Women and the Politics of Empowerment,* edited by Ann Bookman and Sandra Morgen, 297–313. Philadelphia: Temple University Press, 1988.

226   *Battered Women's Justice*

Adams, David. "Treatment Models of Men Who Batter: A Profeminist Analysis." In *Feminist Perspectives on Wife Abuse,* edited by Kersti Yllö and Michele Bograd, 176–99. Beverly Hills, Calif.: Sage, 1988.

Alonso, Ana María. "Gender, Power, and Historical Memory: Discourses of Serrano Resistance." In *Feminists Theorize the Political,* edited by Judith Butler and Joan W. Scott, 404–25. New York: Routledge, 1992.

American Psychiatric Association. *Diagnostic and Statistical Manual of Mental Disorders,* 4th ed. Washington, D.C.: American Psychiatric Association, 1994.

Ardener, Edwin. "The 'Problem' Revisited." In *Perceiving Women,* edited by Shirley Ardener, 19–27. London: Malaby, 1975.

Ardener, Shirley, ed. *Defining Females: The Nature of Women in Society.* New York: Wiley, 1978.

Barone, Michael, and Grant Ujifusa. *The Almanac of American Politics 1988.* Washington, D.C.: National Journal, 1987.

———. *The Almanac of American Politics 1992.* Washington, D.C.: National Journal, 1991.

———. *The Almanac of American Politics 1994.* Washington, D.C.: National Journal, 1993.

———. *The Almanac of American Politics 1996.* Washington, D.C.: National Journal, 1995.

Belknap, Joanne. *The Invisible Woman: Gender, Crime, and Justice.* Boston: Wadsworth Publishing Company, 1996.

Benhabib, Seyla, and Drucilla Cornell. "Introduction: Beyond the Politics of Gender." In *Feminism as Critique,* edited by Seyla Benhabib and Drucilla Cornell, 1–15. Minneapolis: University of Minnesota Press, 1987.

Berk, R., S. F. Berk, D. Loseke, and D. Rauma. "Mutual Combat and Other Family Violence Myths." In *The Dark Side of Families,* edited by D. Finkelhor, R. J. Gelles, G. T. Hotaling, and M. A. Straus, 197–212. Beverly Hills, Calif.: Sage, 1983.

Bernstein, Richard J. Introduction. In *Habermas and Modernity,* edited by Richard J. Bernstein, 1–32. Cambridge, Mass.: The MIT Press, 1985.

Bochnak, Elizabeth, ed. *Women's Self-Defense Cases: Theory and Practice.* Charlottesville, Va.: The Michie Company, 1967.

Bograd, Michele. "Feminist Perspectives on Wife Abuse: An Introduction." In *Feminist Perspectives on Wife Abuse,* edited by Kersti Yllö and Michele Bograd, 11–25. Beverly Hills, Calif.: Sage, 1988.

Browne, Angela. *When Battered Women Kill.* New York: The Free Press, 1987.

Burgess, Robert L., and Patricia Draper. "The Explanation of Family Violence: The Role of Biological, Behavioral, and Cultural Selection." In *Family Violence, Crime and Justice.* edited by Lloyd Ohlin and Michael Tonry, 59–116. Chicago: University of Chicago Press, 1989.

Carden, Maren Lockwood. *The New Feminist Movement*. New York: Russell Sage, 1974.

Cassell, Joan. *A Group Called Women: Sisterhood and Symbolism in the Feminist Movement*. Prospect Heights, Ill.: Waveland Press, Inc., 1977.

Charmaz, Kathy. "The Grounded Theory Method: An Explication and Interpretation." In *Contemporary Field Research: A Collection of Readings,* edited by Robert M. Emerson, 109–26. Prospect Heights, Ill.: Waveland Press, 1983.

Crawford, Alan. *Thunder on the Right: The "New Right" and the Politics of Resentment*. New York: Pantheon Books, 1980.

Collins, Patricia Hill. *Black Feminist Thought: Knowledge, Consciousness, and the Politics of Empowerment*. London: HarperCollins Academic, 1990.

D'Emilio, John. *Sexual Politics, Sexual Communities: The Making of a Homosexual Minority in the United States, 1940–1970*. Chicago: University of Chicago Press, 1983.

Dershowitz, Alan M. *The Abuse Excuse and Other Cop-Outs, Sob Stories, and Evasions of Responsibility*. Boston: Little Brown, 1994.

Dickstein, Leah J., and Carol C. Nadelson. *Family Violence: Emerging Issues of a National Crisis*. Washington, D.C.: American Psychiatric Press, Inc., 1989.

Dobash, R. Emerson, and Russell Dobash. *Women, Violence and Social Change*. New York: Routledge, 1992.

———. "Research as Social Action: The Struggle for Battered Women." In *Feminist Perspectives on Wife Abuse,* edited by Kersti Yllö and Michele Bograd, 51–74. Beverly Hills, Calif.: Sage, 1988.

———. *Violence against Wives: A Case Against the Patriarchy*. New York: The Free Press, 1979.

Echols, Alice. *Daring to Be Bad: Radical Feminism in America, 1967–1975*. Minneapolis: University of Minnesota Press, 1989.

Elshtain, Jean Bethke. *Public Man, Private Woman: Women in Social and Political Thought*. Princeton, N.J.: Princeton University Press, 1981.

Evans, Sara. *Personal Politics*. New York: Vintage Books, 1979.

Ewing, Charles Patrick. *Battered Women Who Kill: Psychological Self-Defense as Legal Justification*. Lexington, Mass.: Lexington Books, 1987.

Faludi, Susan. *Backlash: The Undeclared War against American Women*. New York: Crown, 1991.

Fantasia, Rick. *Cultures of Solidarity*. Berkeley: University of California Press, 1988.

Farganis, James. *Readings in Social Theory: The Classic Tradition to Post-Modernism*. New York: McGraw-Hill, 1993.

Ferree, Myra Marx. "The Political Context of Rationality: Rational Choice Theory and Resource Mobilization." In *Frontiers in Social Movement Theory,* edited by Aldon D. Morris and Carol McClurg Mueller, 29–52. New Haven, Conn.: Yale University Press, 1992.

228   *Battered Women's Justice*

Ferree, Myra Marx, and Beth B. Hess. *Controversy and Coalition: The New Feminist Movement.* Boston: Twayne Publishers, 1985.

Flacks, Richard. *Youth and Social Change.* Chicago: Markham Publishing Co., 1971.

Foucault, Michel. *Discipline and Punish: The Birth of the Prison.* New York: Random House, 1979.

Freeman, Jo. *The Politics of Women's Liberation.* New York: McKay, 1975.

Gamson, William. *The Strategy of Social Protest.* Homewood, Ill.: Dorsey Press, 1975.

———. "The Social Psychology of Collective Action." In *Frontiers in Social Movement Theory,* edited by Aldon D. Morris and Carol McClurg Mueller, 53–76. New Haven, Conn.: Yale University Press, 1992.

Gelles, Richard J. *The Violent Home: A Study of Physical Aggression between Husbands and Wives.* Beverly Hills, Calif.: Sage, 1974.

———. "An Exchange/Social Control Theory." In *The Dark Side of Families: Current Family Violence Research,* edited by David Finkelhor, Richard J. Gelles, Gerald T. Hotaling, and Murray Straus, 151–65. Beverly Hills, Calif.: Sage, 1983.

Gelles, Richard J. and Murray A. Straus. *Intimate Violence: The Causes and Consequences of Abuse in the American Family.* New York: Touchstone, 1988.

Gerlach, L.P., and V. H. Hine. *People, Power, Change: Movements of Social Transformation.* Indianapolis: Bobbs-Merrill, 1970.

Giles-Sims, Jean. *Wife-Battering: A Systems Theory Approach.* New York: Guilford, 1983.

Gillespie, Cynthia K. *Justifiable Homicide: Battered Women, Self-Defense and the Law.* Columbus: Ohio State University Press, 1989.

Gilligan, Carol. *In a Different Voice: Psychological Theory and Women's Development.* Cambridge, Mass.: Harvard University Press, 1982.

Graham, Dee L.R., with Edna I. Rawlings and Roberta K. Rigsby. *Loving to Survive: Sexual Terror, Men's Violence, and Women's Lives.* New York: New York University Press, 1994.

Graham, Dee L.R., Edna Rawlings, and Nelly Rimini. "Survivors of Terror: Battered Women, Hostages, and the Stockholm Syndrome." In *Feminist Perspectives on Wife Abuse,* edited by Kersti Yllö and Michele Bograd. Beverly Hills, Calif.: Sage, 1988.

Habermas, Jürgen. *Theory of Communicative Action.* Boston: Beacon Press, 1984.

———. "Neoconservative Culture Criticism in the United States and West Germany: An Intellectual Movement in Two Political Cultures." In *Habermas and Modernity,* edited by Richard J. Bernstein, 78–94. Cambridge, Mass.: The MIT Press, 1985.

Hall, R., and B. Sandler. *The Classroom Climate: A Chilly One for Women?* Washington, D.C.: Association of American Colleges, 1982.

Harding, Sandra. *The Science Question in Feminism.* Ithaca, N.Y.: Cornell University Press, 1986.

Helfgot, Joseph H. *Professional Reforming.* Lexington, Mass.: Lexington Books, 1981.

Hunt, Scott A., Robert D. Benford, and David A. Snow. "Identity Fields: Framing Processes and the Social Construction of Movement Identities." In *New Social Movements: From Ideology to Identity,* edited by Enrique Laraña, Hank Johnston, and Joseph R. Gusfield, 185–208. Philadelphia: Temple University Press, 1994.

Inglehart, Ronald. *The Silent Revolution: Changing Values and Political Styles among Western Publics.* Princeton: Princeton University Press, 1977.

———. "Political Action: The Impact of Values, Cognitive Level, and Social Background." In *Political Action: Mass Participation in Five Western Democracies,* edited by Samuel H. Barnes, Max Kaase, and Klause R. Allerbeck, 343–80. Beverly Hills, Calif.: Sage, 1979.

———. "Intergenerational Changes in Politics and Culture: The Shift from Materialist to Postmaterialist Value Priorities." In vol. 2, *Research in Political Sociology,* edited by R. J. Braungart. Greenwich, Conn.: JAI Press, 1986.

Jones, Ann. *Next Time She'll Be Dead: Battering and How to Stop It.* Boston: Beacon Press, 1994.

———. *Women Who Kill.* New York: Fawcett Columbine, 1980.

Kanter, Rosabeth Moss. *Men and Women of the Corporation.* New York: Basic Books, 1977.

Kelly, A. *Changing Schools and Changing Society: Some Reflections on the Girls in the Sciences and Technology Project.* New York: The Open University, 1984.

Klandermans, Bert. "The Social Construction of Protest and Multiorganizational Fields." In *Frontiers in Social Movement Theory,* edited by Aldon D. Morris and Carol McClurg Mueller, 77–103. New Haven, Conn.: Yale University Press, 1992.

Klandermans, Bert, and Sidney Tarrow. "Mobilization into Social Movements: Synthesizing European and American Approaches." In vol. 1, *From Structure to Action: Comparing Movement Participation across Cultures, International Social Movement Research,* 1–38. Greenwich, Conn.: JAI Press, 1988.

Klein, Ethel. *Gender Politics: From Consciousness to Mass Politics.* Cambridge, Mass.: Harvard University Press, 1984.

Kramarae, Cheris. *Women and Men Speaking: Frameworks for Analysis.* Rowley, Mass.: Newbury House, 1981.

Laraña, Enrique, Hank Johnston, and Joseph R. Gusfield, eds. *New Social Movements: From Ideology to Identity.* Philadelphia: Temple University Press, 1994.

Lasch, Christopher. *Haven in a Heartless World.* New York: Basic Books, 1977.

Littlejohn, Stephen W. *Theories of Human Communication.* 5th ed. Belmont, Calif.: Wadsworth Publishing Company, 1996.

Martin, Del. *Battered Wives.* San Francisco: Glide, 1976.

McAdam, Doug. *Freedom Summer.* New York: Oxford University Press, 1982.

———. *Political Process and the Development of Black Insurgency, 1930–1970.* Chicago: University of Chicago Press, 1988.

McAdam, Doug, John D. McCarthy, and Mayer N. Zald. "Social Movements." In *Handbook of Sociology,* edited by Neil Smelser. Newbury Park, Calif.: Sage, 1988.

McCarthy, John D., and Mayer N. Zald. *The Trend of Social Movements in America: Professionalization and Resource Mobilization.* Morristown, N.J.: General Learning Corporation, 1973.

Melucci, Alberto. *Nomads of the Present: Social Movements and Individual Needs in Contemporary Society.* Philadelphia: Temple University Press, 1989.

Mies, Maria. "Towards a Methodology for Feminist Research." In *Theories of Women's Studies,* edited by Gloria Bowles and Renate Duelli Klein. Boston: Routledge and Kegan Paul, 1983.

Moore, D.M. "Editor's Introduction: An Overview of the Problem." In *Battered Women,* edited by D. M. Moore, 7–32. Beverly Hills, Calif.: Sage, 1979.

Morgen, Sandra, and Ann Bookman. "Rethinking Women and Politics: An Introductory Essay." In *Women and the Politics of Empowerment,* edited by Ann Bookman and Sandra Morgen, 3–29. Philadelphia: Temple University Press, 1988.

Morris, Aldon D. *The Origins of the Civil Rights Movement: Black Communities Organizing for Change.* New York: The Free Press, 1984.

Morris, Aldon D., and Carol McClurg Mueller, eds. *Frontiers in Social Movement Theory.* New Haven, Conn.: Yale University Press, 1992.

Mouffe, Chantal. "Feminism, Citizenship and Radical Democratic Politics." In *Feminists Theorize the Political,* edited by Judith Butler and Joan W. Scott, 369–84. New York: Routledge, 1992.

Mueller, Carol McClurg. "Collective Consciousness, Identity Transformation, and the Rise of Women in Public Office in the United States." In *The Women's Movements of the United States and Western Europe: Consciousness, Political Opportunity, and Public Policy,* edited by Mary F. Katzenstein and Carol McClurg Mueller. Philadelphia: Temple University Press, 1987.

Neidig, P.H., and D. H. Friedman. *Spouse Abuse: A Treatment Program for Couples.* Champaign, Ill.: Research Press, 1984.

Oberschall, Anthony. *Social Conflict and Social Movements.* Englewood Cliffs, N.J.: Prentice-Hall, 1973.

Pagelow, Margaret Daley. *Family Violence.* New York: Praeger, 1984.

Perrow, Charles. "The Sixties Observed." In *The Dynamics of Social Movements,* edited by Mayer N. Zald and John D. McCarthy, 192–211. Cambridge, Mass.: Winthrop Publishers, 1979.

Phelan, Shane. *Identity Politics: Lesbian Feminism and the Limits of Community.* Philadelphia: Temple University Press, 1989.

Piven, Frances Fox, and Richard A. Cloward. *Poor People's Movements: Why They Succeed, How They Fail.* New York: Random House, 1977.

Pizzey, Erin. *Scream Quietly or the Neighbors Will Hear.* Hillside, N.J.: Enslow Publishers, 1977.

Pizzorno, Alessandro. "Political Science and Collective Identity in Industrial Conflict." In *The Resurgence of Class Conflict in Western Europe Since 1968,* edited by C. Crouch and A. Pizzorno, 277–98. New York: Homes and Meier, 1978.

Pleck, Elizabeth. *Domestic Tyranny: The Making of Social Policy against Family Violence from Colonial Times to the Present.* New York: Oxford University Press, 1987.

———. "Criminal Approaches to Family Violence." In vol. 11, *Family Violence, Crime and Justice: A Review of Research,* edited by Lloyd Ohlin and Michael Tonry, 19–57. Chicago: University of Chicago Press, 1989.

Reineke, M.J. "Out of Order: A Critical Perspective on Women in Religion." In *Women: A Feminist Perspective,* edited by Jo Freeman, 395–413. Mountain View, Calif.: Mayfield Publishing Co., 1989.

Richardson, Laurel. *The Dynamics of Sex and Gender: A Sociological Perspective,* 3d ed. New York: HarperCollins Publishers, 1988.

Rosewater, Lynne Bravo. "Battered or Schizophrenic? Psychological Tests Can't Tell." In *Feminist Perspectives on Wife Abuse,* edited by Kersti Yllö and Michele Bograd, 200–216. Beverly Hills, Calif.: Sage, 1988.

Rosewater, Lynne Bravo, and Lenore E. A. Walker, eds. *Handbook of Feminist Therapy: Women's Issues in Psychotherapy.* New York: Springer Publishing Company, 1985.

Rupp, Leila, and Verta Taylor. *Survival in the Doldrums: The American Women's Rights Movement, 1940 to the 1960s.* Columbus: The Ohio State University Press, 1990.

Saunders, Daniel G., and Sandra T. Azar. "Treatment Programs for Family Violence." In vol. 11, *Family Violence, Crime and Justice: A Review of Research,* edited by Lloyd Ohlin and Michael Tonry, 481–546. Chicago: University of Chicago Press, 1989.

Schechter, Susan. *Women and Male Violence: The Visions and Struggles of the Battered Women's Movement.* Boston: South End Press, 1982.

Sherman, Lawrence W., with Janell D. Schmidt and Dennis P. Rogan. *Policing Domestic Violence: Experiments and Dilemmas.* New York: Free Press, 1992.

Smith, Dorothy E. *The Conceptual Practices of Power: A Feminist Sociology of Knowledge.* Boston: Northeastern University Press, 1990.

Snell, Tracy L. "Women in Prison: Survey of State Prison Inmates, 1991." U.S. Department of Justice, Bureau of Justice Statistics. Washington: GPO, 1994.

Snow, David A., and Robert Benford. "Ideology, Frame Resonance, and Participant Mobilization." In *From Structure to Action: Comparing Social Movements across Cultures,* edited by Bert Klandermans, Hanspeter Kriesi, and Sidney Tarrow, 197–218. Greenwich, Conn.: JAI Press, 1988.

———. "Master Frames and Cycles of Protest." In *Frontiers in Social Movement Theory,* edited by Aldon D. Morris and Carol McClurg Mueller, 133–55. New Haven, Conn.: Yale University Press, 1992.

Sonkin, Daniel Jay, Del Martin, and Lenore E. A. Walker. *The Male Batterer: A Treatment Approach.* New York: Springer Publishing Company, 1985.

Stets, Jan E., and Murray A. Straus. "The Marriage License as a Hitting License: A Comparison of Assaults in Dating, Cohabitating, and Married Couples." In *Violence in Dating Relationships: Emerging Social Issues,* edited by Maureen A. Priog-Good and Jan E. Stets, 4: 161–80. New York: Praeger, 1989.

Straus, Murray A. "Wife Beating: How Common and Why?" In *The Social Causes of Husband-Wife Violence,* edited by Murray A. Straus and Gerald T. Hotaling, 23–38. Minneapolis: University of Minnesota Press, 1980.

Straus, Murray A., and Richard J. Gelles. "How Violent Are American Families? Estimates from the National Family Violence Resurvey and Other Studies." In *New Directions in Family Violence Research,* edited by Gerald T. Hotaling, David Finkelhor, John T. Kirkpatrick, and Murray A. Straus, 14–36. Beverly Hills, Calif.: Sage, 1988.

Strauss, Anselm, and Juliet Corbin. *Basics of Qualitative Research: Grounded Theory Procedures and Techniques.* Newbury Park, Calif.: Sage, 1990.

Straus, Murray A., Richard Gelles, and Suzanne Steinmetz. *Behind Closed Doors: Violence in the American Family.* New York: Harper and Row, 1980.

Steinmetz, Suzanne, and Murray A. Straus. *Violence in the Family.* New York: Harper and Row, 1974.

Tarrow, Sidney. *Struggles, Politics, and Reform: Collective Action, Social Movements, and Cycles of Protest.* Ithaca, N.Y.: Center for International Studies, Cornell University, 1991.

Taylor, Verta. *Rock-a-Bye Baby: Feminism, Self-Help, and Postpartum Depression.* New York: Routledge, 1996.

Taylor, Verta, and Nancy Whittier. "Collective Identity in Social Movement Communities: Lesbian Feminist Mobilization." In *Frontiers in Social*

Movement Theory, edited by Aldon D. Morris and Carol McClurg Mueller, 104–29. New Haven, Conn.: Yale University Press, 1992.

Theberge, N. "Women's Athletics and the Myth of Female Frailty." In *Women: A Feminist Perspective,* edited by Jo Freeman, 507–22. Mountain View, Calif.: Mayfield Publishing Co., 1989.

Tilly, Charles. *From Mobilization to Revolution.* Reading, Mass.: Addison-Wesley Publishing Co., 1978.

———. "Social Movements, Old and New." In *Research in Social Movements, Conflict and Change,* 10: 1–18. Greenwich, Conn.: JAI Press, Inc., 1988.

Walker, Gillian A. *Family Violence and the Women's Movement: The Conceptual Politics of Struggle.* Toronto, Ontario: University of Toronto Press, 1990.

Walker, Lenore. *The Battered Woman.* New York: Harper and Row, 1979.

———. "The Battered Woman Syndrome Study." In *The Dark Side of Families,* edited by David Finkelhor, Richard J. Gelles, Gerald T. Hotaling, and Murray Straus, 31–48. Beverly Hills, Calif.: Sage, 1983.

———. *The Battered Woman Syndrome.* New York: Springer Publishing Co., Inc., 1984.

Walker, Lenore E. *Terrifying Love: Why Battered Women Kill and How Society Responds.* New York: HarperPerennial, 1989.

Whittier, Nancy. *Feminist Generations.* Philadelphia: Temple University Press, 1995.

Younes, L.A. *State Legislative Solutions to the Problem of Family Violence.* Washington, D.C.: Clearinghouse on Family Violence, 1988.

Zald, Mayer N. and Roberta Ash Garner. "Social Movement Organizations: Growth, Decay, and Change." In *Social Movements in an Organizational Society: Collected Essays,* edited by Mayer N. Zald and John D. McCarthy, 121–42. New Brunswick, N.J.: Transaction Publishers, 1987.

Journal Articles

Ahrens, Lois. "Battered Women's Refuges: Feminist Cooperatives vs. Social Service Institutions. *Radical America* 13.4 (1980): 41–9.

Andersen, Erich D., and Anne Read-Andersen. "Constitutional Dimensions of the Battered Woman Syndrome." *Ohio State Law Journal* 53.2 (1992): 363–411.

Appel, Susan D. "Beyond Self-Defense: The Use of Battered Woman Syndrome in Duress Defenses." *University of Illinois Law Review* 4 (1994): 955–80.

Baker, Scott Gregory. "Deaf Justice? Battered Women Unjustly Imprisoned Prior to the Enactment of Evidence Code Section 1107." *Golden Gate University Law Review* 24 (1994): 99–130.

Bates, Jeanne-Marie. "Comment: Expert Testimony on the Battered Woman Syndrome in Maryland." *Maryland Law Review* 50 (1991): 920–44.

Benford, Robert. "Frame Disputes within the Nuclear Disarmament Movement." *Social Forces* 71 (1993): 677–70.

Bird, A.M., and J. M. Williams. "A Developmental-Attributional Analysis of Sex-Role Stereotypes for Sport Performance." *Developmental Psychology* 15 (1980): 319.

Blum, Joanne. "Celeste's Clemency for 25." *Columbus Monthly* (March 1991): 55–58.

Brint, Steven. " 'New Class' and Cumulative Trend Explanations of the Liberal Political Attitudes of Professionals." *American Journal of Sociology* 90 (1984): 30–70.

Browne, Angela. "Exploring the Effect of Resource Availability and the Likelihood of Female-Perpetrated Homicides." *Law and Society Review* 23.1 (1989): 75–94.

———. "Violence against Women by Male Partners: Prevalence, Outcomes, and Policy Implications." *American Psychologist* 48 (1993): 1077–87.

Bush, Diane M. "Women's Movements and State Policy Reform Aimed at Domestic Violence against Women." *Gender and Society* 6.4 (December 1992): 587–608.

Callahan, A. Reneé. "Will the 'Real' Battered Woman Please Stand Up? In Search of a Realistic Legal Definition of Battered Woman Syndrome." *American University Journal of Gender and the Law* 3 (Fall 1994): 117–52.

Caplan, G. "Battered Wives, Battered Justice." *National Review* (24 February 1991): 39–43.

Cohen, Jean L. "Strategy or Identity: New Theoretical Paradigms and Contemporary Social Movements." *Social Research* 52.4 (1985): 869–90.

Creach, D.L. "Imperfect Self-Defense." *Stanford Law Review* 34 (February 1982): 615–38.

Daniels, Arlene Kaplan. "Careers in Feminism." *Gender and Society* 5.4 (1991): 583–607.

Davis, A.J. "Sex-Differentiated Behaviors in Non-Sexist Picture Books." *Sex Roles* 11 (1984): 1–6.

Davis, Nanette J. "Battered Women: Implications for Social Control." *Contemporary Crises* 12 (1988): 345–72.

Dubnos, P. "Attitudes toward Women Executives: A Longitudinal Approach." *Academy of Management Journal* 28.1 (1985): 235–39.

Dutton, Mary Ann. "Understanding Women's Responses to Domestic Violence: A Redefinition of Battered Woman Syndrome." *Hofstra Law Review* 21 (1993): 1191–242.

Eder, Klaus. "The 'New Social Movements': Moral Crusades, Political Pressure Groups, or Social Movements." *Social Research* 52.4 (1985): 869–90.

Edwards, Susan S.M. "A Socio-Legal Evaluation of Gender Ideologies in Domestic Violence Assault and Spousal Homicides." *Victimology: An International Journal,* 10.1–4 (1985): 186–205.

Epstein, Barbara. "Rethinking Social Movement Theory." *Socialist Review* 20 (1990): 35–66.

Ernest, J. "Mathematics and Sex." *American Mathematical Monthly* 83 (1976): 595–614.

Ferraro, Kathleen J. "Processing Battered Women." *Journal of Family Issues* 2.4 (1981): 415–38.

———. "Negotiating Trouble in a Battered Women's Shelter." *Urban Life* 12.3 (1983): 287–306.

Ferraro, Kathleen J., and John M. Johnson. "The New Underground Railroad." *Studies in Symbolic Interaction* 6 (1985): 377–86.

Ferree, Myra Marx, and Frederick D. Miller. "Mobilization and Meaning: Some Social-Psychological Contributions to the Resource Mobilization Perspective." *Sociological Inquiry* 55 (1985): 38–61.

Fine, Michele. "Politics of Research and Activism: Violence against Women." *Gender and Society* 3.4 (1989): 549–58.

Fiora-Gormally, Nancy. "Battered Wives Who Kill: Double Standard Out of Court, Single Standard In?" *Law and Human Behavior* 2.2 (1978): 133–65.

Frank, E.J. "Business Students' Perceptions of Women in Management." *Sex Roles* 19.1–2 (1988): 107–18.

Gagné, Patricia. Appalachian Women: Violence and Social Control." *Journal of Contemporary Ethnography* 20.4 (1992): 387–416.

———. "Identity, Strategy, and Feminist Politics: Clemency for Battered Women Who Kill." *Social Problems* 43.1 (1996): 77–93.

Gelles, Richard J., and Murray A. Straus. "Violence in the American Family." *Journal of Social Issues* 35.2 (1979): 15–39.

Haaken, Janice. "From Al-Anon to ACOA: Codependence and the Reconstruction of Caregiving." *Signs: Journal of Women in Culture and Society* 18 (1993): 321–45.

Hansen, C.H., and R. D. Hansen. "How Rock Music Videos Can Change What Is Seen When Boy Meets Girl: Priming Stereotypic Appraisal of Social Interactions." *Sex Roles* 19 (1988): 287–316.

Herman, Nancy J., and Charlene E. Miall. "The Positive Consequences of Stigma: Two Case Studies in Mental and Physical Disability." *Qualitative Sociology* 13.3 (1990): 251–69.

Jenkins, J. Craig. "Interpreting the Stormy 1960s: Three Theories in Search of a Political Age." *Research on Political Sociology* 3 (1987): 269–303.

Johnson, John M. "Program Enterprise and Official Cooptation in the Battered Women's Shelter Movement." *American Behavioral Scientist* 24.6 (1981): 827–42.

Jones, James T.R. "Battered Spouses' Section 1983 Damage Action against the Unresponsive Police after DeShaney." *West Virginia Law Review* 93 (1991a): 251–357.

————. "Battered Spouses' State Law Damage Actions against the Unresponsive Police." *Rutgers Law Journal* 23 (1991b): 1–78.

Kalmuss, Debra S., and J. A. Seltzer. "Continuity of Marital Behavior in Remarriage: The Case of Spouse Abuse." *Journal of Marriage and the Family* 46 (1986): 11–19.

Lummis, N., and H. W. Stevenson. "Gender Differences in Beliefs and Achievement: A Cross-Cultural Study." *Developmental Psychology* 26.2 (1990): 254–63.

Maguigan, Holly. "Battered Women and Self-Defense: Myths and Misconceptions in Current Reform Proposals." *University of Pennsylvania Law Review* 379 (1991): 414–86.

Margolis, Diane Rothbard. "Redefining the Situation: Negotiations on the Meaning of 'Woman.' " *Social Problems* 32.4 (1985): 332–47.

Mayes, S., and K. Valentine. "Sex-Role Stereotyping in Saturday Morning Cartoon Shows." *Journal of Broadcasting* 23 (1979): 41–50.

McCarthy, John D., and Mayer N. Zald. "Resource Mobilization and Social Movements: A Partial Theory." *American Journal of Sociology* 82.6 (1977): 1212–40.

Melucci, Alberto. "The New Social Movements: A Theoretical Approach." *Social Science Information* 19.2 (1980): 199–226.

————. "An End to Social Movements?: Introductory Paper to the Sessions on New Movements and Change in Organizational Forms." *Social Science Information* 23.4–5 (1984): 819–35.

————. "The Symbolic Challenge of Contemporary Movements." *Social Research* 52.4 (Winter 1985): 789–816.

Miller, Kym C. "Abused Women Abused by the Law: The Plight of Battered Women in California and a Proposal for Revising the California Self-Defense Law." *Review of Law and Women's Studies* 3 (1994): 303–29.

Murphy, Jane C. "Lawyering for Social Change: The Power of the Narrative in Domestic Violence Law Reform." *Hofstra Law Review* 21 (1993): 1243–93.

Offe, Claus. "New Social Movements: Challenging the Boundaries of Institutional Politics." *Social Research* 52.4 (1985): 817–70.

Schneider, Elizabeth M. "Equal Rights to Trial for Women: Sex Bias in the Law of Self-Defense." *Harvard Civil Rights–Civil Liberties Law Review* 15 (1980): 623–47.

————. "Describing and Changing: Women's Self-Defense Work and the Problem of Expert Testimony on Battering." *Women's Rights Law Reporter* 9.3–4 (1986): 195–222.

————. "Resistance to Equality." *University of Pittsburgh Law Review* 57 (1996): 477–524.

Schneider, Elizabeth M., and Susan B. Jordon, with Cristina C. Arguedas. "Representation of Women Who Defend Themselves in Response to Physical or Sexual Assault." *American Journal of Trial Advocacy* 1.19 (1978): 19–46.

Snow, David A., and Richard Machalek. "The Sociology of Conversion." *Annual Review of Sociology* 10 (1984): 367–80.

Snow, David A., E. Burke Rochford Jr., Steven K. Worden, and Robert D. Benford. "Frame Alignment Processes, Micromobilization and Movement Participation." *American Sociological Review* 51 (1986): 464–81.

Thyfault, Roberta K. "Self-Defense: Battered Woman Syndrome on Trial." *California Western Law Review* 20 (1984): 485–510.

Tierney, Kathleen J. "The Battered Women Movement and the Creation of the Wife Beating Problem." *Social Problems* 29.3 (1982): 207–20.

Touraine, Alain. "An Introduction to the Study of New Social Movements." *Social Research* 52.4 (1985): 749–87.

Ulmschneider, Georgia Wralstad. "Rape and Battered Women's Self-Defense Trials as "Political Trials': New Perspectives on Feminists' Legal Reform Efforts and Traditional 'Political Trials' Concepts." *Suffolk Law Review* 29 (1995): 85–124.

Van Cleave, Rachel A. "A Matter of Evidence or of Law? Battered Women Claiming Self-Defense in California." *UCLA Women's Law Journal* 5 (1994): 217–45.

Walker, Lenore. "Battered Women and Learned Helplessness." *Victimology: An International Journal* 2.3–4 (1977–1978): 525–34.

Warshaw, Carole. "Limitations of the Medical Model in the Care of Battered Women." *Gender and Society* 3.4 (1989): 506–40.

Wilmore, J.H. "They Told You, You Couldn't Compete With Men and You, Like a Fool, Believed Them. Here's Hope." *Womensports* (June 1974); 40–43.

Zern, D.S. "Relationships among Selected Child-Rearing Variables in a Cross-Cultural Sample of 110 Societies." *Developmental Psychology* 20.4 (1984): 683–90.

Dissertations

Adams, David. "Empathy and Entitlement: A Comparison of Battering and Nonbattering Husbands." Ph.D. diss., Northeastern University. Boston, 1991.

Gagné, Patricia L. *The Battered Women's Movement in the "Post-Feminist" Era: New Social Movement Strategies and the Celeste Clemencies.* Ph.D. diss., The Ohio State University. Columbus, 1993.

Tierney, Kathleen J. *Social Movement Organization, Resource Mobilization, and the Creation of a Social Problem: A Case Study of a Movement for Battered Women.* Ph.D. diss., The Ohio State University. Columbus, 1979.

Public Documents

U.S. Department of Justice. Bureau of Justice Statistics. "Two-Thirds of
	Women Violence Victims Are Attacked by Relatives or Acquaintances."
	BJS 202–307–0784. Washington: GPO, 1994.
———. "Special Report, Violence against Women: Estimates from the Re-
	designed Survey." Washington: GPO, 1995.
U.S. Department of Labor, Women's Bureau. *1993 Handbook on Women
	Workers: Trends and Issues.* Washington: GPO, 1994.

Index

239

The Author

Patricia Gagné received her Ph.D. from The Ohio State University in 1993 and is assistant professor of sociology at the University of Louisville. She has published several articles and book chapters on wife abuse, the battered women's clemency movement, transgenderism, and qualitative research methods. Her current research focuses on gender and power.

The Editor

Robert D. Benford received his Ph.D. from the University of Texas at Austin in 1987 and is associate professor of sociology at the University of Nebraska–Lincoln. His published works include *The Nuclear Cage* (with Lester Kurtz and Jennifer Turpin) and numerous articles and book chapters on social movements, nuclear politics, war and peace museums, environmental controversies, and qualitative research methods. His current research focuses on the linkages between the social construction of movement discourse, collective identity, and collective memory.